BOOK 3

A MULTI-SENSORY APPROACH
TO LANGUAGE ARTS FOR

SPECIFIC
LANGUAGE
DISABILITY
CHILDREN

A GUIDE FOR ELEMENTARY TEACHERS

BETH H. SLINGERLAND

Educators Publishing Service, Inc.
31 Smith Place, Cambridge, MA 02138-1000

Revised Edition
A Multi-Sensory Approach to Language Arts
for Specific Language Disability Children
A Guide for Elementary Teachers
Book III

By
Marty Aho, Professional Heir
and
The Professional Materials Committee
Slingerland Institute

February 2001 Printing

ISBN 0-8388-1481-6

TO THE MEMORY

of

Anna Gillingham

and

Bessie Stillman

who redirected the course
of my life

and

TO THE MEMORY

of

Mary Persis Winne

whose early recognition of Specific
Language Disability problems in
children made possible my work with
Anna Gillingham and Bessie Stillman

ACKNOWLEDGMENTS

I am especially grateful to and admire the dedicated teachers with whom I have worked and shared over the years. It is they who strengthen the capabilities and enrich the lives of literally hundreds of children with Specific Language Disability. Because of these teachers' activities and understanding adherence to the basic principles of instruction set forth in the Orton-Gillingham approach to language arts, help for these children continues. The children are the inspiration, reason, and purpose for putting my ideas into written words. The teachers bring forth life from the written words; some of them train others, who, by setting up new programs, ensure that SLD children will be helped in the future. These SLD teachers fulfill my own professional life.

CONTENTS

INTRODUCTION TO THE REVISED EDITION

Part of the legacy Beth H. Slingerland left to dedicated teachers of children with dyslexia is found in her three textbooks. Just as Norman Geschwind's article upheld Samuel Orton's original thesis of the brain functions of the dyslexic population, present-day successes attest to the effectiveness of Beth H. Slingerland's contributions to the educational world.

From the very beginning, Mrs. Slingerland made improvements as the need to do so became apparent. She did not intend for her work to become static with the publication of her textbooks. Observations and reports from directors who worked closely with her prompted Mrs. Slingerland to make some changes in procedures only, not the basic principles underlying the approach.

This new edition of Book III includes the changes, variations and uses of crutches that Beth Slingerland transmitted to her professional heir, Marty Aho. Ms. Aho and the Professional Materials Committee worked diligently to retain Beth Slingerland's work in its entirety. Just as Mrs. Slingerland did in person with her protégés, this new edition transmits added clarity, conciseness, and cohesiveness to future users of her materials.

*Month-long, college-accredited summer schools for training teachers to use this multi-sensory method are held each year in various parts of the country (Washington, Oregon, California, Alaska, Utah, Texas, Connecticut, New Hampshire, etc.). For information and brochures write or call The Slingerland Institute at the following address:

One Bellevue Center
411 108th Avenue NE
Bellevue, WA 98004

Telephone: (206) 453-1190
Fax: (206) 635-7762

INTRODUCTION

The instructional procedures presented in this book are for use with children who have a Specific Language Disability and who have had one or two years of previous instruction from the Slingerland adaptation for classroom use of the Orton-Gillingham multi-sensory approach to language arts. While *Book Three* is planned for teachers of children in early-elementary grades, it can be used with older children who are being introduced to the techniques for the first time. It is adaptable to higher elementary levels depending upon the functional use attained by an individual under a teacher's guidance as well as the child's ability to perform independently.

Successful use of the instructional techniques depends upon the teacher's knowledge of language development and understanding of Specific Language Disability with its modality strengths and weaknesses. The contents are organized primarily into structured (not "programmed") steps that depend upon the teacher's training* and sensitivity to the needs of children both in groups and individually. The basic principles underlying this approach and the level of achievement children have reached will help determine the teacher's daily planning for instruction. Basic principles include teaching "through the intellect" and beginning with "single units." Each newly learned unit must be integrated with known material to form a new and more complex unit, which then should be put to functional use before learning and including the next unit. The teacher must structure the lessons to integrate new units with previously learned complex units so that the children will be able to use these language skills independently.

Part 1

BACKGROUND*

LANGUAGE DEVELOPMENT

By the time children reach third grade, usually at eight or nine years of age, they will have passed through the first six years of phenomenal learning of language and, from six to eight or nine years, will have been introduced to the nonphenomenal learning of symbolic language — reading, handwriting, and spelling.

There is beginning to be some evidence** that the neurophysiological brain development in children is rapid with periods of faster and slower growth — extra growth seems to occur from approximately three to ten months, and again from two to four years; slower growth seems to occur from four to six years, followed by a spurt in growth from six to eight or nine years, and then by another period of normal growth. A period of slower brain growth thus occurs at the time children usually are in third and fourth grades. From one to four years, children learn to understand and speak in sentences while from four to six years (during a rest period in brain growth), they put what they have learned into functional use in various ways for speaking and understanding. During the spurt in growth between six and eight or nine years, children usually are ready to be taught how to learn the symbolic language of reading, handwriting, and spelling. When eight- or nine-year-old children reach third and fourth grades, educators should recognize that the years between eight or nine and ten or eleven afford the brain another period of rest, or slow growth. Ample opportunity should be provided for "fixing" and strengthening the newly-learned skills of reading, handwriting, and spelling and for their functional use in written expression. This strengthening period should be in preparation for further growth during the last two years of elementary school (fifth and sixth grades) while horizons of cognitive and learning abilities are widening and extending to receive appropriate teaching and guidance.

The sensory channels that serve the Auditory-Kinesthetic modalities from their preschool initial simultaneous association with the *Visual at the object level* are necessary developments in children during the first six years of learning to understand and use spoken words.

---

*Teachers should read pages 9–14 of the Background in Beth H. Slingerland, *Book Two — Basics in Scope and Sequence of a Multi-Sensory Approach to Language Arts for Specific Language Disability Children: A Guide for Primary Teachers* (Cambridge, Mass.: Educators Publishing Service, Inc., 1976).

**Herman T. Epstein and Conrad F. Toepfer, Jr. have discussed this theory of language development in "A Neuroscience Basis for Reorganizing Middle Grades Education," *Educational Leadership*, Vol. 35, No. 8. (May 1978), pp. 656–660.

From six years on, this same simultaneous Auditory-Kinesthetic association is linked with the *Visual at the symbol level* for reading, handwriting, and spelling. By age twelve, the completion of neurophysiological patterning that serves intake and output for lifetime language development occurs within normal blocks of time. If it does not in otherwise normal children, disability or modality weaknesses should be identified* and recognized as conditions demanding immediate implementation of proper multi-sensory instruction.**

Instruction should be planned:

- to strengthen the weaker modalities by associating them with the stronger;
- to teach children to conceptualize each new learning as it is taught "through the intellect";
- to integrate each new learning with previous learnings; and
- to develop functional use under the guidance of the teacher to build self-confidence and inner motivation resulting from each child's successful performance (not from bribes and material rewards).

Children's disabilities are frequently overlooked or unrecognized until *after* they enter school and fail to learn to read despite intelligence equal to or higher than their classmates' and despite receiving the same kind of instruction to which other children readily respond. In some children the Auditory-Kinesthetic modalities of preschool years may have developed as expected, leading to ability to understand and verbalize without problems, but if Visual modality weakness is present, they may not learn to read, write, and spell as expected or their learning may not be commensurate with their intelligence.

Other children have unrecognized disabilities or developmental lags that occur *before school entry*. Their phenomenal language learning during preschool years may have lagged behind that anticipated and may have been faulty because of a Specific Language Disability. These weaknesses prevent or delay the children's expected progress in perception of spoken language concepts and recall for their own verbal self-expression. SLD children may be considered dull or stupid. As a result, some of them enter school without the secure, simultaneous Auditory-Kinesthetic association of words that is assumed prior to school entry, and they are therefore inadequately prepared to associate Visual symbols with the spoken and understood language they do not have. Their difficulties may be magnified by the time elementary grades are reached.

For still other children, handwriting difficulties prevent success in the written requirements of more advanced grade levels both for writing and copying — Kinesthetic*** modality weaknesses that can stem from two different causes.

---

*Beth H. Slingerland, *Slingerland Screening Tests for Identifying Children with Specific Language Disability*, Forms A, B, C, and D (Cambridge, Mass.: Educators Publishing Service, Inc., 1974).

**Teachers should read pages 2–6 in *Why Wait for a Criterion of Failure* and pages 5–7 in *A Pragmatic Approach to the Evaluation of Children's Performances on Pre-Reading Screening Procedures to Identify First Grade Academic Needs*, Beth H. Slingerland (Cambridge, Mass.: Educators Publishing Service, Inc., 1974 and 1979).

***Kinesthetic* refers to the memory of the sequence of movement involved in:
- use of the speech mechanism to pronounce words, usually in association with the Auditory sensory channel, for recall of sound symbols; and
- use of the arm and hand, usually in association with the Visual sensory channel, for recall of the appearance of sight symbols.

Without secure, automatic, correct recall of the necessary movement or "feel," voluntary motor function cannot be triggered to bring about the desired response in the speech mechanism or in the hand for writing.

Some children are clumsy or lack skill in small muscle control. They have difficulty recalling *sequential movement* patterns, such as those needed to skip, hop, dance, draw, and use pencils or crayons, etc. This clumsiness is apt to interfere with the necessary kinesthetic-motor movements of the hand in writing — a difficulty akin to agraphia.

If, instead, recall of the Visual *appearance* of the letters of the alphabet and/or words is lacking, sequential movement is lost or confused in spite of possible good motor control, and handwriting suffers — a difficulty akin to dyslexia.

It is for teachers of these children, regardless of which of the three sensory channels is weak — Auditory, Visual, or Kinesthetic — that this book is written.

RATIONALES

FOR RECOGNITION OF CHILDREN WITH SPECIFIC LANGUAGE DISABILITY

Specific Language Disability children are those with average to superior intelligence whose achievement in language skills — reading, penmanship, spelling, and oral and written expression — is not commensurate with their intelligence in spite of educational opportunities, socioeconomic background, and even the desire to learn. They are not mentally deficient, brain damaged, or primarily emotionally disturbed nor do they have learning disabilities per se. Their difficulties are specific to language skills and in no way global in nature. They are responsive to multi-sensory instruction by trained teachers. Their learning depends upon the degree of the disability, the time when instruction begins, native intelligence, and the skill of the teacher — all reasons for early identification of the problem and implementation of a multi-sensory approach to learning.

FOR ADMINISTRATIVE SUPPORT OF SLD CLASSROOM PROGRAMS

Some fifteen to twenty percent of children who have mild to severe degrees of Specific Language Disability usually do not get the help they need. They are the ones who are unresponsive to conventional teaching, despite exposure to what would be considered excellent teaching and effective methods for the majority of children.

A classroom of children taught with a multi-sensory approach offers supplementary support to a school system having special education programs for the children who have problems of a different nature, such as mental deficiency, brain damage, or primary emotional disturbance and for whom special help is given out of the classroom or in very small groups. Regular classrooms of identified SLD children, organized at each grade level, operating within the domain of regular education are able to provide for the children who otherwise would be overlooked in spite of their equal right to the specific instruction they require. Such SLD classrooms are like other classrooms in most respects; only the instruction for language skills is different and should be offered in a specific way by teachers trained to do so.

No large sums of additional taxes and no additional teachers are needed for an SLD program. However, one of the teachers at each grade level needs to have special training in use of multi-sensory techniques. Extra books or equipment for the children are unnecessary because techniques are devised for use with any of the good, conventional basic readers and spellers.

FOR THE INSTRUCTIONAL APPROACH

Children are taught "through the intellect" to develop "patterns of thought" and procedures for conceptualizing. They learn to use conscious effort to do what children who do not have a disability are able to do without the same conscious effort and self-direction.

FOR INTEGRATING NEW WITH PRECEDING LEARNINGS

Instruction begins with single alphabetic units which, when combined to form word units and word-plus-suffix units, prepare the way for phrase units. Phrasing, as the first step in writing, leads to sentence and paragraph units. Guided functional experience with each new learning (such as different ways of spelling, capitalizing, punctuating, etc.) used in sentence and paragraph units widens the integrative power which must expand for upper-elementary and intermediate-grade compositions since their paragraph units form the complex units of essay writing.

When word units are combined to form phrase units that convey fragmentary thoughts, the first step in reading begins. Unlocking single words is no more than word naming, *a skill* to be integrated into phrase and sentence reading. Paragraph comprehension depends on having previously learned to read sentences for comprehension of single thoughts. Combining those single thoughts forms a paragraph unit. Each new step within the growing language structure depends upon the previous learnings put to functional use under a teacher's guidance during the elementary grades, the time when basic skills should be taught and practiced for later independent needs.

FOR PSYCHOLOGICAL BENEFITS

When children begin to acquire the language skills, the lack of which have caused academic failure or inadequate performance, their personalities are affected positively. A change in attitude, first noticed by parents, is an early indication of a child's recognition of independent ability to learn, regardless of the grade level at which the learning skills take place. While praise and encouragement are helpful, it is the child's own inner recognition of successful performance that inspires self-confidence and restores or develops the desired self-image.

FOR USE OF THE DAILY FORMAT TO PLAN INSTRUCTION*

The same format used for planning daily lessons in primary grades should be used with children in the continuing elementary grades. What they are to be taught in each section of The Daily Format will be different depending upon their levels of previous achievement.

A teacher's planning for THE AUDITORY APPROACH for children's verbal and written expression should be done with the understanding that Auditory precepts and inner thought call forth the initial Auditory stimuli for speaking and for writing something readable. Planning for THE VISUAL APPROACH for children's learning to read the thoughts previously expressed by another in written form begins from Visual stimuli. With this in mind THE AUDITORY and VISUAL APPROACH lesson plans should be made as separate units of instruction.

The goals should be understood by the teacher and made clear to the children. In THE AUDITORY APPROACH, learning to write and spell and to use words in phrases and sentences enables an individual's thoughts to be expressed in written form that can be read by others. In THE VISUAL APPROACH, learning to copy and to read what already has been written enables each individual to share the thoughts of another as expressed in writing.

Proposing what one wishes to say in writing (propositional writing)** begins with inner thoughts expressed with words heard inwardly that must be associated with their Visual symbols and then with the Kinesthetic memory of their "feel" before voluntary motor function can serve the hand for handwriting. Writing requires simultaneous Auditory-Visual-Kinesthetic or multi-sensory association for:

- learning to write letters of the alphabet automatically as single units of sound-sight-feel;
- associating the names and sounds of the letters with their equivalent Visual symbols;
- using Auditory symbols blended to form new word units — simultaneous A-V-K association for spelling and handwriting; and
- learning to use phrases and sentences to express thought.

Deriving meaning from writing begins when minds are ready to perceive the thoughts written by another. To read, the child with a Specific Language Disability must perceive Visual symbols and simultaneously associate them with the Auditory sounds, grouped in phrases and sentences that convey the meaning — a Visual-Auditory association for silent reading and a Visual-Auditory-Kinesthetic association for oral reading.***

The LEARNING TO WRITE section in The Daily Format serves a need in both THE AUDITORY and VISUAL APPROACHES. Using the letters for handwriting and spelling is necessary in THE AUDITORY APPROACH. Using the letters for copying and for recognition of words is necessary in THE VISUAL APPROACH.

Instruction for handwriting and THE AUDITORY APPROACH appears on the white pages in Part 3, and for copying and THE VISUAL APPROACH, on the green pages in Part 4.

*Refer to Slingerland, *Book Two — Basics in Scope and Sequence*, pp. 9–14.

**Propositional writing expresses the children's ideas in their own words — not in a "creative" sense and not written from dictation, but "proposed" in each one's own way.

***The Kinesthetic sensory channel plays only a small part in silent reading. In teaching SLD children to read, there should be much oral reading if the teacher is to know what each child is doing and where specific help is needed — help requiring the child to make a complete V-A-K multi-sensory association.

FORMAT FOR PLANNING DAILY PERIODS OF INSTRUCTION

For Written Work and for Reading in Primary and Intermediate Grades

LEARNING TO WRITE
An Auditory-Visual-Kinesthetic Approach as the first "unit" of sight-sound-feel.
1. Teaching new letters of the alphabet (lower case and upper case)
2. Practice new letters after teaching
3. Reviewing letters taught
4. Learning how to connect cursive letter forms

THE AUDITORY APPROACH

A—ALPHABET CARDS
Name or *Sound* is spoken as an initial auditory stimulus for complete simultaneous A-V-K association for a given stimulus.

B—BLENDING
Teaching and practice for phonetic encoding (blending) as the next larger "unit"—a "word unit"—the first functional use of letters of the alphabet for *spelling*.

C—SPELLING
Teaching (Green Flag) words, non-phonetic (Red Flag) words, ambiguously spelled (Yellow Flag) words put to use in:
   Suffix usage with concept
   Phrases
   Sentences—**paragraphs** and, in due time, **compositions** in which the "units" become increasingly larger

THE VISUAL APPROACH

A—ALPHABET CARDS
Card is exposed as an initial visual stimulus for complete simultaneous V-A-K association for a given stimulus.

B—UNLOCKING
Teaching and practice for phonetic decoding (unlocking) as next larger "letter unit"—a "word unit"—the first functional use of letters to form words for *naming*.

C—PREPARATION FOR READING—Practice with phrases and sometimes words alone.
Phrases
1. Teacher reads phrase; Children repeat for complete A-V-K association.
2. Teacher reads phrase; A child *finds* and *reads*; Class repeats-auditory stimulus for A-V-K association.
3. Teacher asks a child to *find* and *read* the phrase that gives the meaning expressed by the teacher—requiring auditory perception and concept with understanding for complete A-V-K association and performance.
4. Children given turns to read the 6–8 phrases and class repeats after each phrase is read—for complete A-V-K association.

D—DICTATION

Continued use of already *learned* words and new words *taught*, including suffixes, to write *phrases* and *sentences*.

Paragraph study for dictation begins in Grade 2.

Refer to Bk. 2—pgs. 157–189 and Bk. 3—pgs. 116–144 for directions.

E—THE GOAL:
INDEPENDENT WRITING

For Answering questions, propositional writing, and creative expression

D—READING FROM THE BOOK

Teacher follows structured steps, as follows:

1. *Structuring*. Refer to Bk. 3, pgs. 249–250.
2. *Studying aloud* by having individual children study aloud and make corrections before *rereading* for all to hear and follow.
3. *Studying silently* a paragraph or two, or a page followed by individuals taking turns to read orally a part of the studied assignment.
4. *Independent study* followed by oral reading from which the teacher determines success with:
   1. phrasing
   2. attacking unfamiliar words
   3. conceptualizing
   4. independence in study

Refer to Bk. 3, pgs. 251–255 and pgs. 256–257

E—THE GOAL:
INDEPENDENT READING

Reading material at or below instructional level, or for individual selection.

***THE DAILY FORMAT FOR PLANNING INSTRUCTION
FOR WRITTEN WORK AND FOR READING**

LEARNING TO WRITE
A Visual-Auditory-Kinesthetic-motor Approach
- Learning new letters of the alphabet
- Reviewing letters already learned
- Learning capital letters
- Learning how to connect cursive letter forms

COPYING—A Visual-Kinesthetic Approach
- Learning to copy groups of letters, words, phrases, and sentences
- Learning to copy as a functional skill

THE AUDITORY APPROACH	*THE VISUAL APPROACH*
A—ALPHABET CARDS *Name* or *sound* is given as an initial auditory stimulus.	*A—ALPHABET CARDS* Card is exposed as an initial visual stimulus.
B—BLENDING Teaching and practice for encoding.	*B—UNLOCKING* Teaching and practice for decoding.
C—SPELLING Phonetic, or *Green Flag* words, Nonphonetic, or *Red Flag* words, Ambiguous, or *Yellow Flag* words, put to functional use with: Suffixes, Phrases, Sentences. Rules (in intermediate grades).	*C—PREPARATION FOR READING* Practice with *words* or *phrases* 1. Teacher names, children repeat (V-A-K Association). 2. Teacher names; a child finds and names; the class repeats (A—A-V-K Association). 3. Teacher asks child to *find* and *name* the word or phrase that gives the meaning expressed by teacher (*A—concept*—A-V-K). 4. A child reads the word or phrase, and the class repeats (V-A-K Association).
D—DICTATION Phrases and sentences. Paragraphs (beginning in the second year of the primary level).	*D—READING FROM THE BOOK* Teacher structures part of the lesson for: 1. Phrasing. 2. Learning to attack unfamiliar or unrecognized words. 3. Conceptualizing. 4. Learning how to study, etc.
E—THE GOAL: *INDEPENDENT WRITING* Answering questions. Propositional writing. Creative expression.	*E—THE GOAL:* *INDEPENDENT READING* Material at or below instructional level, or for individual independent selection.

*This format was revised by Beth Slingerland in 1982. See revised format on pages 8 and 9.

Part 2

SUPPLEMENTARY MATERIAL

In addition to this book, the following supplementary material should be available if the teacher is to use the instructional techniques correctly and with understanding. It can be purchased* or, in some cases, made by the teacher.

REQUIRED

6219 Slingerland, *Small Manuscript Alphabet Cards* (shown on *Chart Holder*, page 16)
1662 Slingerland, *Teacher's Hand Pack for Classroom Use*

1682 Slingerland, *Yellow Card Pack*

*Materials are available from Educators Publishing Service, Inc., 75 Moulton Street, Cambridge, Mass. 02238. Numbers preceding each item are catalog numbers for convenience in ordering.

1663 Slingerland, *Card Packet for Introducing Spelling Rules*

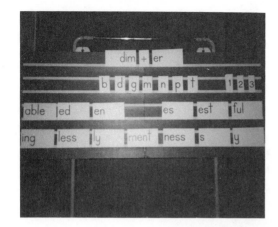
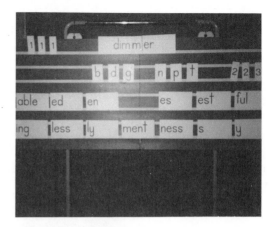

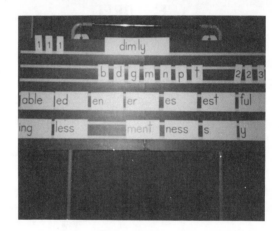

1-1-1 Rule

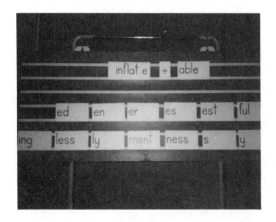
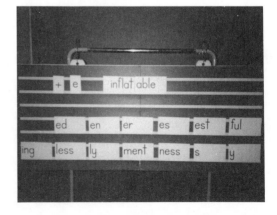

Silent-*e* Rule

218 Slingerland, and Murray, *Teacher's Word Lists For Reference Revised, 1987.*

1664 Slingerland, *Phonogram, Suffix, and Prefix Kit.*

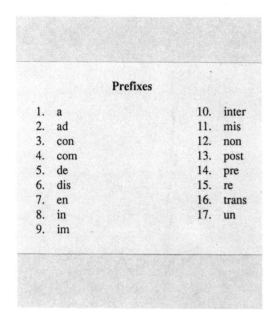

Prefixes

1.	a	10.	inter
2.	ad	11.	mis
3.	con	12.	non
4.	com	13.	post
5.	de	14.	pre
6.	dis	15.	re
7.	en	16.	trans
8.	in	17.	un
9.	im		

Suffixes

1.	able	10.	ist
2.	ed	11.	ive
3.	en	12.	less
4.	er	13.	ly
5.	es	14.	ment
6.	est	15.	ness
7.	ful	16.	ous
8.	ing	17.	s
9.	ish	18.	y

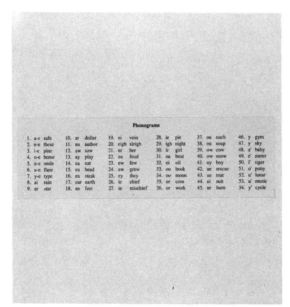

Phonograms

1. a-e	safe	10. ar	dollar	19. ei	vein	28. ie	pie	37. ou	ouch	46. y	gym
2. e-e	these	11. au	author	20. eigh	sleigh	29. igh	night	38. ou	soup	47. y	sky
3. i-e	pine	12. aw	saw	21. er	her	30. ir	girl	39. ow	cow	48. a'	baby
4. o-e	home	13. ay	play	22. eu	feud	31. oa	boat	40. ow	snow	49. e'	meter
5. u-e	mule	14. ea	eat	23. ew	few	32. oi	oil	41. oy	boy	50. i'	tiger
6. u-e	flute	15. ea	head	24. ew	grew	33. oo	book	42. ue	rescue	51. o'	pony
7. y-e	type	16. ea	steak	25. ey	they	34. oo	moon	43. ue	true	52. u'	lunar
8. ai	rain	17. ear	earth	26. ie	chief	35. or	corn	44. ui	suit	53. u'	music
9. ar	star	18. ee	feet	27. ie	mischief	36. or	work	45. ur	burn	54. y'	cycle

Refer to the Phonogram, Suffix and Prefix Kit, 1993 for current key words.

1482 Slingerland, *Cursive Letter Wall Cards*

1483 Slingerland, *Permanent Cursive Patterns for Tracing the Alphabet*

*The key word for *i* is now inch.

69   Chart Holder*

Chart Holders, shown with *Small Manuscript Alphabet Cards*

9219   Handschug, *Manuscript Alphabet Wall Cards* (first through third grades)

*Chart Holder refers to the *Pocket Wall Chart* which can be purchased from Educators Publishing Service, Inc. Many classrooms are already provided with such charts.

1484 Slingerland, *Alphabet Wall Chart* (The word for "I" has been changed to inch)

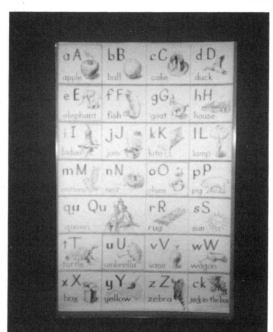

OPTIONAL (OR ACCESSIBLE FOR REFERENCE)

217 Slingerland, *Phonetic Word Lists for Children's Use* (A classroom set of one per child)

1480 Slingerland, *Book Two—Basics in Scope and Sequence of a Multi-Sensory Approach to Language Arts for Specific Language Disability Children: A Guide for Primary Teachers* (accessible for reference)

1685 Slingerland, *A Pragmatic Approach to the Evaluation of Children's Performances on Pre-Reading Screening Procedures to Identify First Grade Academic Needs* (accessible for reference)

PAPER NEEDS

Newsprint, twelve-by-eighteen inches
Composition Paper, 1-, 1/2-, and 3/8-inch lined

Part 3

TEACHING PROCEDURES FOR LEARNING TO WRITE AND THE AUDITORY APPROACH TO SPELLING AND WRITTEN EXPRESSION

LEARNING TO WRITE
A Visual-Auditory-Kinesthetic-motor Association

INTRODUCTION

Whether children with a Specific Language Disability are in the third grade and have been following this continuum or are being introduced to this multi-sensory approach to cursive handwriting at any grade level for the first time, the same basic instructional techniques are required. The same writing techniques can be, and are being, applied with young people at the junior and senior high school levels. When handwriting is not functional, children should not be expected to "hurdle" the steps in learning, nor should they be expected to "pick it up on their own." They require specific instruction and guidance as offered in Orton-Gillingham approaches in which learning to read, spell, and *write* begin with single units of sight-sound-feel, i.e., letters of the alphabet. The instruction for learning handwriting should include help in forming legible letters that can be recalled automatically and written correctly from any sensory stimulus. Handwriting should then be used functionally in propositional writing with the teacher's help in establishing performance patterns.

In the third year of this approach, an initial step is making the transfer from manuscript to cursive writing, the letter forms of which generally are used throughout the country from third grade on. How to do this is explained in this book. The process of learning to write is not part of phenomenal development and should be taught as a basic skill. As the cursive form of each letter is introduced, review time should be planned for strengthening the Visual-Auditory-Kinesthetic (VAK) associations of *sight-sound* (grapheme-phoneme)-*feel* (hand and mouth) of each letter as it is named.

Essentially the same procedures are used to teach cursive writing as well as manuscript writing.* Children following this continuum presumably can be expected to have learned the

*Beth H. Slingerland, *Book One — A Multi-Sensory Approach to Language Arts for Specific Language Disability Children: A Guide for Primary Teachers* (Cambridge, Mass.: Educators Publishing Service, Inc., 1971), pp. 40–76 and Slingerland, *Book Two — Basics in Scope and Sequence*, pp. 29–43.

names of the letters. Nevertheless, it is the current teacher's responsibility to check what children do and do not know, and to begin at the level children have attained, not at the level they are supposed to have reached. All of the learners will need to acquire new associations — the Visual *appearance* and the Kinesthetic-motor *feel* associated automatically with the Auditory *sound* of the name of the cursive letter forms.

The purpose of the structured organization in the daily LEARNING TO WRITE lessons is to provide practice with cursive letters and immediate use of them in the A—Alphabet Cards and B—Blending lessons before real need occurs in the written work of C—Spelling, D—Dictation, and E—Propositional and Creative Writing (the independent written expression that spontaneously follows).

For the first four to six weeks of the third year, it is advisable to *emphasize* learning the cursive forms as soon as possible (but without undue pressure or demand in written work before the letters have been learned well enough for functional use). In this way, future recall will not be confused. *Written requirements* in all subjects for the first three or four weeks of the school year should be *deemphasized* until children can form cursive letters automatically. Until the handwriting is sufficiently good to be included for complete A-V-K-m association, teaching can focus on Auditory-Visual association in B—Blending and the *Yellow Card Pack* and use of the Chart Holder for oral spelling.

Copying is triggered from Visual stimuli and should not be expected or required until automatic recall of cursive letter forms is securely established. *How to copy* will be explained in THE VISUAL APPROACH on the green pages. Its introduction begins with single units, two-letter units, and three-letter units, and progresses to word, phrase, and sentence units.

Teaching handwriting to children should not be confused with teaching phonics or spelling. Handwriting must become automatic if it is to be functional for spelling words (from Auditory stimuli) or for copying words (from Visual stimuli). Children should be taught that handwriting is a basic skill that is needed throughout life, regardless of an individual's divergent interests and purposes.

OBJECTIVES FOR LEARNING TO WRITE

For the third year of the continuum or for children at any grade level entering an SLD program for the first time,* the objectives are:

- to teach cursive writing in both lower- and uppercase letters of the alphabet;
- to teach relative letter size and alignment;
- to teach letter connections;
- to foster automatic rhythmic flow in moving from one letter to the next;
- to develop automatic writing skills to such a degree that they serve functionally for written expression and for copying; and
- to teach and give directed practice in transcribing visually presented symbols of manuscript, and other scripts, to cursive.

*The same techniques are applicable to fifth- and sixth-year girls and boys and to those of higher grade levels when their writing skills are not satisfactory or functional.

LETTER FORMS

LOWERCASE CURSIVE LETTER FORMS

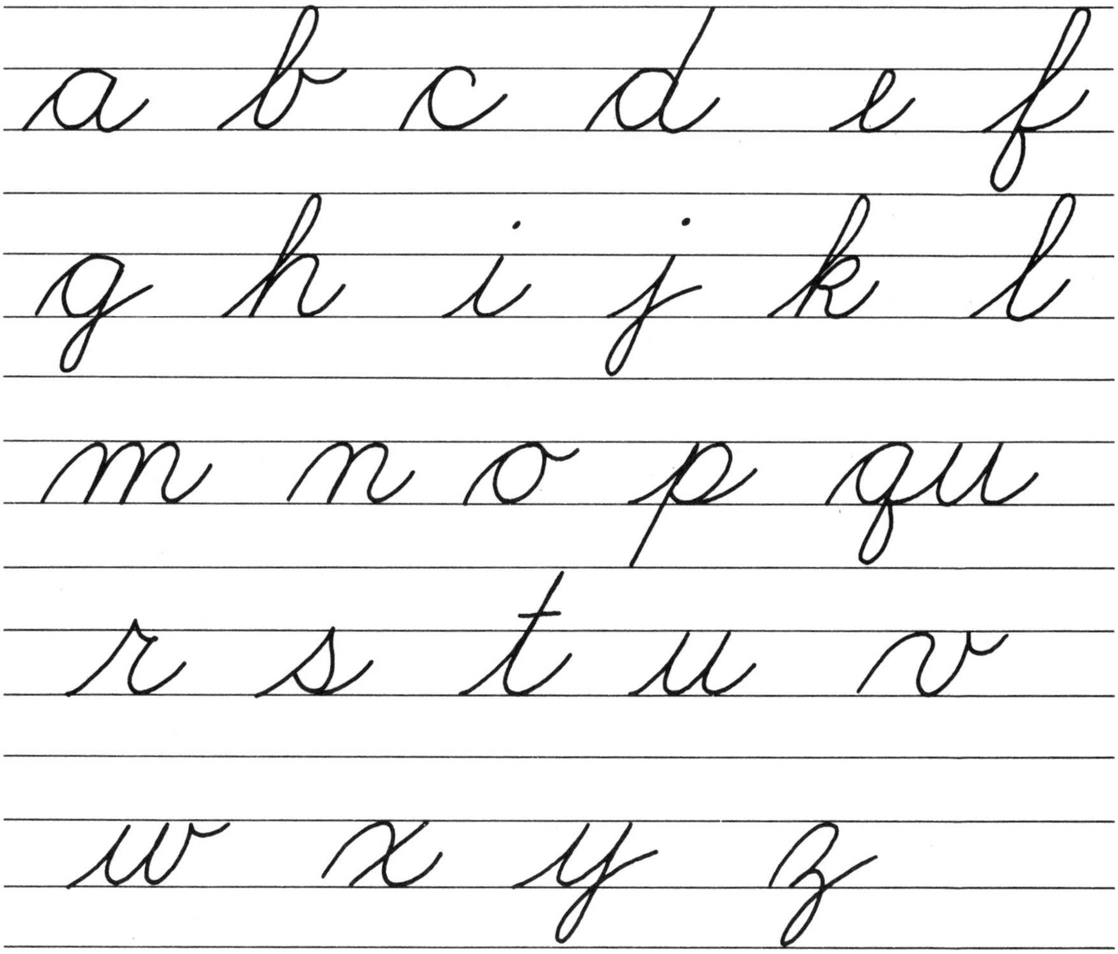

a b c d e f

g h i j k l

m n o p qu

r s t u v

w x y z

Some school systems prefer the letter forms shown below.

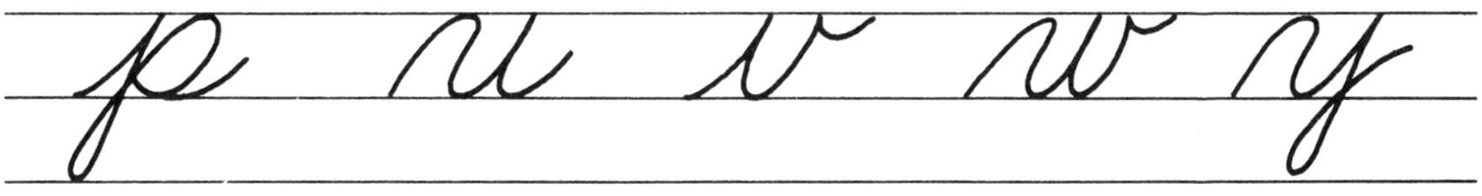

p u v w y

UPPERCASE CURSIVE LETTER FORMS

LOWERCASE CURSIVE LETTER FORMS THAT BEGIN WITH SIMILAR STROKES

UPPERCASE CURSIVE LETTER FORMS
THAT BEGIN WITH OR CONTAIN SIMILAR STROKES

$$A \quad C \quad O \quad E \quad D \quad L \quad \mathcal{Lu}$$

$$B \quad H \quad K \quad P \quad R$$

$$T \quad F \quad G \quad S \quad I \quad J$$

$$M \quad N \quad \mathcal{Lu} \quad U \quad V \quad W$$

$$X \quad Y \quad Z$$

Some letters having the same below-the-line strokes are:

$$g \quad j \quad y \quad p \quad z$$

Two letters having different below-the-line strokes from the preceding ones are:

They swing around in the direction that is "out from my body" (right-handed children) or "across my body" (left-handed children).*

Letters in lowercase cursive writing all end at the writing line with the exception of *b, o, v,* and *w* and they end at the midline.

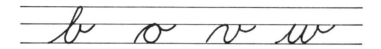

Those that end at the writing line are easily connected with succeeding letters, but the four that end at the midline require special teaching. (Refer to page 44.)

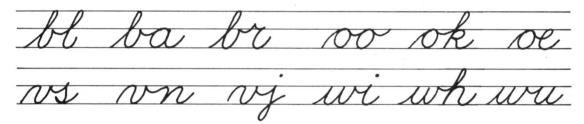

The letter *x* also requires special teaching both for its formation and for its connection with other letters in words. (Refer to page 45.)

MATERIALS

FOR GROSS MOTOR MOVEMENT

PERMANENT PATTERNS—LOWERCASE

Permanent Cursive Patterns for tracing lowercase cursive letter forms are used with children when they are being introduced to cursive writing, and for children at any grade level who have Kinesthetic-motor weakness or disability. The lowercase letters should be made at least eight, nine, or ten inches high to allow for free arm swings from the shoulder while practicing. The practice should be for gross motor movement and not necessarily for letter-size

*Slingerland, *Book One — A Multi-Sensory Approach*, p. 62.

relationship until memory of the movement involved can be retained for easy recall. (Refer to pages 32-33.) Permanent Patterns often are made on school reproducing equipment and can be kept from year to year, or they can be purchased.*

EXPENDABLE PATTERNS—LOWERCASE

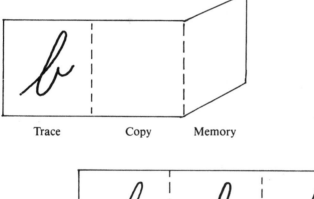

Trace   Copy   Memory

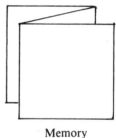

Memory

Review

Back of paper to be used for recall of letters already learned as dictated by the teacher.

As soon as the gross motor movement of a letter has been learned, teacher-made Expendable Patterns for tracing, copying, and writing from memory should be given to the children for practice—explained on pages 34-35. The back of the paper can be used for review of letters as dictated by the teacher. While learning the gross motor movement, no particular attention need be given to letter-size relationship.

The Expendable Patterns can be discarded after use. Some of them can be saved for comparison or display at some future date to show improvement.

*Beth H. Slingerland, *Permanent Cursive Patterns for Tracing the Alphabet* (Cambridge, Mass.: Educators Publishing Service, Inc., 1981).

FOR LETTER-SIZE RELATIONSHIP

PERMANENT PATTERNS—LOWERCASE

Children beginning the third year of this program, and others having difficulty at any level, should be given Permanent Patterns for tracing letters made with correct spacing that shows letter-size relationship. All such children require review, strengthening, or teaching supervised by a teacher to aid their automatic recall of the "feel" of the letters.

Fold margins top and bottom. Then fold into thirds upward. Place a dot on the writing line, being sure to leave a full space below the writing line.

The Permanent Patterns can be kept from year to year because the children use only their fingers or the blunt ends of their pencils for tracing to acquire the feel of the letter forms in association with their appearances and names. Pencil *points* should be used on the Expendable Patterns shown on the following pages.

As soon as children have mastered the gross motor movement, they should be given patterns for letter-size relationship, as shown above, to learn relative letter size.

PERMANENT PATTERNS—UPPERCASE

In the third year, emphasis should be placed on learning only the capital letters needed for some particular purpose. From the fourth year on, all capital letter forms should become "fixed" in memory for instant retrieval in functional use. All of the capital letters should be reviewed and practiced with a teacher's guidance and supervision.

Fold margins top and bottom. Then fold into thirds. Place a dot on the writing line, being sure to leave a full space below the writing line.*

*Sometimes newsprint can be purchased already lined to specification. If so, it is highly recommended.

Cursive Letter Wall Cards should be placed on the wall for easy reference of children at any time throughout the year.

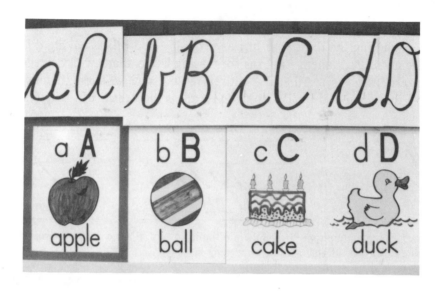

EXPENDABLE PATTERNS FOR TRACING, COPYING, AND WRITING FROM MEMORY

After letters have been introduced on Permanent Patterns (shown on previous pages) for relative size, Expendable Patterns should be made on twelve-by-eighteen-inch newsprint. Paper folding always should be done *by the teacher* and not by the children. Several sheets, but not more than three or four, can be folded at one time to show the creases clearly.*

The letter form in the first space is for tracing and should be made by the teacher. The second space is for copying, and the last panel is for writing from memory by folding the first panel to cover the second. Spaces on the back of the paper should be used for review writing and tracing letters dictated by the teacher, as shown below.

Trace	Copy	Write from memory	Some schools prefer

Fold margins top and bottom. Fold into fourths upward. Open papers. Fold into thirds crosswise. Open.

*Expendable Patterns may be run off on school reproducing equipment.

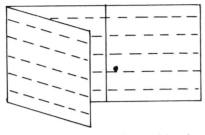

Back of paper may be used for review.

Fold to cover pattern when writing from memory.

EXPENDABLE PATTERNS FOR PRACTICE

Patterns for additional practice should be made *by the teacher* on twelve-by-eighteen-inch newsprint as shown below. (Refer to page 37.)

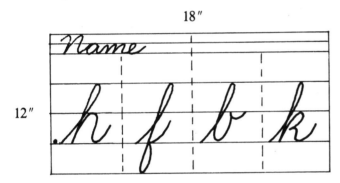

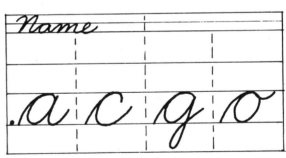

Fold margin at top for writing name. Fold in fourths lengthwise. Open papers. Fold in fourths crosswise. Open papers. Both sides of the paper should be used.

FOR RHYTHMIC FLOW FROM LETTER TO LETTER

EXPENDABLE PATTERNS FOR PRACTICE

These patterns are the same as those for letter-size relationship in the preceding section.

FOR REDUCING LETTER SIZE

EXPENDABLE PATTERNS FOR PRACTICE

If commercially-lined newsprint is not available, twelve-by-eighteen-inch newsprint can be folded to permit reducing the size of the letters. The teacher should fold the papers as explained and illustrated below.

Fold top margin line on which names are written. Fold in half lengthwise; then fold in thirds. Open papers.

PROCEDURES

GROSS MOTOR MOVEMENT

LEARNING CURSIVE LETTER FORMS

The children should be introduced to lowercase cursive letter forms before being expected to learn the capitals. Whenever a cursive letter is to be taught, a card such as the ones shown on page 30 should be placed above (or below) the *Manuscript Alphabet Wall Card* on which the corresponding letter form appears in manuscript. The cursive sample should be left on the wall for reference throughout the year.

>   NOTE: After six or seven letters have been taught and their cursive cards placed
>   on the wall, all of the cards can be placed in their permanent positions.

When introducing the cursive forms of letters, the following procedure should be used. The teacher should expose the card on which the cursive form appears and give its *name*. Presumably, children will have learned the name and also its sound. The teacher should:

1. Write the letter on the chalkboard, making it at least nine to twelve inches high.
2. Point out where the first stroke begins.

3. *Trace* lightly over the pattern several times while *naming* the letter each time it is traced for the class to *see and hear. The sound of the letter should not be given — only the name.*

Next, the children should be given Permanent Patterns. (Refer to pages 27-28.) The sitting position should be discussed and checked — back straight, both feet on the floor, and both arms on the desk or table. Position of the paper on the desk should be shown, and thereafter checked for a comfortable slant before each lesson begins. For right-handed children the top right corner of the paper should be toward the top right corner of the desk, and for left-handed children the top left corner of the paper should be toward the top left corner of the desk.

Pencils should be held comfortably with fingertips *not* extending below the colored, unsharpened end of the pencil. The sharpened portion should never be grasped since the fingers will interfere with clear vision of what is being written.

Practice should begin with the first two fingers tracing over the patterns until the movement becomes rhythmical. Then the blunt end of the pencil should be used while the letter is *named* at the same time that it is being traced.

The teacher should move among the children to give help where needed. For a child with Kinesthetic-motor weakness, the teacher should place a hand over that of the child, telling him or her to relax while allowing the arm to be pushed by the teacher through the movement that forms the letter. This requires no effort on the part of the girl or boy.

Teacher: "I'll do the work of moving your arm; you do the *feeling* as I guide your hand. *Name* the letter with me as it is formed."

NOTE: The letter *should not be drawn*. It should be formed with a free arm swing from the shoulder to make sure the *total gross movement* is felt rhythmically.

PRACTICING CURSIVE LETTER FORMS

After sufficient practice has been given tracing newly-introduced letters with the first two fingers and the blunt end of the pencil, Expendable Patterns on twelve-by-eighteen-inch newsprint should be provided for each child. (Refer to page 28.) The paper should be folded vertically in thirds with the letter pattern made by the teacher in the first panel.

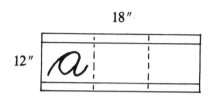

The children should trace over the pattern, first with two fingers, and then with the blunt end of the pencils. When directed, they should trace lightly with their pencil points, always using free arm swings and never drawing the letter form.

As the *feel* of the letter form becomes secure, it should be copied in the second space. The teacher should use a red pencil to reinforce or correct a child's pattern, if needed, before giving a nod of approval for the child to trace over his or her own copied pattern. The children should be reminded that they are tracing letters in order to *learn*, and that the red marks do not necessarily indicate mistakes. Instead, they will help the children strengthen their strokes and practice correctly. Do not seek perfection — only the correct arm movement.

For the final step, the children fold the first panel over the second (copying space), and write the letter from memory in the third panel. (Refer to page 28.) The teacher is responsible for checking each child's performance and not allowing any child to be the sole judge of his or her performance. A child with severe disability may need to return to the tracing pattern for further practice in order to become sure of the *feel* of the letter.

Each child should be given an Expendable Pattern which he or she should:

1. *Trace* while naming the letter in the first box. (The letter sound should *not* be given.) Tracing should continue until the child is directed to copy. (With experience, many of the children become able to judge when they are ready to move on to copying.)
2. *Copy* the letter in the second space, *naming* it *while* it is being formed. When "okayed" by the teacher, the child should trace the letter until directed to write it from memory.
3. *Write* from memory in the third space after the paper has been folded to cover the first two patterns. (Refer to pages 28 and 30-31.) When the teacher's nod or word of approval has been given, each child should continue tracing over the pattern written from memory.

The teacher should circulate about the room and, where need is evidenced, give immediate help with the letter strokes for rhythmic arm movement. The children should understand that the papers are only "practice papers" used for learning, not tests. The red marks made by the teacher "show up" against pencil marks.

NOTE: New letter forms should be practiced for gross motor movement. In lessons in which letters are being introduced, the known letters can be practiced for secure recall or for letter-size relationship, which will be explained below.

The Daily Format should include the following:
1. introduction of an unlearned cursive letter form;
2. review practice of letters already learned; and, as soon as letter-size relationship has been included,
3. practice for uniform letter-size relationship.

LETTER-SIZE RELATIONSHIP

LEARNING LOWERCASE LETTER FORMS

As soon as approximately five or six lowercase letters have been learned for gross motor movement, their relative letter size should be introduced. Practice should be on Permanent Patterns as shown on page 29. When a letter is introduced, explain that its first stroke begins on the writing line (sometimes spoken of as the base, lower, or foot line), and that letters are one or two spaces above the writing line or have strokes that extend below the writing line — corresponding to most manuscript forms. The *Cursive Letter Wall Card*, shown on page 30, already should be in place above or below the *Manuscript Alphabet Wall Card*, where it should remain as a constant reference point throughout the year.

NOTE: Children who have been following the continuum usually need practice with no more than five or six Permanent Patterns before they are ready to learn each newly introduced letter on the Expendable Patterns *for letter-size relationship*. Children who are being introduced to this multi-sensory approach for the first time may require practice with many of the letters on Permanent Patterns before they are ready to move to the Expendable Patterns. Children with Kinesthetic disabilities may need to practice each new letter on Permanent Patterns for gross motor movement whether they have been following the continuum or are beginners in this approach, no matter what their grade levels. In order to plan wisely, teachers must rely on their judgment of the degree of the disability, *the amount of previous successful experience*, and the time at which the child came into an SLD program.

By the time approximately a dozen letters have been introduced and practiced on Permanent and Expendable Patterns for relative letter size, children probably will have acquired the "pattern for learning," with cognition of letter-size relationship which usually enables them to learn newly-introduced cursive letter forms more rapidly than at first. Thereafter, and depending upon the teacher's judgment, it is possible to move directly:

- from the Permanent Patterns for gross motor movement to Permanent Patterns for relative letter size; or
- to learning the "feel" of the letter form on Permanent Patterns for letter-size relationship (page 29), and from there to varying procedures, which will be explained below.

NOTE: Not more than one to three letters should be introduced for initial learning in any day's lesson; nor should a new letter necessarily be introduced every day. However, these limitations should not apply to letters being reviewed.

As soon as a letter has been taught for letter-size relationship, it should be included regularly in lessons for review practice to make sure its correct recall becomes automatic.

LEARNING GROUPS OF LETTERS
THAT BEGIN WITH SIMILAR STROKES

Tracing over Letters on the Chalkboard

The teacher should place lines spaced for letter-size relationship on the board and then write letters that begin with the same strokes on the lines as the children watch.

Point out each letter's like and unlike strokes and whether the letter is one or two spaces high.

For practice, several groups of letters that begin with similar strokes should be written on the board by the teacher.

Children should be given turns going to the board, and with chalk, tracing lightly over the *letter named by the teacher.*

Teacher: "Form the *k* with a free arm swing while looking at it. Tell how many spaces high it is. Stand back from the board and keep your back to the class to prevent your writing from appearing backward to those who are watching. Now trace the *k*."

NOTE: After this initial direction, the children should understand, and it should not be necessary to give the same direction each time these letters are made. After tracing once with arm swings, the correct letter should be traced over the teacher's pattern on the board.

Children at the board: Trace over the letter pattern named by the teacher.
Children at their seats: Form the same letter with free arm swings.

The same procedure should be followed with other groups of children to give them turns tracing over the *named letter(s)* after stating whether the letter is one or two spaces high.

Tracing over Letters on Expendable Patterns

Each child should be given an Expendable Pattern made on twelve-by-eighteen-inch newsprint. (Refer to pages 30-31.) For practice, follow the procedures explained on pages 34-35.

RHYTHMIC FLOW FROM LETTER TO LETTER

TRACING FOR RHYTHMIC FLOW

Children should be given letter patterns made by the teacher for tracing. (Refer to page 31.) Before children start to trace, they should name all of the letters. Then the teacher should direct the class to trace over whichever letter the teacher names. Children should continue tracing in good rhythm until directed to trace the next named letter.

The same procedure should be continued with each of the letters, not necessarily named in the order in which they appear on the page.

> Teacher: "Trace the *g*."
> Class: Names the letter each time it is formed in tracing, continuing to do so until the next letter is named. There should be no break in rhythmic performance from one letter to the next.

The teacher should skip around from one letter to another, pacing performance to allow for no more than three or four tracings of each letter before naming the next one.

DOTTING THE WRITING LINE

The children should be given blank newsprint, folded as shown on page 31. They should be taught to dot the writing line as follows:

> Teacher: "Count the top (margin) line on which you write your name as *line one.* Place your finger on that line and count down to the third line. Keep your finger on *line three.*" (Have the children keep their fingers on *line three* until checked.) "Put a dot on *line three* to show that it is to be the writing line" (sometimes called the base line or the foot line).

The teacher should check to make sure dots are correctly placed and then show the children how to find the next writing line.

> Teacher: "Beginning on the *next line,* count it as *one* and count down to the third line. Put a dot on the third line to show it is to be another writing line."

There should be two writing lines on the page, with spaces arranged to prevent stems that go below the line from overlapping tall stems of the letters written below.

> NOTE: Experienced teachers are not surprised when confusion is evidenced by SLD children over this simple act of organizing line arrangement for writing. Teachers should provide guidance in developing ability to organize for any kind of written work. Organization for varying purposes in writing arrangements should be taught.

USING LETTERS JUST PRACTICED FOR MEMORY AND TRACING

> Teacher: "Write *a*. Remember how many spaces it takes. Trace lightly over your pattern as I check your writing."

To prevent any unnecessary errors, children should be reminded at the beginning of the lesson to refer to the letter on the wall if their memory of the appearance is uncertain. Otherwise, they should try to remember without looking.

> Class: Writes and traces the *a*, saying "*a*" each time it is formed.
> Teacher: "Write *c*."
> Class: Writes and traces the *c*, naming it softly each time it is formed.
> Teacher: "*O*."
> Class: Writes and traces.

The same procedure should be followed with each named letter. There should be no pause between naming of the letter and performance and naming of the next letter, and so on.

> NOTE: At the same time as letter-size relationship is being practiced, new letters can be introduced for gross motor "feel" with Permanent Patterns. (Refer to page 29.) After a letter form has been learned, the letter-size relationship should be explained and used with letters already being practiced for this relationship. As the children learn all of the letters in cursive, the teacher should be:
> • introducing new letter forms with practice for gross motor movement;
> • carrying the letters over into correct letter-size relationship with practice for automatic recall;
> • reducing letter size to bring about small muscle control; and
> • affording functional use of letters that have been learned in experiences that will be explained later in sections A—Alphabet Cards and B—Blending of THE AUDITORY APPROACH.

All of the letter forms usually can be learned for simultaneous Visual-Auditory-Kinesthetic association in four or five weeks if this plan of instruction is followed each day. Thereafter, each day's allowance of time for LEARNING TO WRITE should be devoted to practicing good lowercase and capital letters, letter connections, automatic recall, and rhythmic flow from one letter to the next, all of which develop the handwriting skills necessary for written expression.

REDUCING LETTER SIZE

Reduction in letter size should be done in preparation for using letters functionally for written association in A—Alphabet Cards and in learning letter connections needed for writing words in B—Blending of THE AUDITORY APPROACH.

PRACTICING AUTOMATIC RECALL

Children should be given blank newsprint, folded as shown on page 32. The teacher should dictate letters for the children to write and trace until the next letter is named. While the children are so engaged, the teacher should move about, giving help where it is needed. A red pencil should be used to show where improvement in letter formation can be made. Giving immediate help ensures correctly made letter forms for tracing and prevents practice with incorrectly made letters.

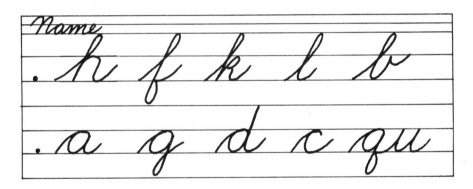

Practice in moving from one letter to the next named letter smoothly (but with no pressure to hurry) helps develop a rhythmic tempo or pacing without any break between hearing and forming one dictated letter, tracing, and writing, and tracing the next one as soon as it is named by the teacher.

> NOTE: This automatic recall and rhythmic movement from one letter to the next should precede functional use of letters for writing words. To write words requires concentration on how *words are spelled* rather than on trying to recall how *letters are formed*. Written spelling should not be hampered by inability to write automatically, insofar as possible. Therefore, controlled guidance and practice are essential.

If a teacher has moved too quickly with previous steps, the children — or a particular child — may falter at this point, which should *indicate to the teacher* that he or she should give more practice in letter formation.

PRACTICING RHYTHMIC FLOW

After the children can automatically recall most of the letters, they should be given practice in moving from one letter to the next as follows:

Teacher: Names a letter.
Class: 1. Repeats the name of the letter.
          2. Immediately writes the letter on papers.
          3. Traces lightly over the letter, naming it softly each time it is traced until the next letter is named.
Teacher: While the children are tracing, names the next letter.
Class: As each child completes the letter being traced, immediately names, writes, and traces, as explained above, until the teacher names the next one.

The same procedure should be followed with many letters, often with fifteen, twenty, or as many as can be written on the page.

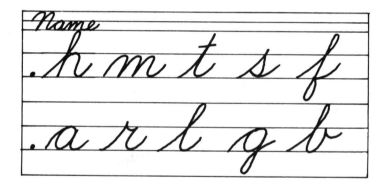

CONFUSING LETTER FORMS

By teaching "through the intellect," children usually can be helped to tell themselves how to recall confusing letters.* When uncertain, children should learn to tell themselves what to do before beginning to write the letter. All children should be given practice in verbalizing self-direction before performing. The usual Permanent and Expendable Patterns should be used.

RIGHT-HANDED CHILDREN

    b and *d***
    "*B* — tall stem up, down, turn *out from my body*, up, and out."
    "*D* — round like an *a*, straight up, down, and out."

*It has been noted that the older and more intellectually motivated children are more apt to use suggestions to aid recall than are younger children who have not experienced the same degree of failure and, therefore, do not feel the same need to depend upon themselves.

**Slingerland, *Book One — A Multi-Sensory Approach*, pp. 62-63.

f and *qu*
>"Only *f* and *qu* have stems below the line that turn *out from my body*, up, and out."
>"*F* — up like an *l*, down below the line, turn *out from my body*, up, and out."
>"*Qu* — round like an *a*, stem below the line, turn *out from my body*, up, and out."

p
>"*P* — up to the midline, down below the writing line, up to the midline, round *out from my body*, and out."

LEFT-HANDED CHILDREN

b and *d*
>"*B* — tall stem up, down, turn *across my body* (or toward my other arm), up, and out."
>"*D* — round like an *a*, straight up, down, and out."

f and *qu*
>"Only *f* and *qu* have stems below the line that turn *across my body*, up, and out."
>"*F* — up like an *l*, down below the line, turn *across my body*, up, and out."
>"*Qu* — round like an *a*, stem below the line, turn *across my body*, up, and out."

p
>"*P* — up to the midline, down below the writing line, up to the midline, round *across my body*, and out."

CAPITAL LETTERS

LEARNING CAPITAL LETTER FORMS

The same procedure explained for lowercase letters should be followed for teaching uppercase forms. (Refer to pages 24, 26, and 29.)

ASSOCIATING CAPITAL AND LOWERCASE LETTER FORMS

After a capital letter has been learned, it should be associated with its lowercase form as shown on the cursive cards on the wall. (Refer to page 30.) For the practice, each child should be given folded or lined paper.

Teacher: "Make small *m* and capital *m*."
Class: "*M*, capital *m*," naming the letters as they are formed. Tracing should continue until the next letters are named by the teacher.

Sometimes the teacher should reverse the order by naming the capital letter and then the lowercase letter.

m M t T S s b B

When reasonable skill has been achieved in automatic formation of capital letters — or the capitals that have been taught — the teacher should name different letters to be written as "double-letter units" but *not* as connected letters.

> Teacher: "Do not connect the letters that I name, but keep them close together. Write capital *c* and small *t*. Put a one-finger space between the two letters I name. Capital *m* and small *f*; small *g* and capital *s*; capital *d* and small *l*."

C t M f g S D l

> NOTE: The goal of this practice is to strengthen Auditory perception and brief recall for Auditory-Visual-Kinesthetic-motor performance. Writing letters as they are dictated is a less complicated step than writing words and sentences.

LETTER CONNECTION

As already explained, the teaching of relative letter size will have started before all of the letter forms have been taught. After the gross motor movement is learned, followed by relative letter size, and then reduced letter size, the same procedure should be continued for teaching letter connections. They should be taught before expecting children to group letters functionally for writing words — the purpose being *to prevent mistakes* in the mechanics of handwriting before they are allowed to occur.

> NOTE: Learning "through the intellect" can be fostered at the outset of teaching letter connections by explaining to the children that all of the lowercase letters begin and end at the writing line with the exception of four letters. Those four begin at the writing line but they end *at the midline*. Letters that are completed at the writing line can be joined easily with other letters that begin at the writing line. But the four letters that end, instead, *at the midline*, must be connected in special ways. Those four letters are *b, o, v,* and *w*. The teacher should demonstrate on the chalkboard and tell the children that they will be taught how to connect the *b, o, v,* and *w* with all other letters and with each other.

PRACTICING SIMPLE CONNECTING STROKES ON THE CHALKBOARD

On the writing lines made by the teacher on the chalkboard, single letters with uncomplicated connecting strokes should be joined to show children how they form two-letter units or three-letter units, and that when grouped to spell words, such units are thought of as word units. A word such as *ham* should be written to illustrate this.

Children should be given turns tracing over letter patterns made by the teacher on the chalkboard while the children at their seats form the letters with free arm swings. (The arm should be comfortably bent at the elbow and *not held straight out* in an unnatural position.)

Avoid using letter connections such as *bo* until the difficult connecting strokes have been taught.

PRACTICING SIMPLE CONNECTING STROKES ON NEWSPRINT

Newsprint such as the children have been using should be given to each child. They should make dots on the writing lines.

> NOTE: Some children with especially weak Kinesthetic-motor modalities may need to be given teacher-made patterns to trace. Others, by now, may be able to make good letters and to connect them without difficulty. However, *all of the children* should be introduced to letter connections and guided by the teacher.

Teacher: "Write *l l* as a two-letter unit and trace."
Class: Forms the letters with arm swings before writing on its papers.

Traces over its individually-made patterns.
Teacher: Moves about the room, checking performances and helping where there is need. "Leave a two-finger space and write *l k*."
Class: Writes the letters and traces.

The same procedure should be followed with other letters named by the teacher. When dictating three-letter units, the teacher should say, "Write *t l t, m f c, p a b*," and others.

The children should repeat, forming the letters with free arm swings first and then writing on papers. By repeating and forming the letters with arm swings, simultaneous A-V-K-m association is experienced before written performance with real words begins. The sounds of the letters should *not* be given, *only the names.*

Examples

tlt mfc pab sho

PRACTICING MORE DIFFICULT CONNECTING STROKES
(b, o, v, and w)

The letter connection strokes that are more difficult often require patterns for tracing. They should be introduced *before* they are needed in writing words or immediately preceding need if they have not been taught.

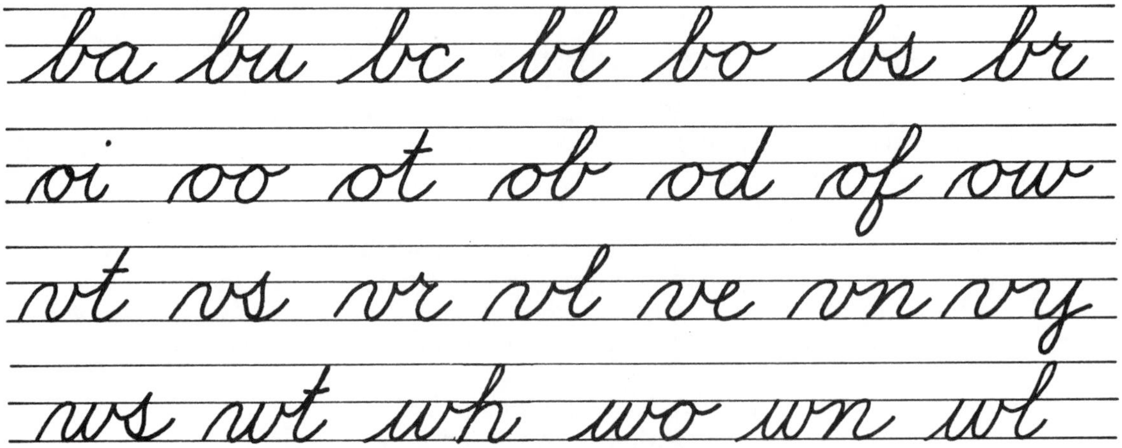

ba bu bc bl bo bs br

oi oo ot ob od of ow

vt vs vr vl ve vn vy

ws wt wh wo wn wl

The same procedures should be followed with capital letters that have strokes ending at the writing line or at some other point, such as *h* and *p* at the midline or *d, o, v,* and *w* at the top line.

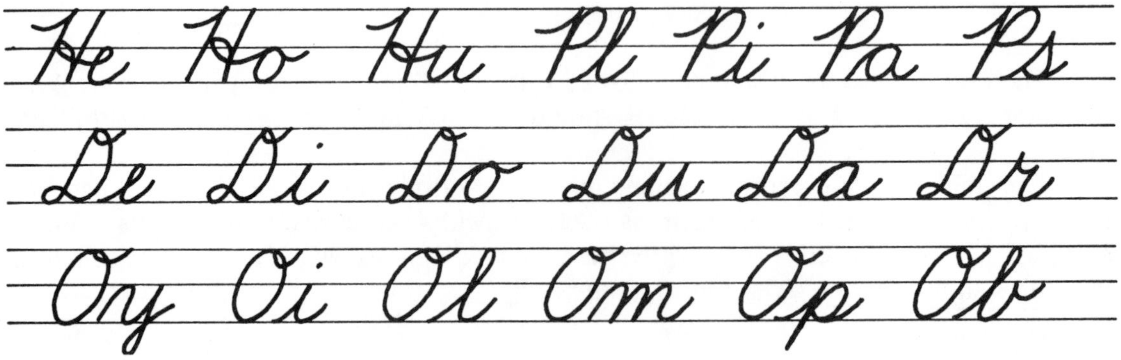

He Ho Hu Pl Pi Pa Ps

De Di Do Du Da Dr

Oy Oi Ol Om Op Ob

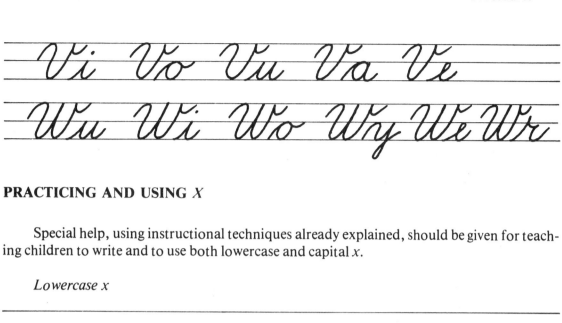

PRACTICING AND USING *X*

Special help, using instructional techniques already explained, should be given for teaching children to write and to use both lowercase and capital *x*.

Lowercase x

Capital x

Using the x

REDUCING LETTER SIZE TO COMPOSITION-PAPER SPACING

To secure small-muscle control, children should begin to reduce letter size as soon as gross motor movement and rhythmic flow from one letter to the next have brought about their Auditory-Visual-Kinesthetic-motor recall. This readiness usually occurs with the letters learned first and before all of the cursive forms have been taught or, if taught, before the gross motor movement in letter-size relationship for all of them is automatic.

During the daily period of guidance, LEARNING TO WRITE lessons should include:

- learning a letter that has not been taught (refer to pages 32-35);
- review of learned letters for practice in automatic recall and/or letter-size relationship (refer to page 39); and
- practice on 1-inch- or 1/2-inch-spaced composition paper for reducing the size of the *learned letters*.

Composition paper should be used for the children's first practice in reducing the size of the letters to 1 inch, then 1/2 inch, and, when the letters can be well made, to 3/8 inch. Eventually, lined paper of the standard spacing used by the school district can be successfully used. *Two spaces* — not one space — should continue to be used for letter formation until upper-elementary grades are reached. Reducing the letter size should come *after* letter-size relationship becomes automatic and *before* letters are put to functional use in C—Spelling, D—Dictation, or E—Propositional and Creative Writing.

The smaller letters permit complete phrases to be written on one line, enabling the children to perceive phrases as whole units, and not as individual words written on different lines. This perception adds to "phrase unit" cognition.

PRACTICING SINGLE LETTERS

Usually paper used in schools has lines arranged as shown below.

If not, the writing lines should be indicated with dots. (Refer to pages 37-38). Tall letters should be two spaces and the others, one space.

The teacher should dictate individual letters as explained on page 40. Sometimes the children should trace lightly over their own patterns until the teacher names the next one. As the children's recall of letter forms becomes automatic, the tempo of dictation should be increased *but not hurried*, to avoid frustrating the children or causing poor performance. The flow of rhythmic movement from one letter to the next should lead to the kind of performance that is needed for writing words. The sounds should not be given — only letter names should be spoken. Unless the teacher specifically asks for the dictated letters to be capitalized, they should be made in lowercase.

> NOTE: The teacher should circulate about the room to make sure that children are succeeding and working up to standard. That standard will be no higher than the teacher expects, and it cannot be attained if the teacher stands at the front of the class without closely viewing individual performances, seating positions, how pencils are held, etc. Moving about enables him or her to give assistance, commendation, and encouragement. *Practice is never meant to serve as speed drill*, but, instead, is intended to develop uninterrupted, individual, rhythmic tempos of movement from one letter to the next and from one performance to the next.

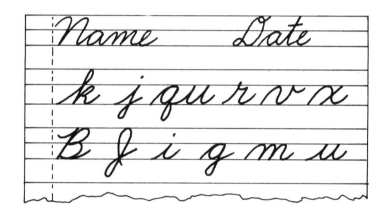

PRACTICING DOUBLE- OR TRIPLE-LETTER UNITS

Practice for rhythmic flow from one dictated single-letter unit to the next should have prepared children to write two- or three-letter units that require connections. Initial practice should require simple letter connections only, such as:

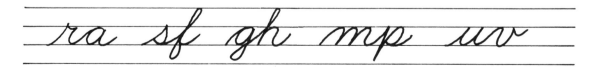

The teacher should tell the children to listen to the named letters, to repeat them orally while writing them with free arm swings, and then to write them on their papers. They should continue tracing their own patterns until the next letters are named. There should be no interruption between one performance and the next.

Forming the letters with arm swings before writing on papers should be eliminated as soon as the teacher judges that the children are ready. That step is meant only to serve as a crutch to prevent their making mistakes in written performance.

After two-letter units, three-letter units should be dictated. Again, no difficult letter connections should be required until connections of letters ending at the midline have been taught and practiced.

Teacher: "Write *s t r* together as one unit of letters."
Class:
1. Writes *s t r*, naming each letter as it is formed.
2. Traces lightly over its patterns, naming each one as it is traced until the next letters are dictated.
3. Leaves a two-finger space, writes the next letters and traces, following the usual procedure, and with no interruption between the different letter-writing performances.

When letters with more difficult connections are to be dictated, the teacher should tell the children to *think first* before beginning to write and to *remember* that letters ending at the midline connect with other letters at the midline and not at the writing line as do most of the other letters. The letter connections should have been practiced as explained on pages 43 and 47 before rhythmic flow is practiced.

Examples

Instructional techniques for integrating the teaching and practicing of handwriting will be presented in THE AUDITORY APPROACH.

NOTE: The desired goal in early-elementary grades is for children to attain automatic writing skills to use for any written requirements at any elementary grade level, on composition paper of approximately 3/8-inch spacing. Practice for legibility and good letter formation should be kept in mind even as individuality in handwriting evolves. Writing from teacher-dictation (Auditory stimulus) prepares the way for self-direction in copying (Visual stimulus), as well as for propositional writing for self-expression.

As handwriting progresses into an automatic basic skill, it should be put to use from:

an AUDITORY stimulus associated with the Visual-Kinesthetic sensory channel, enabling the student to write from dictation by another or from self-proposed individual thought and understanding.

a VISUAL stimulus associated with the Kinesthetic (and possibly Auditory) sensory channel, enabling written or printed material of another (or of self) to be copied with, or even without, understanding the meaning or ability to read what is being copied.

THE AUDITORY APPROACH TO SPELLING AND WRITTEN EXPRESSION

Lessons in THE AUDITORY APPROACH should be given at a separate time of the day from those in THE VISUAL APPROACH.

The goal of THE AUDITORY APPROACH is to aid in the development of skills for individual *output* or verbalized and written thought and ideas that originate from *inner* stimuli. It is the opposite of THE VISUAL APPROACH, in which the goal is to aid in the development of skills for individual *input* from the written thought and ideas of others which originate from *outer* stimuli.

Before using the multi-sensory approach, teachers should read Part 1, Background. It explains how to follow The Daily Format and how to integrate new material with that previously learned. Practice is directed toward independent functional use of basic language skills.

A—Alphabet Cards

INTRODUCTION

When children have not been following the continuum and are beginning this multi-sensory approach for the first time, reference should be made to A—Alphabet Cards of the earlier books in this series.* Omitting or slighting any previous steps may confuse students. Children at the third year and beyond, regardless of grade level, should start at the same point as first-year children — with the smallest units of sight-sound-feel (letters of the alphabet). However, older children can be expected to have had some previous exposure to letters of the alphabet, and with their added maturity to make progress at rates of input and output different from those of first-year beginners. Unfortunately, the failures and inadequacies in achievement and overall cognition of older children may result in negative attitudes and self-images, thereby introducing obstacles not present in the younger children. For these reasons, if for no others, it is imperative that teachers structure lessons for successful performances in such a way that each step becomes firmly implanted and integrated with previously learned steps before moving ahead to the new ones.

Practice for phoneme-grapheme (sound-symbol) perception, recall, and association of "letter units" must precede their use for blending and unlocking words. Instant, automatic, intersensory association from any given Auditory, Visual, or Kinesthetic stimulus is to be striven for — structured in THE AUDITORY APPROACH for Visual association of the written symbol when *hearing* its name and/or sound, and in THE VISUAL APPROACH for Auditory association of its name and sound when *seeing* its written form.

---

*Slingerland, *Book One — A Multi-Sensory Approach,* pp. 85, 88, 91, 98 and *Book Two — Basics in Scope and Sequence,* pp. 44–54.

With the A—Alphabet Cards of THE AUDITORY APPROACH, a short practice for sound-symbol (phoneme-grapheme) association should precede the day's lesson in B—Blending; similarly, in THE VISUAL APPROACH, a short practice for symbol-sound (grapheme-phoneme) association should precede decoding words in the B—Unlocking division of The Daily Format. (Refer to page 66 and THE VISUAL APPROACH.) Practice from Auditory stimuli prepares the way for automatic sound-to-sight symbol associations for the task of spelling whole words. *Therefore, children's success — their ability to perceive and simultaneously make Auditory-Visual-Kinesthetic associations — depends upon the teacher's learning the correct sounds and clearly enunciating single letters, phonograms (diphthongs and digraphs), and letter combinations.*

By the time the second and third years of the continuum are reached, spelling is complicated because some sounds are spelled in more than one way and all possible ways must be learned.

Common spellings for the long *a* sound,* for example, include:

a	eigh
a-e	ey
ai	ei
ay	ea

Choosing the correct grapheme *for spelling* a given sound may be difficult, yet, when *reading* is the task, there may be no more than one or two sounds for the symbol that is *seen*. For reading, the diphthongs *ai* and *ay* each say /ā/. The *ea* has three sounds — /ĕ/, /ē/, /ā/ — which require more memory but not as much as the eight spellings for the sound of the long *a*.

For the above reason, many graphemes introduced in the second year should not be employed as phonemes for blending until they have been introduced and practiced in the A—Alphabet Cards time of both THE AUDITORY and VISUAL APPROACHES and in the B—Unlocking time of THE VISUAL APPROACH. They are easier to use in reading than in spelling and, therefore, should be introduced for reading before being introduced into the steps for spelling. However, each phonetic element can and should be included in the practice *with cards* of both approaches. (Refer to pages 213-215.)

Any phonetic element that was introduced only for reading during the second year should be taught for spelling during the third year, and its use should be extended in consecutive years. This means a child must learn the different ways of spelling any given sound, and then put this learning to meaningful, functional use in spelling and written work with guidance from the teacher.

OBJECTIVES FOR A—ALPHABET CARDS

Phoneme-grapheme (sound-symbol) associations for which to strive are:
1. Consonant sounds spelled with single consonants, digraphs (*ck, ph, ch, kn, wr*), trigraphs (*dge*), *qu* and *cks,* (refer to page 54 for clarification of cks sound.), and the soft sounds of *c* and *g* when followed by *e, i* or *y.*
2. Short vowels.

*Beth H. Slingerland and Carol Murray, *Teacher's Word List for Reference, Revised Edition*, 1987.

3. Long-vowel sounds spelled with vowel-consonant-*e* (*v-e*), vowels at the end of accented (open) syllables, diphthongs (*ai, ea, ie*), and vowel digraphs (*ee, ea, ie*).
4. Various vowel sounds spelled with phonograms.
5. Consonant-vowel "sound units" spelled with letter combinations (*ink, ung, tion, sion, ple, tle*).
6. Consonant sounds spelled with digraphs (*sh, ch*) or trigraphs (*tch*).

Not all phoneme-grapheme units shown below will be, nor should have been, taught during the second year of the continuum. Those that have been, should be reviewed, retaught, and introduced to newcomers in an SLD classroom. Some of them, shown with asterisks, are not meant for presentation until children reach upper-elementary or junior high levels, but teachers should be familiar with them for unexpected or exceptional needs that may arise. To teach superfluous concepts is to confuse and distort children's "thought patterns" when they are putting these "sound-symbol units" to use in spelling words.

PHONEMES AND GRAPHEMES FOR AUDITORY-VISUAL-KINESTHETIC ASSOCIATION

Phoneme or Sound*	Key Word**	Grapheme or Symbol
1. Consonants		
/b/, not /bŭh/	ball	b
/k/, not /kŭh/	*c*ake	c
	*k*ite	k
	Ja*ck*	ck (consonant digraph) Appears only at the end of words and follows a single vowel.
	***Christmas	ch
/d/, not /dŭh/	duck	d
/f/, not /fŭh/	fish	f
	*ph*one	ph (consonant digraph)
/g/, not /gŭh/	goat	g
/h/, not /hŭh/	house	h

Only air is expelled. Walls of throat do not touch.

*Diacritical markings are based on *Webster's New Collegiate Dictionary* (Springfield, Mass.: G. & C. Merriam Co., 1958). Because of the variations in conversational language with the diacritical marks used in the dictionary cited, an explanation should be given to the children about the ongoing changes in our written and spoken language.

**Most of the key words are the same as those used on the Handschug *Manuscript Alphabet Wall Cards*, available from Educators Publishing Service, Inc. A few key words listed here differ from those printed in *Teacher's Word Lists*. For various reasons, different school systems may choose different key words. The important point is that a word selected should be used consistently for that particular grapheme by all of the teachers throughout the grades.

***Words with asterisks can be introduced for spelling in upper-elementary grades and junior high but not in third grade, except in rare instances. Many of the grapheme counterparts *can be learned for reading* long before they should be expected to be used in spelling. If needed for spelling, they can be learned as Red Flag words.

Phoneme or Sound	Key Word	Grapheme or Symbol
/j/, not /jŭh/	jam	j
	gem	g (sometimes soft, followed by *e, i,* or *y*)
	bri*dge*	dge (trigraph) Appears only at the end of words and follows a single vowel.
/l/, not /lŭh/ not /ŭl/	lamp	l

The /l/ sound can be *felt* if prolonged until the throat opens on the short *a* sound of *lamp*.

| /m/, not /mŭh/ | mittens | m |

For /m/ the lips stay closed.

/n/, not /nŭh/	nest	n
	*kn*ife	kn (consonant digraph)
/p/, not /pŭh/	pig	p
/kw/, not /kwŭh/	*qu*een	qu In our language, *q* generally is followed by *u* and should not be learned as *q* alone but as a single unit, *qu*.
/r/, not /rŭh/ not /ûr/	rug	r

The /r/ can be felt if prolonged until the throat opens on the short *u* of *rug*.

	*wrist	wr (consonant digraph)
/s/, not /sŭh/	sun	s
	*c*inch or i*c*e	c (soft, followed by *e, i,* or *y*)
/t/, not /tŭh/	turtle	t
/v/, not /vŭh/	vase	v (Refer to page 207.)
/w/, not /wŭh/	wagon	w

First, say *agon*, and by contrast, the /w/ sound can be heard and felt when the whole word *wagon* is pronounced.

---

*Words with asterisks can be introduced for spelling in upper-elementary grades and junior high but not in third grade, except in rare instances. Many of the grapheme counterparts *can be learned for reading* long before they should be expected to be used in spelling. If needed for spelling, they can be learned as Red Flag words.

Phoneme or Sound	Key Word	Grapheme or Symbol
/ks/, not /ĕks/	bo*x*	x In our language, *x* saying /ks/ is never found at the beginning of words or syllables, only at the end.
	jac*ks*	cks Can be confused with *x* when the *s* is a suffix or forms the plural when the word ends in the /k/ sound.
/y/, not /yŭh/ Instead of saying *yellow*, first say *ellow*; the sound and feel of the *y* can be perceived when included in the whole word *yellow*.	yellow	y
/z/, not /zŭh/	zebra wa*s* or ro*s*e	z s

2. *Vowels (short)*

/ă/	apple	a
/ĕ/	elephant	e
	head	ea
/ĭ/	inch	i
	*g*y*m* or c*y*nic	y
	*misch*ie*f	ie
/ŏ/	olives	o
/ŭ/	umbrella	u
(same as schwa sound)	*h*o*ney	o

3. *Vowels (long)*

	*p*a*rade′	a (end of unaccented syllable)
/ā/	b*a*by	a (end of accented syllable)
	r*ai*n	ai (diphthong)
	pl*ay*	ay
	s*a*f*e*	a-e (*a*-consonant-*e*)
	sl*eigh*	eigh
	st*ea*k	ea (diphthong)
	*th*ey*	ey
	*v*ei*n	ei

*Words with asterisks can be introduced for spelling in upper-elementary grades and junior high but not in third grade, except in rare instances. Many of the grapheme counterparts *can be learned for reading* long before they should be expected to be used in spelling. If needed for spelling, they can be learned as Red Flag words.

Phoneme or Sound	Key Word	Grapheme or Symbol
/ē/	meter	e (end of accented syllable)
	th*ese*	e-e
	feet	ee (vowel digraph)
	eat	ea (digraph)
	chief	ie (digraph)
/ī/	t*i*ger	i (end of accented syllable)
	p*ine*	i-e
	*pie	ie (diphthong)
	*sky or cycle	y (end of accented syllable)
	*t*y*pe	y-e
/ō/	p*o*ny	o (end of accented syllable)
	h*ome*	o-e
	boat	oa
	snow	ow
/ū/	m*u*sic	u (end of accented syllable)
	m*ule*	u-e
	few	ew
	*resc*ue*	ue
	*feud	eu
	*suit	ui

4. Various Vowel Sounds Spelled with Phonograms

Phoneme or Sound	Key Word	Grapheme or Symbol
/o͞o/	moon	oo
	grew	ew
	fl*ute*	u-e
	l*u*nar	u (end of accented syllable)
	*soup	ou
/o͝o/	book	oo
/ou/	ouch	ou
	cow	ow
/oi/	oil	oi
	boy	oy
/ô/	saw	aw
	author	au
/är/	star	ar
/ôr/	corn	or
/ûr/	her	er
	girl	ir
	burn	ur
	*ear*th	ear
	w*o*rk	or (preceded by *w*—wor)

*Words with asterisks can be introduced for spelling in upper-elementary grades and junior high but not in third grade, except in rare instances. Many of the grapheme counterparts *can be learned for reading* long before they should be expected to be used in spelling. If needed for spelling, they can be learned as Red Flag words.

Phoneme or Sound	Key Word	Grapheme or Symbol
/ẽr/	*dollar	ar
	*visitor or educator	or

5. Letter Combinations as "Single Units"

Phoneme or Sound	Key Word	Grapheme or Symbol
/ĭng/	sing	ing
/ŭng/	sung	ung
/ĭngk/	think	ink
/ăngk/	thank	ank
/shŭn/	nation	tion
	*mission	sion
/zhŭn/	*vision	sion
/p'l/	purple	ple
/t'l/	little	tle

(Refer to THE VISUAL APPROACH, page 223.)

6. Consonant Digraphs

Phoneme or Sound	Key Word	Grapheme or Symbol
/ch/, not /chŭh/	chair	ch
	match	tch (trigraph)

(Refer to THE VISUAL APPROACH, page 208.)

Phoneme or Sound	Key Word	Grapheme or Symbol
/sh/	ship	sh
	*chef	ch
	*partial	ti
	*social	ci
	*ocean	ce
/th/, not /thŭh/	thimble	th
/t̶h̶/, not /thŭh/	this	th
/hw/, not /hwŭh/	wheel	wh

Blow out, as in blowing out a candle.

MATERIALS

Teacher's Hand Pack for Classroom Use
Yellow Card Pack
Phonogram, Suffix and Prefix Kit

*Words with asterisks can be introduced for spelling in upper-elementary grades and junior high but not in third grade, except in rare instances. Many of the grapheme counterparts *can be learned for reading* long before they should be expected to be used in spelling. If needed for spelling, they can be learned as Red Flag words.

PROCEDURES

Before letters of the alphabet can be used functionally in spelling and writing words, there must be automatic, simultaneous A-V-K association from any one of the three sensory stimuli. When the stimulus is Auditory, as it is in THE AUDITORY APPROACH, the children *should not see the symbol* while hearing its sound given by the teacher. Practice with the letters provides *output* for the performing child and *input* for the class, and complete *review* of simultaneous multi-sensory Visual-Auditory-Kinesthetic association for all of the children when they *repeat*. The time devoted to A—Alphabet Cards of THE AUDITORY APPROACH is for strengthening and reinforcing Visual-Kinesthetic association from *Auditory stimuli* — a language skill required in encoding words for spelling.

There should be a short daily practice (four to seven minutes) preceding the encoding of the B—Blending period to ensure simultaneous associations without hesitation or need of prompting.

During the transition from manuscript to cursive, the children should be expected to use cursive for the letters that they have learned in LEARNING TO WRITE and to use manuscript for those that they have not been taught. After learning all the letters, they should be expected to use cursive entirely and not to mix cursive and manuscript letter forms while carrying out a single task.

> NOTE: After a class has been following the continuum for two or three years, it should not be necessary for the entire group to repeat after each child's performance. The teacher, however, should be sure to expose the card at the conclusion of each child's performance for complete and correct Visual-Auditory association. Also, a child who has just entered the group should repeat after each performance to reinforce perception and recall.

USING THE TEACHER'S HAND PACK

To begin, the *Teacher's Hand Pack for Classroom Use* should be arranged in two packs — one composed of the sight-sound units known to all of the children and the other of the units yet to be taught and transferred to the pack of learned units. How long it will take to consolidate the two packs will depend upon the children's abilities to perceive, store, and recall, which in turn will depend largely on the regularity of daily practice and the skill of the teacher.

Only the teacher should hold the Hand Pack. He or she should give the sound correctly and audibly. The card should not be exposed until the child's performance is completed.

The Auditory sound should be associated with its Visual and Kinesthetic counterparts when the child *names* the letters visualized internally and, with arm swings, forms the letter(s) as visualized. When correctly done, the teacher must expose the card to reinforce Auditory-Visual-Kinesthetic association.

To introduce the lesson, the teacher should say: "I will give the sound, and call upon someone to spell it. Then the class will repeat unless a mistake is made. If so, *be silent and I will not expose the card* until the child I called upon has corrected the mistake if he or she can. If not, another one of you will be asked to do so. When the right spelling is given, I will expose the card, and all of you will repeat.''

NOTE: After no more than two such introductions, the teacher seldom needs to do more than say, ''I will give the sound for you to tell about and to spell.''

Examples

Teacher:	Gives a sound, such as /kw/.
Child:	''*Q-u*,'' forming letters with arm swings, ''queen, /kw/.''
Teacher:	Exposes card.
Class:	Repeats, ''*Q-u*,'' using arm swings, ''queen, /kw/.''
Teacher:	''/oi/, as in boy.''*
Child:	''*O-y*,'' using arm swings, ''boy, /oi/.''
Teacher:	Exposes card.
Class:	Repeats.
Teacher:	''/oi/, as in oil.''
Child:	''*O-i*,'' using arm swings, ''oil, /oi/.''
Teacher:	Exposes card.
Class:	Repeats.
Teacher:	''/är/.''
Child:	''*A-r*,'' using arm swings, ''star, /är/.''
Teacher:	Exposes card.
Class:	Repeats.
Teacher:	''/ŭng/.''
Child:	''*U-n-g*,'' using arm swings, ''sung, /ŭng/.''
Teacher:	Exposes card.
Class:	Repeats.
Teacher:	''/ā/, as in rain.''
Child:	''*A-i*,'' using arm swings, ''rain, /ā/.''
Teacher:	Exposes card.
Class:	Repeats.
Teacher:	''/ā/, as in sleigh.''
Child:	''*E-i-g-h*,'' using arm swings, ''sleigh, /ā/.''
Teacher:	Exposes card.
Class:	Repeats.
Teacher:	''/ū/, as in mule.''
Child:	''*U*-consonant-*e*,'' using full arm swings to form the *u* and *e* and a left-to-right dash to stand for the word *consonant*, ''mule, /ū/.''
Teacher:	Exposes card.
Class:	Repeats.

*Refer to Slingerland, *Phonogram Chart*. The key word for the ''sound unit'' must be given because there is more than one way to spell /oi/ — *oi* and *oy*. Unless they know which spelling is expected, the children might not use the right phonogram.

Teacher: "/hw/, as in wheel" (being sure to *blow* the sound out).
Child: "*W-h*," using arm swings, "wheel, /hw/."
Teacher: Exposes card.
Class: Repeats.

Examples of phonemes to be used in a day's lesson

/ōō/	as in *grew*	*ew*
/ôr/	as in *corn*	*or*
/ō/	as in *home*	*o–e*
/ou/	as in *ouch*	*ou*
/ou/	as in *cow*	*ow*
/ô/	as in *author*	*au*
/ă/	as in *apple*	*a*
/ē/	as in *these*	*e-e*
/ûr/	as in *burn*	*ur*
/shŭn/	as in *nation*	*tion*
/ăngk/	as in *thank*	*ank*
/ē/	as in *chief*	*ie*
/y/	(consonant sound)	*y*
/ĕ/	as in *head*	*ea*

Examples (including some of the more difficult phonemes) for children at more advanced levels

/t'l/	as in *little*	*tle*
/n/	as in *knife*	*kn*
/z/	as in *zebra*	*z*
/z/	as in *rose*	*s*
/ū/	at the end of an accented syllable	*u*
/k/	as in *chorus* or *Christmas*	*ch*
/k/	as in *Jack*	*ck*
/v/	as in *vase*	*v*
/ch/	as in *chair*	*ch*
/b/	as in *ball*	*b*
/kw/	as in *queen*	*qu*

/t̶h̶/	as in *this*	th
/ch/	as in *match*	tch
/ō/	as in *boat*	oa
/j/	as in *bridge*	dge
/j/	as in *jam*	j
/o͞o/	as in *flute*	u-e

USING THE YELLOW CARD PACK

The *Yellow Card Pack* should be brought into use as soon as the children begin to learn more than one way to spell a given sound. (Refer to pages 52-56.) This first occurs in the first grade with the sound /k/, spelled with *c, k,* or *ck*. At the upper-elementary or secondary levels, the *ch* will be added for words such as *chorus, choir, school, architect, chrome, chlorine,* and *Christmas* (from Latin derivation).

When more than one way of spelling a given sound is being learned and put to functional use, the *Yellow Card Pack* should be used during the time devoted to A—Alphabet Card practice of THE AUDITORY APPROACH. (The *Yellow Card Pack* is not intended for use in THE VISUAL APPROACH.)

Example

Teacher: "Tell all the ways you know to spell the sound /oi/."
Child: "*O-i*, oil, /oi/ and *o-y*, boy, /oi/."
Teacher: Exposes the Yellow Card.
Class: Repeats the spelling as shown on the card to strengthen simultaneous Auditory-Visual-Kinesthetic association as the teacher points to each grapheme while it is being spelled.

NOTE: The letters should be made with free arm swings. Boys and girls who are being taught in very small groups or as individuals at the *secondary level* may use the first two fingers to write with free arm swings on desks for the tactile sensation it provides. In classrooms, the teacher would not be able to observe children's performances satisfactorily if done in that way. Therefore, forming letters on desks is discouraged.

Teacher: "Tell all the ways you know for spelling the sound /ĕ/."
Child: "*E*, elephant, /ĕ/ and *e-a*, head, /ĕ/."
Teacher: Exposes the Yellow Card.
Class: Repeats as the teacher points to each grapheme while it is being spelled.

Teacher: "Tell all the ways you know of spelling /o͞o/."
Child: "*O-o*, moon, /o͞o/; *u* at the end of a syllable, lunar, /o͞o/; *u*-consonant-*e*, flute, /o͞o/; *e-w*, grew, /o͞o/."
Teacher: Exposes the Yellow Card.

Class: Repeats in the order the spellings appear on the card while the teacher points to each grapheme as it is named.

Teacher: "The sound /ē/."

Child: "*E* at the end of a syllable, meter, /ē/; *e*-consonant-*e*, these, /ē/; *e-e*, feet, /ē/; *e-a,* eat, /ē/; *i–e*, chief, /ē/; *y*, candy, /ē/."

Teacher: Exposes the Yellow Card.

Class: Repeats in the order in which the spellings appear on the Yellow Card (not necessarily in the order the child may have given them).

The children should be expected to give only the spellings that they have been taught for a given sound. They should understand that any spellings which have not been taught, but which appear on a card, are to be omitted until they have been introduced. The unlearned spellings on the card will be taught at a later time. (Some of the children learn them on their own as they master the concept of ambiguously spelled words.)

PRACTICE TO REINFORCE RECALL OF AMBIGUOUS SPELLING

After children have learned different ways of spelling a given sound, they enjoy this practice. One child should be asked by the teacher to stand at the front of the room with his or her back to the class. The teacher should stand facing the class but where the child "having the turn" cannot see the *Yellow Card Pack* held in the teacher's hands. The teacher should expose a Yellow Card for the class to see while the child is asked to tell all the different known ways to spell the sound given by the teacher.

1. The performing child should not be able to see the card but from the Auditory stimulus given by the teacher should make the simultaneous Auditory-Visual-Kinesthetic associations from memory alone. Without this memory, the different spellings cannot be used functionally.

2. The teacher should point on the Yellow Card to the grapheme spelled by the child while the class watches and listens.

3. The class always can associate the spelling by the performing child with the grapheme pointed to by the teacher as the child spells — an *output* for the individual child and a complete *input* for the children in the class.

Teacher: Exposes the Yellow Card on which the different ways of spelling a sound, such as /n/, are shown for the class, but not the performing child, to see. Says, "/n/."

Child: "*N*, nest, /n/ and *k-n*, knife, /n/," forming each letter with arm swings as it is named.

The teacher and the class say, "Right," or "OK," as the teacher exposes the card for the child to see as he or she turns around — a Visual reinforcement for the child such as the class had while he or she was performing. Then the entire class repeats for further reinforcement as the teacher points to each grapheme while it is being spelled. Another child is chosen and the same procedure is followed.

Teacher: Exposes a Yellow Card for only the class to see. "Spell all the ways you know for the sound /ō/."

Child: "*O* at the end of a syllable, pony, /ō/; *o-w*, snow, /ō/; *o-a*, boat, /ō/." (If another learned way cannot be recalled, the teacher should give the *key word* to assist memory by saying, "*O* as in home." Usually that triggers recall and the child will say, "*O-consonant-e*, home, /ō/."

Teacher: Exposes card for the child, as well as the class, to see.

Class: Repeats each spelling, using full arm swings as the teacher points to each spelling on the card.

Teacher: "Spell /ûr/."

Child: "*E–r*, her, /ûr/; *i–r*, girl, /ûr/; *u-r*, burn, /ûr/." forming each letter as it is named.

Teacher: Exposes card for the child, as well as the other children, to see.

Class: Repeats as teacher points to each grapheme while it is being spelled.

NOTE: If upper levels have learned *a-r*, dollar, /ēr/ and *o-r*, visitor or educator, /ēr/, they should be included.

WRITING FROM
AUDITORY (PHONEME)–VISUAL (GRAPHEME) ASSOCIATION

The procedures described above and the *Teacher's Hand Pack for Classroom Use* or the *Yellow Card Pack* should be used for writing the letters on lined paper. This practice also gives good experience in the organization and functional use of automatic writing skills, provided the teacher has given appropriate preparation and has instilled in the children high standards of performance in learning handwriting.

At this level of achievement, the lesson periods for LEARNING TO WRITE and A—Alphabet Cards can be combined into an integrated lesson for practice in simultaneous association of a given sound with its corresponding Visual symbol and its Kinesthetic-motor "feel" for formation of letters as described in the sample lessons below.

NOTE: The teacher must be sure that every letter to be used has been taught, with practice for its automatic recall, in previous LEARNING TO WRITE lessons.

SAMPLE LESSON USING THE TEACHER'S HAND PACK

Each child should be given composition paper with 1-, 1/2-, or 3/8-inch spacing, depending on how far advanced each is in learning cursive forms and their letter connections. The papers should be folded into columns to allow graphemes to be written one under the other. Also, it helps to have the writing lines numbered.

Teacher: "What says /ûr/ as in burn?"

Child: "*U-r*, burn, /ûr/," forming letters with arm swings.

Teacher: Exposes the card.
Class: Repeats, "*U-r*, burn, /ûr/," forming letters with arm swings. Writes *u r* on papers, softly naming each letter as it is formed.

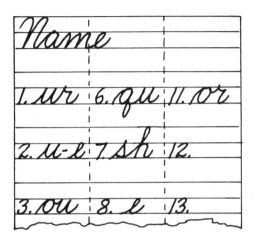 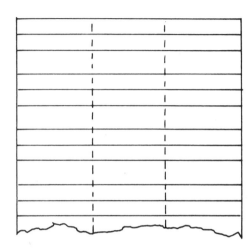

As the children begin to make automatic associations, *"crutches" may be withdrawn.* The teacher should 1) give the sound (and the key word when needed), 2) call upon a child to give the answer for the class to hear, 3) expose the card, and then, 4) have the class write directly on their papers, eliminating the repetition and arm swings as shown in the previous example.

Teacher: "/ī/, as in pine."
Child: "*I-consonant-e*, pine, /ī/," forming letters with arm swings.
Teacher: Exposes card.
Class: Writes directly on papers, softly naming each letter as it is written.

Eventually, practice procedure can be changed to require greater memory of letter formation by exposing the card after the class has written the letters.

Teacher: "/är/, as in star."
Child: "*A-r*, star, /är/."
Class: Writes on paper.
Teacher: Exposes the card where it can be seen by all of the children. Moves about the room checking children's work.

If guidance is to be effective, the teacher must give meaningful help at the moment of need and before the lesson is concluded.

SAMPLE LESSON USING THE YELLOW CARD PACK

When the children understand that often there is more than one way to spell a given sound, especially vowel sounds, the teacher should give the sound only — no key words —

and an individual child should tell all of the different ways that have been learned by spelling each one, naming each key word, and giving the sound of each one. Then the Yellow Card should be exposed for the children in the class to see; they should repeat and write the spellings. To develop memory, the card should *not* be left exposed.

Teacher: "Tell all the ways you know to spell the sound /j/."
Child: "*J*, jam, /j/; *d-g-e*, bridge, /j/; and sometimes *g* followed by *e, i,* or *y.*"
Teacher: Exposes card.
Class: Repeats as the teacher points to each grapheme as it is being spelled.
Teacher: Removes card from sight.
Class: Writes each spelling on papers — on the same line, one after the other.
Teacher: Moves about the room to make sure performances are correctly done, and then exposes the card for a final check.

NOTE: As the children write their answers one after the other on the line, the teacher has the opportunity to show how well-made commas or dashes can be used to separate each spelling, as with the *j* sound: *j, dge* or *j — dge.*

Follow the same procedure for other spellings.*

Teacher: "The sound /ē/."
Child: "*E* at the end of a syllable, *me*ter, /ē/; *e-e*, feet, /ē/; *e–a*, eat, /ē/; *e*-consonant-*e*, these, /ē/; *i–e*, chief, /ē/."

NOTE: If the *y* has not yet been learned, it should be omitted; otherwise, it should be included, the child saying, "*Y*, candy, /ē/." Until recently the /ē/ sound for *y* was not recognized; only the short *i* sound, /ĭ/, was acceptable.

Letters should be placed on the children's papers as follows:

Name   *Date*

j, dge

e, ee, ea, e-e, y, ie

ar

---

*Slingerland, *Teacher's Word Lists*, p. 1.

Examples of other phoneme spellings

/är/	as in *star*	*ar*
/ch/	as in *chair*	*ch*
	as in *match*	*tch*
/b/	as in *ball*	*b*
/ăngk/	as in *thank*	*ank*
/oi/	as in *oil*	*oi*
	as in *boy*	*oy*
/ou/	as in *ouch*	*ou*
	as in *cow*	*ow*
/o͞o/	as in *moon*	*oo*
	as in *flute*	*u*-consonant-*e*
	as in *lunar*	*u* at the end
	or *ruby*	of syllable
	as in *soup*	*ou*

The children should be expected to give only the spellings they have been taught for a given sound. Gradually withdraw "crutches" as explained for the practice with the Teacher's Hand Pack. (Refer to page 63.)

> NOTE: The practice explained above serves as recall-output from an Auditory stimulus for the performing child and more input for the listeners, with review in multi-sensory association, including Kinesthetic-motor movement required for writing.

Learning the different ways of spelling a single unit or sound serves as an initial structured step for beginning functional use of the dictionary *before* its independent use can be expected.

Phonograms, diphthongs, digraphs, and letter combinations usually are introduced in THE VISUAL APPROACH and are put to immediate use in unlocking words as a reading skill before they are carried over to THE AUDITORY APPROACH for encoding of ambiguous or Yellow Flag words as a spelling skill.

B—Blending

INTRODUCTION

Blending is a basic skill which leads into spelling (encoding), an essential skill for written expression. It should precede the more complicated and demanding steps in learning to spell, which will be elaborated on in C—Spelling. Within The Daily Format, B—Blending is essentially a time to teach that the letters have no meaning other than their names until they become integral parts of "word units." (Words, of course, are the smallest units of speech that have meaning when taken by themselves.) It provides time for *input* as well as *output* under the teacher's direction and guidance. It also affords a definite time to introduce, review, and practice phoneme-grapheme association, an integral step in word formation.

Many of the phonemes may have been introduced as graphemes in B—Unlocking of THE VISUAL APPROACH and practice on them may have been given in A—Alphabet Cards for associations from either Visual or Auditory stimuli. The children who are new to the program require specific teaching by the teacher, but experience has shown that they also learn from observing, hearing, and repeating the classroom practice of their more experienced peers. Children who have been continuously enrolled in this multi-sensory approach can be expected to have learned in the first year the blending technique, which is the same with phonograms (diphthongs and vowel digraphs), letter combinations, and vowel-consonant-*e* as with short vowels. This blending technique is the same as the one taught in the primary grades.* Additional ways of spelling and using the phonemes with different vowels, consonants, letter combinations, and vowel-consonant-*e* patterns in words should now be taught. The new letter units should be explained and integrated with the known units under the guidance of the teacher. Both oral and written blending should be included in THE AUDITORY APPROACH of The Daily Format.

> NOTE: Children who have been in primary SLD classrooms which follow this multi-sensory approach can be expected to have learned to blend words by using some of the long and short vowels, phonograms (diphthongs and digraphs), vowel-consonant-*e*, and letter combination sounds for spelling words. However, to assume that they have learned all of them or can recall and use them securely at this time would be a mistake on the part of the teacher.

While the teaching of cursive writing is being emphasized, written work should be de-emphasized until the children can form the new letters and their connections automatically. Therefore, before they are expected to write the words that they blend in oral practice, the children should form the words on the Chart Holder. By doing so, they review letters and phonograms taught in the second year of the continuum and learn to blend new ones. Known suffixes and those to be introduced should be added, extending the suffix concept that was developed in the first years to individual verbalized and written self-expression.

*Slingerland, *Book Two — Basics in Scope and Sequence*, pp. 54–81.

Blending on the Chart Holder ensures that the correct thought pattern for blending is being followed by each child. (Refer to pages 69-72.) Also, this practice allows the children to experience a gross motor body movement for correct letter sequencing when they form words with the *Small Manuscript Alphabet Cards.*

The initial stimulus for encoding is auditory. The word pronounced by the teacher can be *heard* but not seen. The end result should be a word that can be *seen* after its Auditory perception has been associated with its Visual counterpart. Oral spelling alone, without seeing the word formed either with cards or in handwriting, is not enough and fails to serve the complete, simultaneous multi-sensory association needs of the SLD child. Therefore, while cursive handwriting is being learned, use of the Chart Holder enables practice in Auditory-Visual association while reviewing known phonograms and introducing new ones. When the children repeat the word and write it, Auditory-Visual-Kinesthetic multi-sensory association is strengthened.

Next, words containing letters that have been taught in cursive writing can be blended orally and then in written form without waiting for the entire alphabet to be learned in cursive. In the beginning, writing and blending should be kept as two distinct skills that SLD children must learn through conscious effort. After both the handwriting and blending have been made reasonably secure as separate tasks, they should be combined. Children usually do this without difficulty. By eliminating the need to concentrate on how to form a letter and/or how to blend the word, concentration can be focused on the word itself and written blending approached as a single task.

Each day's lesson plan should include a time both for review and/or introduction of new concepts. Often, a newly introduced phoneme should be practiced on the Chart Holder for a lesson or two before it is practiced in writing. This procedure ensures that the children understand what they are doing and avoids confusion and unnecessary mistakes.

The blending practice given herein should prepare the way for the more complex steps necessary for learning to spell and for propositional writing. It also provides for review and "overteaching" to strengthen recall and automatic performance.

OBJECTIVES FOR B—BLENDING

The objectives listed below are those that can be followed with children who have been in the first and second years of the continuum and are ready for the third year. *The objectives extend into upper-elementary grades four, five, and six.* How far a third-year child can progress depends upon his or her prior learning and experience, the degree of individual disability, and the teacher's education and experience in teaching Specific Language Disability children.

As already mentioned on page 65 of A—Alphabet Cards, the "single units" of sight-sound-feel to be taught for blending should be introduced in THE VISUAL APPROACH and practiced for simultaneous association from either Visual or Auditory stimuli in both THE VISUAL and THE AUDITORY APPROACH of the A—Alphabet Card time of each day's lesson plan. Instructional techniques for blending are explained in the Procedures section. Lists of words for quick reference can be found in *Teacher's Word Lists for Reference** (*TWL*).

*Slingerland and Murray, *Teacher's Word Lists Revised*

The children should be able to blend the following new Auditory-Visual (phoneme-grapheme) "sound units" with units that have already been learned:

One-syllable phonetic, short-vowel words (Green Flag),* such as r*i*b, r*a*nt, bl*u*nt, cl*e*ft, and cl*o*mp (*TWL*, pages 6-14).

One-syllable phonetic words that contain diphthongs and digraphs (Yellow Flag),* such as str*ai*n, t*oa*st, str*ee*t, h*ou*nd, sw*oo*p, p*oi*nt, br*igh*t, sl*eigh*, and qu*oi*ts (*TWL*, pages 23-33).

One-syllable phonetic words that contain vowel-consonant-*e* (v-*e*) such as br*a*v*e*, th*e*s*e*, str*i*p*e*, cr*a*z*e*, sh*o*r*e*, including both sounds of *u*-consonant-*e* (*u*-*e*): /ū/ as in p*u*r*e*, m*u*l*e*, c*u*b*e*, and /o͞o/ as in fl*u*t*e*, r*u*l*e*, and r*u*d*e* (*TWL*, pages 37-38).

One-syllable phonetic words that contain letter combinations, such as r*ing*, sl*ang*, th*ink*, s*unk*, fl*ung*, and dr*ank* (*TWL*, pages 35-36).

One-syllable phonetic words that contain consonant digraphs, such as hu*sh*, *sh*ed, *wh*en, mir*th*, *th*irst, *wh*ich, *wh*ite, *ch*urn, *kn*ow, *kn*ee, *ph*one, *Ph*il, *th*is, brea*th*, *wr*ite, and *wr*ing (*TWL*, pages 15-17).

One-syllable phonetic words that contain phonograms, such as c*ar*t, t*or*n, j*er*k, b*ur*st, squ*ir*m, and f*or*k. With upper-grade children, *ear* /ûr/ as in *ear*n, l*ear*n, and *ear*th; and *or* when preceded by *w* /ûr/, as in (w)*or*m, (w)*or*th, (w)*or*k, (w)*or*d, (w)*or*st, and (w)*or*ld (*TWL*, pages 21-22, 30-31).

One-syllable phonetic words that contain one vowel followed by the trigraphs *tch* and *dge*, such as bu*dge*, scra*tch*, pi*tch*, lo*dge*, cru*tch*, swi*tch*, fu*dge*, and e*dge* (*TWL*, pages 15, 18).

One-syllable phonetic words that contain *c* with a soft sound and *g* with a soft sound *sometimes* when followed by *e, i,* or *y,* such as *c*ell, spru*c*e, ri*c*e, flee*c*e, *c*inch, *c*ent, *g*ym, *g*em, *c*ite, wa*g*e, and gor*g*e (*TWL*, pages 55-56).

Two-syllable phonetic words that contain short vowels in each syllable with two like consonants in the medial position, such as ten-n*i*s, rab-b*i*t, m*u*f-f*i*n, pol-len, gos-sip, hap-pen, and *a*n-ne*x* (*TWL*, pages 45, 46, 48).

Two-syllable phonetic words that contain short vowels in each syllable with two unlike consonants in the medial position, such as ban-y*a*n, *a*n-v*i*l, c*a*t-nip, pl*a*s-tic, sus-pend, im-press, and c*a*m-p*u*s (*TWL*, pages 45, 46, 48.)

Two-syllable phonetic words that contain a short-vowel syllable (vowel followed by one or more consonants) and a silent-*e* syllable, such as ruf-*fle*, dim-*ple*, bub-*ble*, smug-*gle*, daz-*zle*, tus-*sle*, top-*ple*, and thim-*ble* (*TWL*, pages 45, 46, 47).

Two-syllable phonetic words that contain a short-vowel syllable and a vowel-consonant-*e* syllable, such as in-h*a*le, c*a*s-cade, gr*a*n-ule, sun-shade, em-pire, cos-tume, wish-bone, and st*a*m-pede (*TWL*, pages 45, 46, 49).

Two-syllable phonetic words that contain a short-vowel syllable and a phonogram syllable, such as ex-pl*oi*t, hor-net, mar-mot, whip-cord, Nor-man, mas-toid, with-out, and saw-dust (*TWL*, pages 45, 46, 49).

Two-syllable phonetic words that contain an accented long-vowel syllable (an open syllable, e.g., one with a vowel at the *end*) and a syllable that contains a previously learned "vowel-sound unit," such as r*i*-val, r*i*-*fle*, tu-nic, tr*i*-pod, to-tem, pro-file, t*i*-rade, se-quel, fra-cus, Ve-nus, and no-*ble* (*TWL*, pages 45, 46, 50).

---

* Refer to page 95 for definitions.

Two-syllable phonetic words that contain a syllable with soft *c* or soft *g*, such as *gen-tle, cen-sus, gi-rate, ci-der, cir-cus, ac-cept, voy-age, in-dulge,* and *ad-vance* (*TWL*, pages 55-56).

Two-syllable or multisyllabic phonetic words that contain short-vowel syllables and a letter combination, such as *men-tion, suc-tion, ten-sion, sus-pen-sion, in-ven-tion, con-struc-tion, af-flic-tion,* and *con-nec-tion* (*TWL*, pages 51, 52).

Two-syllable or multisyllabic phonetic words that contain one syllable with a letter combination, such as *blank-et, trink-et, em-bank-ment, yank-ee,* and *sunk-en* (*TWL*, pages 35, 36).

Two-syllable or multisyllabic phonetic words that contain long-vowel syllables and a letter combination, such as *lo-tion, na-tion, mo-tion, sta-tion, so-lu-tion, pro-fu-sion, in-clu-sion,* and *e-va-sion* (*TWL*, pages 35, 36).

One-syllable, two-syllable, or multisyllabic phonetic words that contain prefixes, such as *dis-like, re-did, re-surge, mis-fit, mis-step, mis-treat, re-lo-cate, mis-fire, dis-o-bey, re-pol-ish, dis-em-bark, dis-en-chant, re-e-lect, mis-re-port, mis-shape, mis-han-dle,* and *mis-judge* (*TWL*, pages 43-44).

Multisyllabic phonetic words that contain any unit already learned, such as *ven-ti-late, gran-u-late, min-i-mum, man-do-lin, in-ter-lude, in-fec-tion, re-se-clude, leath-er, por-trait,* and *dis-taste-ful* (*TWL*, pages 44, 49, 51, 53).

MATERIALS

Chart Holder and *Small Manuscript Alphabet Cards*
Teacher's Hand Pack for Classroom Use
Teacher's Word Lists for Reference Revised
Phonogram, Suffix, and Prefix Kit
Composition paper

PROCEDURES

ONE-SYLLABLE WORDS

BLENDING ORALLY USING THE CHART HOLDER

The Chart Holder should be placed where it can be seen readily by all of the children. A four-by-five-inch card strip (blue, green, or yellow) should always be kept on the left side of the top line of the Chart Holder. On the right side of the top line, but clearly separated from the smaller strip, should be a four-by-twelve-inch card strip of the same color. Sizes are approximate but the strips should be large enough to form a background for the three-by-four-inch *Small Manuscript Alphabet Cards,* as shown in the illustration.

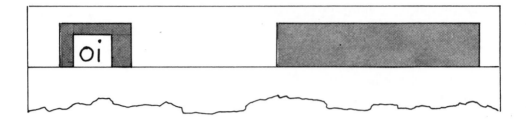

The first step in this blending practice is to identify the vowel sound, select its *Small Manuscript Alphabet Card*, and place it in front of the smaller colored strip where the child and the class can see this vowel and distinguish it from all other letters on the chart. The longer colored strip should serve as the background for the word that is to be blended.

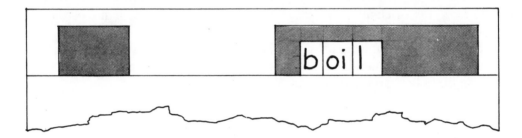

NOTE: Most children in the third or fourth year of the continuum will have acquired the blending technique as an automatic skill, but teachers should not assume that this is true for all children, and, therefore, review should be provided. Children entering the program require specific teaching. They benefit greatly from the repetitious performance in the practice of the more-experienced children.

The blending technique should be followed consistently to establish the thought pattern as an automatic performance requiring no prompting by the teacher. The teacher should pronounce the word for all to hear. A child should be chosen to go to the Chart Holder and blend the word with *Small Manuscript Alphabet Cards* as follows:

1. Repeats the word so that the *vowel sound* can be *heard* and felt;
2. Gives the *vowel sound*; and
3. Names the letter(s) that spells the vowel sound and places the card(s) on the smaller colored strip.

Now the word is ready to be blended and the child should continue.

4. Repeats the word to ensure its correct recall and pronunciation; and
5. Spells the word by placing and *naming each letter as its card is placed* on the longer colored strip.

If, however, children are not ready to drop the crutches which helped blending become securely established,* it may be necessary to revise Step 5:

*Slingerland, *Book Two — Basics in Scope and Sequence*, pp. 58–59.

a. Gives the initial consonant sound(s) that precedes the vowel sound and names the consonant(s) (*without naming the key word*) while forming them with arm swings and then placing the card(s) on the longer colored strip.

b. Gives the vowel sound and names the corresponding sight symbol(s) (no key word) as the card(s) is transferred from the colored background strip into correct sequential position within the word being blended.

c. Gives the last sound(s) and names the letter(s) (no key word) while forming it with arm swings before the card(s) is placed in correct position to complete the word.

When the performance is completed, the child should step to the side (keeping his or her back to the class) to make the word visible to all of the children. With the entire class joining in, the child should repeat the word and spell it, forming each letter with full arm swings as it is named.

As blending becomes secure, "crutches" as outlined in Steps a, b, and c should be dropped one at a time, first by omitting arm swings as the initial and final consonants are named and placed, then by omitting sounds of the initial and final consonant(s) as they are named and placed. *Steps 1 through 5 should not be omitted*, however, in this blending practice.

The goal for the child is to use the technique with as few steps as possible when spelling an unknown phonetic word. In class practice with the teacher, practice in "patterning"* or "computerizing"** should not be eliminated.

The teacher should take advantage of the time during the first several weeks of school while the children are learning cursive writing to *review* known spellings of vowel sounds and

*"Patterning" is learning the thinking process through conscious effort for carrying the Visual (or Auditory or Kinesthetic) message over its sensory channel to the brain for perceptual-conceptual integration.

**"Computerizing" is securing a particular "patterning" on the brain to enable it to be used with automatic ease and without the same conscious effort required in "patterning."

to *introduce* new ones for blending on the Chart Holder. The "three-fold language pattern"* is completed for oral blending when the word is *felt* in pronouncing the *heard* word and *seen* when formed with cards on the Chart Holder.

The teacher should determine which short vowels, letter combinations, and phonograms the children have learned for instant Auditory-Visual recall. Those cards should be placed in the Teacher's Hand Pack and in the pack of *Small Manuscript Alphabet Cards* used on the Chart Holder. In addition to the alphabet cards, no more than five or six of the known phonogram cards should be placed on the Chart Holder at any one time — because it is important to avoid cluttering the Chart Holder and interfering with easy perception. The known phonogram cards should be changed from day to day as needed for the day's lesson in blending.

> NOTE: Sometimes when a child needs a phoneme spelled with two or three letters, no card for this will appear on the Chart Holder. Children usually discover for themselves that single letter cards on the holder can be arranged in an overlapping fashion to create the needed phoneme.

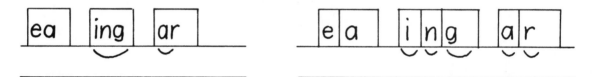

Children should be told that phonemes spelled with two or three letters are placed together on one card to aid their Visual perception and recall. Until their recall is automatic, the phoneme has not been learned as a part of the computerizing process in their own brains.

Innumerable phonetic words**can be blended with the known spellings of given short-vowel and consonant sounds, for example:

–v–	jam	consonant-vowel-consonant	(3 sounds)
–v––	mast		(4 sounds)
––v–	slab		(4 sounds)
––v––	brand or clasp		(5 sounds)
—v–	*th*in	digraph-vowel-consonant	(3 sounds)
–v—	di*sh*		(3 sounds)
—v—	*wh*i*ch*		(3 sounds)
––v–—	brun*ch*		(5 sounds)
–––v—	spla*sh*		(5 sounds)

Short Vowels

The teacher pronounces a word such as *draft*. (Refer to *TWL*, pages 5-18.) A child is

---

*Anna Gillingham refers to this as the "language triangle." Anna Gillingham and Bessie W. Stillman, *Remedial Training for Children with Specific Disability in Reading, Spelling, and Penmanship* (Cambridge, Mass.: Educators Publishing Service, Inc., 1960), p. 40.

**Refer to the word lists found in Slingerland and Murray, *Teacher's Word Lists Revised.*

chosen to go to the Chart Holder to encode the word with cards on the Chart Holder while the class watches. The child should repeat the word, "Draft."

> NOTE: The word must be repeated clearly and loudly enough for the entire class to hear. If the child mispronounces or inserts or deletes one of the sounds, the teacher should say, for example, "I did not say *draf*; I said *draft*," and the child should repeat correctly and begin again to encode the correctly pronounced word.

Teacher: "Draft."
Child: "Draft, /ă/, *a*," using arm swings, and then placing the card on the small colored strip.

> NOTE: Until cursive writing has been learned and automatic recall of cursive is reasonably functional, only manuscript should be used.

Having determined the vowel spelling, the child should be ready to spell the word.

Child: "Draft, *d-r-a-f-t*," naming each letter as its card is placed on the long strip above. Steps to the side and facing the Chart Holder, spells the word orally, forming each letter with arm swings.
Class: "Draft, *d-r-a-f-t*," forming letters with arm swings in manuscript until cursive has been learned and the teacher directs the children to use cursive.
Teacher: "Strict."
Child: "Strict, /ĭ/, *i*," using arm swings, and then, placing card on colored strip, repeats, "Strict, *s-t-r-i-c-t*," naming each letter as it is placed on the long colored strip. Steps to side, with back to class, and repeats the word; spells orally using arm swings.
Class: "Strict, *s-t-r-i-c-t*," naming each letter as it is formed with arm swings.
Teacher: "Which (not *w*ich)."
Child: "Which, /ĭ/, *i*," placing card on small strip. "Which, *w-h-i-c-h*," naming each letter as it is placed on the long strip. Repeats and spells orally, using arm swings.
Class: "Which, *w-h-i-c-h*," naming each letter as it is formed with arm swings.
Teacher: "Twist."
Child: "Twist, /ĭ/, *i*," placing card on small strip. "Twist, *t-w-i-s-t*," placing cards on long strip, spells orally using arm swings.
Class: Repeats and spells orally.

Letter Combinations

Teacher: "Swing."
Child: "Swing, /ĭng/, *i-n-g*," placing card on small strip. "Swing, *s-w-i-n-g*," placing each card on long strip, spells orally using arm swings.
Class: "Swing, *s-w-i-n-g*," using arm swings.

Teacher: "Chunk."

Child: "Chunk, /ŭngk/, *u-n-k*," placing card on small strip. "Chunk, *c-h-u-n-k*," naming while placing each card on long strip. Steps aside and spells orally.

Class: "Chunk, *c-h-u-n-k*," using arm swings.

Teacher: "Strength (not stre*n*th)."

Child: "Strength, /ĕng/, *e-n-g*," placing card on small strip. "Strength, *s-t-r-e-n-g-t-h*," naming while placing each card on long strip. Spells orally as class watches.

Class: "Strength, *s-t-r-e-n-g-t-h*," using arm swings.

Phonograms

NOTE: The *Phonogram Chart* shown below should be left on the wall where it can be seen throughout the year. Strips from the Phonogram, Suffix, and Prefix Kit should be placed on the wall as they are taught.

Refer to the Phonogram, Suffix, and Prefix Kit for the current key words.

For reteaching and introducing new phonograms, the teacher should determine which phonograms are known and which must be taught. When a new phonogram is introduced, it should be used in many different words for practice before it is mixed with others in blending practice. Its card should be included in the Teacher's Hand Pack from then on.

Examples of words with a new phonogram for the teacher to dictate and the children to spell orally:

ie, /ē/

chief	grief
thief	shriek
shield	brief
pier	piece*

(*TWL*, page 28.)

*The *ce* makes this a Yellow Flag word because the spelling of the sound after /ē/ must be remembered as *ce* and not *s*.

Review Words

Examples of words to be dictated for reviewing phonograms, short vowels, letter combinations, and a newly taught phonogram:

str*ay*	ch*unk*	sp*or*t
sc*out*	str*ai*n	k*e*lp
h*oi*st	cr*u*nch	br*ie*f
qu*e*nch	t*oy*	sn*ea*k
c*ou*ch	s*ou*th	sc*ar*f
p*ier*	bl*u*nt	shr*ie*k
sn*or*t	qu*e*st	st*ar*t

(*TWL*, pages 21-33.)

Teacher: "Stray."

Child: "Stray, /ā/, *a-y*." If the child knows several ways of spelling the /ā/ sound and is not sure which is the right one, he or she should say, "Is it *a-y* or *e-i-g-h*?" (The teacher should give the answer.) "Stray, *s-t-r-a-y*," placing cards on the long strip as they are named. Repeats *stray*, and spells orally.

Class: Repeats *stray*, and spells orally, "*S-t-r-a-y*," using arm swings.

NOTE: Unless the word is encoded on the Chart Holder where it can be seen, Auditory-Visual-Kinesthetic association, or integration, for Visual reinforcement is lost. The children who are watching will *hear*, but not *see*, in an exercise intended to strengthen Auditory-Visual-Kinesthetic integration necessary for spelling.

Teacher: "Scout."

Child: "Scout, /ou/, <u>*o-u*</u>," placing *ou* card on the short strip. "Scout, *s-c-<u>o-u</u>-t*," placing cards on the long strip. Repeats *scout* and spells orally.

Class: Repeats *scout* and spells, "*S-c-o-u-t*" orally, forming each letter with arm swings as it is named.

Teacher: "Quest."

Child: "Quest, /ĕ/, *e*," placing the *e* card on the short strip. "Quest, *<u>q-u</u>-e-s-t*," placing each card on the long strip as it is named. "Quest, *q-u-e-s-t*," spelling orally.

Class: "Quest, *q-u-e-s-t*," while writing with arm swings.

Teacher: "March."

Child: "March, /är/, *a-r*. March, *m-a-r-c-h*," placing cards on the Chart Holder. "March, *m-a-r-c-h*."

Class: "March, *m-a-r-c-h*."

Before the third year ends, all of the phonograms listed in A—Alphabet Cards, pages 52-56, and shown on the *Phonogram Chart*, page 74, usually will have been taught except to children who entered the program late.

During the first few weeks, while cursive writing is being taught, an opportunity is provided for reviewing and/or learning how to blend with phonograms, vowels, and letter combinations (also vowel-consonant-*e*, which will be explained later), before a child is asked to put blended words to more functional use in C—Spelling and D—Dictation.

BLENDING ORALLY AND ON PAPER IN CURSIVE WRITING

It is unnecessary to wait until all cursive letters have been learned before having the children omit the Chart Holder and begin to write words directly on their papers after they blend them orally.

It is necessary to use words (and real syllables) that:
- contain only the letters that have been learned, and
- contain only the letter connections that have been taught. (The teacher should be sure to use letters that connect at the writing line before using those that connect at the midline. Refer to LEARNING TO WRITE, pages 42-45.)

All words should be written within two spaces on composition paper to ensure letter-size relationship and alignment. *Children's standards of penmanship will be no higher than their teacher's standards and expectations for children's performances.*

The preparation in B—Blending and C—Spelling is given to establish cognition of word formation and use of penmanship as a skill basic to independent, individualized written expression.

Oral blending should precede written blending to prevent mistakes in letter sequencing.

Teacher: "Lack." Chooses a child to blend orally.
Child: "Lack, /ă/, *a*," with back to class. "Lack, *l-a-c-k*," naming each letter as it is formed and connected in cursive writing with arm swings.
Class: Repeats by naming and spelling *lack*, using arm swings. *Writes on composition paper*, softly naming each letter as it is formed.

Words should be written one under the other in columns as shown on page 77.

Examples of words with learned cursive letters to be dictated by the teacher, blended orally, and written on composition paper by the children:

cab	lag	gab
lack	clack	hal (as in halibut)

left	sash	cash	kelp	rug
hash	desk	red	fad	rust

Examples of words with a newly-introduced letter, such as *qu*, for the teacher to dictate and the children to blend orally and write on composition paper:

qu

quit	quack	quilt	qu*ee*n
squint	squelch	squish	squid
squ*ea*k	squ*ea*l	squ*ir*t	

When the teacher foresees that a particular letter or letters such as *s* and *p* (made with the same beginning stroke) will be needed for written blending, the letters should be taught ahead of time in LEARNING TO WRITE and practiced in written A—Alphabet Cards (pages 62-63). By then their use should be nearly automatic, enabling the child to concentrate on sequencing the letters in blending.

Vowel-Consonant-*e* Words (v-*e*)

NOTE: At some time during the third year of this program, children usually are ready to comprehend explanations for modification of vowel sounds. Vowels may be modified when followed by a consonant or when the word ends with a silent *e*.

When a vowel occurs at the end of a word or a syllable, its sound is usually the same as its name and is called a *long-vowel sound*. Words which fall into this group include g*o*, p*o*-ny, m*o*-tor, sh*e*, m*e*-ter, s*e*-quel, and c*u*-pid. By placing a consonant after the vowel in a word or syllable, the long-vowel sound is modified, usually to its *short-vowel sound* as in m*e* — m*e*t, g*o* — g*o*t, fr*a*-cus — fr*a*n-tic, P*o*-lish — p*o*l-ish, s*i*-lent — s*i*l-ver, and r*i*-val — r*i*v-er.

If a word with three sounds, such as *ride*, were blended according to its three sounds, it would be spelled *rid*. However, it would be pronounced /rĭd/, not /rīd/, because the *i* followed by a consonant becomes /ĭ/. By adding a silent *e* the vowel can be returned to its long sound, and *ride* will be pronounced as desired, /rīd/.

This explanation for teaching "through the intellect" already should have been given in B—Unlocking of THE VISUAL APPROACH before it is brought over for encoding to spell. Its application for functional use is much more difficult for spelling than for reading because of ambiguities in spelling. If not known, the word *ride* might have been spelled r*igh*d or r*ie*d. (Refer to pages 213-236.) For decoding, perception of *i-e* /ī/ immediately unlocks the word as /rīd/.

When they practice blending v-*e* words, the children should be told that all of the dictated words are to be spelled with vowel-consonant-*e*, and only two or possibly three vowel sounds will be used. They are to listen for the long-vowel sound and, after blending orally, they are to write the word in the appropriate column. (Classification is a task added to blending and writing for widening integrated performances — something children with SLD often struggle to accomplish, if not given help.)

Children should head their papers as shown below before beginning.

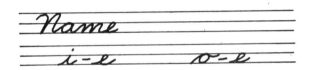

Words for the teacher to dictate: *shine, grope, stove, strive, stroke, quite, quote, doze, spine, choke,* and *Mike*.

Teacher: "Shine." Chooses a child to blend orally.
Child: "Shine, /ī/, *i*-consonant-*e*," forming each letter as it is named and using a horizontal stroke (—) for the word *consonant*. Repeats *shine* and writes s-h-i-n-e using arm swings.
Class: "Shine, s-h-i-n-e," naming each letter as it is formed with arm swings. Writes *shine* in the appropriate column, naming each letter softly as it is formed.

The teacher should move about the room checking to make sure that performances are correct for encoding, placement, and letter connections.

Teacher: "Grope."
Child: "Grope, /ō/, *o*-consonant-*e*. Grope, g-r-o-p-e."
Class: "Grope, g-r-o-p-e." Writes in the appropriate column.

The teacher may remind the children how to connect the *o* with the *p, v, k, t,* and *z*. Continue with the same procedure.

Example of *i-e* and *o-e* placement on paper:

Name	
i-e	*o-e*
shine	grope
strive	stone
quite	stroke
spine	quote

Words can be written on the back of the paper after columns are properly headed.

U-Consonant-*e* Words

Special explanations and practice should be given for *u-e* with its two sounds — /ū/ and /o͞o/. (Refer to *TWL*, page 38.) It is difficult to pronounce the long-*u* sound after *j, r,* and sometimes *l*. For the sake of euphony the *u* is pronounced /o͞o/ rather than /ū/ in some words, e.g., *rude, jute, June,* and *plume.* The blending technique is the same. Words such as the following should be dictated by the teacher: *cute, cure, prune, rule, June, pure, cube,* and *brute.* The written performance should be arranged as shown below.

u-e /ū/	u-e /o͞o/
cute	prune
cure	rule

Review of Vowel-Consonant (v-) and Vowel-Consonant-*e* (v-*e*) Words

Sometimes the children should write the dictated words in columns, and children at the third-year and more advanced levels should be asked to indicate the kinds of words they are. Examples of words to be dictated are shown below.

drive	*i-e*	blaze	*a-e*	crate	*a-e*	clove	*o-e*
slump	*u-*	whisk	*i-*	these	*e-e*		
bunch	*u-*	craft	*a-*	those	*o-e*		

At times, for independent work, the words should be copied from the most recently completed written performance into columns classified "vowel-consonant" and "vowel-consonant-*e*."

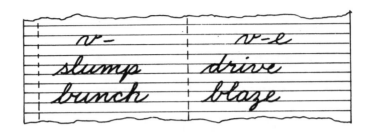

Letter Combinations

Each letter combination should be learned as a unit and the blending technique should be the same as with other units of sound.

Teacher: "Chunk."
Child: "Chunk, /ŭngk/, *u-n-k*; chunk, *c-h-u-n-k*."
Class: "Chunk, *c-h-u-n-k*," writing with arm swings. Writes on paper, softly naming each letter as it is written.

The same procedure should be followed with other words containing letter combinations such as those listed below.

sling	thank		bank	(ănk)
clank	think		trunk	(ŭnk)
drink	length	(ĕng)	fling	(ĭng)
string	slung		swing	(ĭng)

Mixed word lists such as the following may be used for reviewing vowel-consonant, vowel-consonant-*e*, letter combination, and phonogram words:

trust	(u-)	thud	(u-)
yank	(ank)	sling	(ing)
*screen	(ee-)	*blame	(a-e)
*coast	(oa-)	*sprite	(i-e)
sprig	(i-)	*duke	(u-e)
hung	(ung)	blink	(ink)
*sprain	(ai)	*point	(oi-)
*flee	(ee)	*stray	(ay)

*If the spelling is ambiguous, the children should be encouraged to ask which of the known ways is the correct spelling, e.g., "Screen, /ē/. Is /ē/ spelled *e-e, e-a*, or *i-e*?" The teacher should say, "*E-e*."

Phonograms

ar and *or*

The blending technique is the same as that used for vowel-consonant-*e* words, i.e., "Start, /är/, *a-r*; start, *s-t-a-r-t*."

ar

chart	spark	farm
scarf	smart	bark
march	lark	harp

(Refer to *TWL*, page 30.)

or

north	sport	porch
born	scorn	forth
thorn	stork	storm

(Refer to *TWL*, page 30.)

er, ir, and *ur*

While the blending technique remains the same for words with the phonograms *er, ir,* and *ur*, the words may be ambiguously spelled. The correct spellings must be determined.

er	*ir*	*ur*
her	swirl	turn
verb	chirp	burst
perch	first	church
stern	girl	curve**
serf*	mirth	

(Refer to *TWL*, page 31.)

Ambiguously Spelled /ûr/ Words***

fern	skirt	birth*
thirst	third	berth*
birch	churn	surf*
curl		

*Explain meaning.

**Children should be reminded that words ending with the /v/ sound must have *v* followed by silent *e*.

***If the spelling is ambiguous, the children should be encouraged to ask which of the known ways is the correct spelling, e.g., "Her, /ûr/. Is /ûr/ spelled *e-r, i-r,* or *u-r*?" The teacher should say, for example, "*E-r* for the word *her*."

ear, and *or* Preceded by *w*

As the children advance, they should be taught how to blend words with the /ûr/ sound spelled *ear*. Such words are among the ambiguously spelled words — not difficult for unlocking but requiring recall of the several possibilities and exact memory of which one is right for encoding. (Refer to A — Alphabet Cards, page 55.)

	ear	
earn	search	heard
earth	learn	hear*se*

These are words to be integrated into spelling practice which will be explained in C—Spelling.

When *or* is preceded by *w*, (*w*)*or*, its sound is /ûr/. The decoding technique is the same as that described previously.

Teacher: "Work." (When this blending practice is introduced, the teacher should say, "Think what sound you hear just before the /ûr/ sound.")

Child: "Work, /ûr/, *o-r* preceded by /w/, *w-o-r-k*. Work, *w-o-r-k*," writing with full arm swings.

Class: Repeats *work*, spells orally, and writes on paper.

The same procedure should be continued with *worth, word, world, worst,* and *worm,* followed by their integration into functional use as shown in C—Spelling.

Digraphs and Trigraphs

Children following the continuum will have learned to perceive and recognize both digraphs and trigraphs in THE VISUAL APPROACH for decoding to read words. While the sounds may be perceived, the spelling may be ambiguous for encoding. The several possibilities must be recalled — one of the reasons for practice with the Yellow Cards — to enable the children to find the correct spelling in the dictionary or from an authoritative source.

To familiarize children with the use of digraphs and trigraphs, words should be dictated for oral and written blending as shown below. (Refer to *TWL*, pages 16, 17, 18.)

/n/ — *gn*

Teacher: "Some words beginning with the sound /n/ are spelled *gn*. The ones I will dictate for you to blend and write are worked out in the same way we blend other words. Gnarl."

Child: "Gnarl, /är/, *a-r*; gnarl, *g-n-a-r-l*."

Class: "Gnarl, *g-n-a-r-l*"; then writes on papers.

Teacher: "If you are not sure how the beginning /n/ sound is spelled, be sure to ask if it is spelled with *n* or *gn* and I will tell you."

At any grade level, if the need is immediate, the child may ask, "Is /n/ spelled with *n* or *gn*?" (Asking, "How is /n/ spelled?" would not be a satisfactory thinking process for the child.) Children at upper-elementary levels may refer to the dictionary.

The same procedure should be continued with one-syllable words, such as *gnaw, gnat, gnome*, and *gnash*. How to put the words into functional use is explained in C—Spelling.

/f/ — *f, ph*

Both *f* and *ph* appear at the beginning and end of words and syllables. One approach for blending with them is to have the children's composition papers divided into two columns headed *f* and *ph*. After noting the one sound /f/ for both spellings, the teacher should dictate words from a list such as the one shown below. A child should be asked to blend orally (presuming use of the Chart Holder is no longer necessary except for teaching something new). If the child is not sure whether *f* or *ph* is the right spelling, he or she should ask, as already explained. If, however, the child makes a mistake before asking, the teacher should say, "The word sounds right with your spelling, but that is not the way it is spelled." The child should make his or her own correction before again spelling orally. When the word is correctly blended, the class should repeat, and all of the children should write the word in the correct column.

Words such as the following may be dictated by the teacher:

fled	flame
phone	Phil ("a boy's name")
fill	graph
phrase	phlox* ("a kind of flower")

NOTE: Many more words containing *ph* can be used when practicing blending with two-syllable or multisyllabic words, but they should not be used until after the digraph *ph* has been practiced in single-syllable words and the technique for blending two-syllable or multisyllabic words has been reviewed and enlarged upon in the directed functional use given in C—Spelling.

/ch/ — *ch* and *tch*

The sound /ch/ is spelled with the digraph *ch* and the trigraph *tch*, but the *tch* is not used at the beginning of words. It is used at the end of a word following a single vowel, as in *catch*, except for a few common words — *such, much, rich*, and *which*. For practice in blending with *ch* and *tch*, the composition paper should be folded into two columns and headed as shown below.

*If the child spells the final sound /ks/ with *cks* or *cs* or *ks*, the teacher should say that any one of them would give the correct sound, but another single letter that is used only at the end of words or syllables, as in *tax, mix, box*, etc., is the right spelling. This is said to the child to aid recall of the *x* with its /ks/ sound.

It should be explained to the children that *ch* is used at both the beginning and the end of words and syllables, but *tch*, with only a few exceptions, usually comes at the end of a single-vowel word. The teacher's explanation will be understood more easily after the written blending is completed because the organization of the written words will afford a complete Auditory-Kinesthetic-Visual association.

Teacher: "Match. Where do you hear the /ch/ sound? . . . Yes, at the end. How will the vowel sound be spelled? . . . Yes, with *a*. Then, how will the /ch/ after a single vowel be spelled? . . . Yes, with *tch*."

Child: "Match, /ǎ/, *a*; match, *m-a-t-c-h*."

Class: "Match, *m-a-t-c-h*" (first orally and then written on papers in the correct column).

Teacher: "Chain. Where do you hear the /ch/? . . . Yes, at the beginning. What does that tell you about its spelling? . . . Yes, it will be with *ch* because *tch* is not used at the beginning of words.

"Peach. Where do you hear the /ch/? . . . Yes, at the end. How is the vowel sound spelled? . . . Yes, with two vowels, *ea*. What does that tell you about spelling /ch/? . . . Yes, *ch* is the right spelling because *tch* is not used after two vowels, only one."

After the initial steps above, only the usual procedure should be followed for written blending unless some particular need is evidenced and then help should be given *at the moment of need*.

Words such as the following should be dictated by the teacher:

ditch	fetch	march	couch
clutch	hatch	stretch	lunch
chum	church	Dutch	pooch
chunk	grouch	porch	churn
clinch	quench	scratch	blotch

NOTE: In the words *porch, church, grouch*, etc., the *vowel sound* is spelled with *two letters* and not with a single vowel.

Papers should look like the illustration shown below.

Exceptions

In a separate lesson, teach the several exceptions to *tch* spelling — *much, such, rich,* and *which* — and carry them forward in the same day's lesson for integration into phrase and sentence writing in C—Spelling.

Ambiguously Spelled /s/ and /j/

/s/ — *s,* and *c* When Followed by *e, i,* or *y*

In blending, /s/ is usually spelled with *s,* but *c* followed by *e, i,* or *y* is sometimes the right spelling. Because such words are "caution" or Yellow Flag (ambiguously spelled) words, their spelling must be *learned and remembered.* Therefore, groups of such words should be dictated for written blending with the teacher's guidance and carried forward for integrating into suffix, phrase, and sentence writing in the period allowed in C—Spelling, in D—Dictation, and eventually in E—Propositional and Creative Writing.

It should be explained that the letter *c* has no sound of its own but uses the *k*'s sound /k/ for its *hard sound* and the letter *s*'s sound /s/ when followed by *e, i,* or *y* for its *soft sound.* It is with the soft sound /s/ that practice in blending should be given.

The following words should be dictated by the teacher:

rice*	brace*	fleece	piece
race*	twice*	choice	cell
ace*	ice*	cinch	cent
place*	cite*	peace	

Two-syllable words containing soft *c* should not be dictated for blending until practice has been given with other two-syllable and multisyllabic words.

/j/ — *j, dge,* and Soft *g* When Followed by *e, i,* or *y*

When the sound /j/ occurs at the beginning or end of words and syllables, the letter *j* is used most commonly. When the sound /j/ occurs at the end of one-syllable, short-vowel words, the trigraph *dge* /j/ usually is used, as in *fudge, ridge,* and *edge.* In still other words, sometimes *g* followed by *e, i,* or *y* gives its soft sound /j/ (required for blending an ambiguously spelled word), for example, *page, wage, legion,* and *orgy.*

Because of the ambiguity, groups of words using the different spellings should be practiced for written blending and integrated into suffix, phrase, and sentence writing as explained in C—Spelling.

Examples of /j/ — *ge* at the end of one-syllable words:

cage	gorge	surge	rage
gage	large	huge	lunge

*The teacher should point out that the silent *e* serves two purposes in the vowel-consonant-*e* words to make the vowel say its own name and to cause the *c* to have its soft sound /s/.

Examples of /j/ — *j* used in regularly spelled words:

joke	jail	jam	Jill
Jack	jay	jade	jeep
just	Jake		

Examples of /j/ — *dge*:

ridge	fudge	ledge	badge
budge	judge	nudge	dodge
wedge	lodge		

Mixed lists of words such as the following can be used to review the sound of /j/:

smudge	page	joke	wage
charge	bridge	cringe	range
drudge	barge	judge	join

To avoid errors, a child should spell each word orally in the usual way before writing it.

TWO-SYLLABLE WORDS

Children probably will have learned how to unlock two-syllable or multisyllabic words in THE VISUAL APPROACH during the second year of the continuum and to blend some of them in THE AUDITORY APPROACH.*

It should be explained to children that the number of vowel sounds required in pronouncing a word usually determines the number of syllables it must have. They should understand the basics of syllable division and spelling in blending phonetic words. (Refer to the note on page 122.)

1. Every syllable must have a vowel, as in c*a*t n*i*p, *i*n d*e*nt, and even in the syllable *fle* in r*u*f *fle* where the *e* is silent.
2. *Placement* of the vowel within a syllable usually determines vowel sound. For example, in *Po lish*, the vowel *o* has a long sound at the end of an accented (open) syllable, and in *pol ish*, the *o* has a short sound because it is followed by a consonant.
3. *Accent* also determines vowel sound and placement:
   a. At the end of the *accented syllable*, the vowel usually has a long sound, as in *tu' lip, fra' cus, mu' sic*, and *a' pron*.
   b. At the end of an *unaccented syllable*:
      e, o, and *u* usually have a half-long (lightly-stressed) sound, as in *re gard', pro vide'*, and *u nite'*;
      i usually has a short sound, as in *Ti bet', di vine'*, and *in vi ta' tion*; and
      a usually has an obscure or schwa sound, as in *a bode', ca det', a way'*, and *pa rade'*.

*Slingerland, *Book Two — Basics in Scope and Sequence*, pp. 75–81.

NOTE: Commonly used words having vowels followed by consonants that modify, but do not shorten, vowel sounds are *was, watch, wash, want, wall,* and *walk.* They must be practiced, over-learned, and put to functional use in phrase and sentence writing in C—Spelling.

The teacher should introduce or review accent by writing several words on the chalkboard and placing the accent mark before pronouncing the words for the children to hear and see. For a child who has difficulty hearing accent — and many do have difficulty — taps on the child's shoulder for the "feel" as the word is pronounced, or taps where the sound can be heard in association with seeing the accent mark, are helpful.

TWO MEDIAL CONSONANTS

Blending Orally Using the Chart Holder

NOTE: The Chart Holder should be used for blending while a child is learning to use cursive writing. However, blending with the cards should not continue beyond its temporary service as a "crutch" while something new is being introduced and review of syllable division is practiced. The Chart Holder serves as a means for Visual sensory linkage or association with the Auditory-Kinesthetic sensory channels used for oral blending. Eventually it should be eliminated in favor of writing the words on the chalkboard. This, in turn, should be dropped when the children are ready to move directly to written blending on paper.

The children should be told why colored card strips are placed in the top pocket of the Chart Holder — one strip for each syllable of the word to be blended — as shown below.

With two-syllable, short-vowel phonetic words having two consonants in the medial position, the procedure should be as follows:

Teacher: "Talcum, tal-cum" (emphasizing each syllable the second time the word is spoken).
Child: "Talcum, tal, /ă/, *a,*" (placing the vowel *a* card below the first card strip).
"Talcum, cum, /ŭ/, *u,*" (placing the vowel *u* card below the second card strip).

Having accomplished the difficult step of hearing the vowel sound in association with its
Visual symbol, the child should be ready to blend the word.

Child: "Talcum, tal, *t-a-l*," placing and naming each consonant, including the
vowel card, as it is placed on the colored strip. "Talcum, cum, *c-u-m*,"
placing and naming the letters. Pushes the two strips and cards together to
form the word *talcum*.

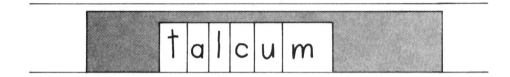

Steps to the side to enable all to see and writes *talcum* with arm swings,
always naming each letter.

Class: Repeats the word and writes with arm swings.

NOTE: Manuscript letter forms should be used until cursive forms have been
learned with correct letter connections. *Using both manuscript and cursive in the
same word should never be permitted.*

The same procedure should be followed to allow other children to have turns with words
such as *plas tic, lin den, ban dit, gob let, gob lin,* and *ton sil.* (Refer to *TWL*, page 48.)

Blending in Cursive Writing on the Chalkboard

The chalkboard should be used while the children are learning to write with cursive letter
forms and to blend different syllable spellings for two-syllable words. Lines on which to write
each syllable and a single line on which to write the completed word should be drawn on the
chalkboard. The same procedure as that used with cards on the Chart Holder should be followed by having the vowel, or phonetic element, written below each syllable line before blending and writing the syllables.

Using two-syllable, short-vowel phonetic words with two like consonants in the medial
position, the procedure should be as follows:

Teacher: "Muffin, muf fin," overemphasizing the /f/ sound in the second syllable.

Child: "Muffin, muf, /ŭ/, *u*," writing *u* below the first syllable line. "Fin, /ĭ/, *i*,"
writing *i* below the second syllable line.

After completing the steps shown above, the child should be ready to write each syllable and know that hearing the vowel sound in association with its vowel symbol(s) (the most difficult part of encoding words) has been accomplished.

Child: "Muffin, muf, *m-u-f*," naming each letter as it is written on the first syllable line. "Muffin," (if repeating helps) "fin, *f-i-n*," naming each letter as it is written on the second syllable line. Rewrites both syllables to form the complete word on the longest word lines, always naming letters as they are formed.

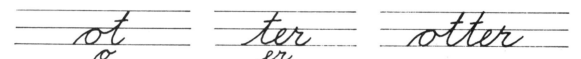

Child steps to the side, ready to write the word with the class.

Class: Repeats *muffin* and writes with full arm swings, naming each letter as it is formed and connected with succeeding letters.

The same procedure should be followed to allow other individuals to have turns with words such as *nob bin, hap pen, gos sip, ten nis, pip pin, an nex, rab bit, fos sil,* and *pol len.* (Refer to TWL, page 48.)*

The same procedure should be followed with words in which the last syllable ends with *er.* The phonogram *er* should be written below the second syllable line as in the following words: *ot ter, but ter, trig ger, lad der, blot ter, rub ber, dip per, ham mer,* and *zip per.* (Refer to TWL, page 48.)

Blending in Cursive Writing on Composition Paper

When the children have learned cursive letter forms well enough to use them independently and functionally (after five or six weeks if writing has been taught as explained in LEARNING TO WRITE), the following procedure should be used. The teacher should name the word and then pronounce each syllable clearly. On composition paper, the children should draw two short lines on which to write each syllable and one longer line on which to write the whole word.

One child should be called upon to work out the vowel-sound spelling for each syllable, and the entire class should write the correct vowel spellings below the syllable lines they have made. An example is shown for the word *linden.*

*Most children can successfully use the following procedure after the concept for syllables has been internalized: Teacher pronounces the word, "cactus". Child repeats "cactus" *cac,* /ă/ a", naming letter as it is formed with full arm swing; "*cac* c-a-c", naming each letter as it is formed with full arm swing, "*tus*", /ŭ/ u", naming letter as it is formed with full arm swing; "*tus,* t-u-s," naming each letter as it is formed with full arm swing. Child repeats "*cactus,* c-a-c-t-u-s," naming each letter as it is formed with full arm swing. Class repeats word, names each letter as it is formed with full arm swing; repeats word and writes word on paper, naming each letter as it is written.

_i_   _e_

The performing child should blend the first syllable orally and, with the class, write it on the first syllable line. The same child should blend the second syllable and, with the class, write it on the second syllable line. As the last step, the word should be repeated and, with the class, written with free arm swings before the whole word is written on their papers.

lin   _den_   _linden_
_i_   _e_

SILENT-_e_ SYLLABLES

fle, tle Endings

Children who are working in this continuum will have already acquired understanding of the silent-_e_ syllables _fle, tle, kle_, etc., as three-letter units. This understanding is part of learning to decode in B—Unlocking of THE VISUAL APPROACH.

> NOTE: Syllables such as _dle, fle, zle, kle_, etc., are referred to as silent-_e_ syllables because they have no vowel sounds, but to be syllables, they must contain vowels. The silent _e_ is used in such syllables. The vowel _e_ frequently serves the purpose in visual, but soundless, ways as in vowel-consonant-_e_ words (_lake, cube_), when following a _v_ at the end of a word (_have, dove_), in causing the letters _c_ and _g_ to have soft sounds (_cell, race, gem, page_), and in silent-_e_ syllables (_puzzle, bubble_).

Because a silent-_e_ syllable is a complete three-letter unit, it should be written on the writing line immediately after it is perceived, and not written below the line, as shown below for the word _candle_.

_a_   _dle_

> NOTE: Instead of drawing lines on which to place written syllables, the children may fold the papers into three columns — two columns for the syllables, and one wider one for the whole word.

The teacher should dictate words such as the following: _can dle, dim ple, hum ble, sim ple, crum ble_, and _trem ble_. (Refer to _TWL_, page 47.)

Teacher: "Candle, can dle."
Class: "Candle, can dle," drawing two lines for the two syllables.

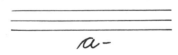

Teacher: Asks a child to blend the word *candle*, as already explained.
Child: "Candle, can, /ă/, *a*," and, with the class, writes *a* under the first syllable line. "Candle, /d'l/, *d-l-e*," and, with the class, writes *dle* on the second syllable line. Spells the whole word orally, "Candle, *c-a-n-d-l-e*," naming each letter as it is formed with arm swings.
Class: Repeats *candle* and writes, first with arm swings and then on papers, naming each letter softly as it is written.

During teaching and practicing time, the teacher should circulate about the room to check children's work as they are performing. Help given at such times is most effective.

Single Consonant Sounds in Medial Positions

As children progress through the third year and/or lower-intermediate grades, they should understand that hearing a short-vowel sound means that a consonant follows. A word such as *grand* should be blended by saying, "Grand, /ă/, *a* followed by a consonant," and for written blending practice, *a-* should be written below the syllable line with the horizontal stroke standing for the word *consonant*.

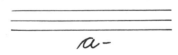

As a result of their experience in unlocking words in THE VISUAL APPROACH, children should already have been taught how a vowel sound is modified from a long sound, usually to a short sound, when followed by a consonant in a word or syllable. Therefore, two-syllable words such as *ruffle, fiddle,* and *nibble*, with single consonant sounds in the medial positions, require two like consonants. In *ruffle*, the first *f* modifies the vowel *u* to its short sound, and the second *f* is part of the three-letter, silent-*e* syllable unit.

Words such as the following should be dictated by the teacher: *puz zle, top ple, sad dle, ap ple, cud dle,* and *smug gle*. (Refer to *TWL*, page 47.)

The teacher may need to overemphasize the pronunciation to help children hear consonants in both syllables and remember that the short-vowel sounds require that a consonant follow.

Long-Vowel Sound in First Syllables

When silent-*e* syllables have long-vowel sounds in the first syllable, they are usually spelled with single vowels at the end of the syllable. They should be blended as follows: "Cradle, cra dle; cra, /ā/, *a* at the end of a syllable; dle, *d-l-e*."

The teacher should dictate words such as the following: *bu gle, ma ple, ti tle, ta ble, no ble*, and *ri fle*. (Refer to *TWL*, page 47.)

All of the words above have the accent on the first syllable; therefore, the long-vowel sounds are spelled with vowels at the end of the syllable. (If the first syllable of the word *bugle* ended with a *g*, it would be pronounced /bŭggle/, not /būgle/.)

Words with first syllables containing phonograms, such as the following, should be dictated by the teacher: *poo dle, gar gle, nee dle, tur tle, mar ble, stee ple, gar ble, pur ple*, and *whee dle*. (Refer to *TWL*, page 47.)

The teacher should refer to page 47 in *Teacher's Word Lists for Reference* for silent-*e*-syllable words containing letter combinations such as *ank* and *ing*, and the consonant digraph *ck*. There are letter combinations in which the *g* and *k* do "double duty," as in *jingle* and *twinkle*. The digraph *ck* serves in two ways — the *c* in the first syllable to shorten the vowel sound and the *k* in the second syllable as part of the three-letter, silent-*e* syllable.

ONE MEDIAL CONSONANT

When the children are ready to practice blending words containing only one medial consonant, they should be told that only one consonant will be in the medial position. An explanation, as part of teaching "through the intellect," should be given about placement of that medial consonant.

When only one consonant occurs in the medial position, the vowel sound of the first syllable determines placement of that consonant, either in the first or the second syllable. If the vowel sound is short, *the vowel* must be followed by the consonant to make it a *vowel-consonant syllable*, as in *rob in*. If the vowel sound is long, *the vowel* must occur at the end of the first syllable to make it a *vowel-at-the-end, or open, syllable*. The consonant belongs in the second syllable, as in *ro bot*.

In initial lessons, the teacher should have the children blend words with short-vowel sounds in the first syllables; in succeeding lessons, they should blend words with long-vowel sounds in the first syllables. Eventually the children should blend both types of words after discriminating vowel sounds for themselves.

The usual blending procedure should be followed as explained previously. Words such as the following should be dictated by the teacher.

Medial Consonant in First Syllable and Accent on First Syllable

frol ic	sev en	spin et	hab it
fam ish	cab in	clos et	gran ule
ban ish	prof it	mim ic	stam pede

(Refer to page 86 and *TWL*, page 50.)

> Teacher: "Frolic, frol ic."
> Child: "Frolic, frol ic. Frol, /ŏ/, *o* followed by a consonant, *f-r-o-l*; ic, /ĭ/, *i* followed by a consonant, *i-c*. Frolic, *f-r-o-l-i-c*."

Medial Consonant in Second Syllable and Accent on First Syllable

ro tate	o zone	cli max	lo tus
si lent	fe line	tri sect	ba con

(Refer to page 86 and *TWL*, page 50.)

> Child: "Rotate, ro tate; ro, /ō/, *o* at the end of a syllable. Ro, *r-o*; tate, /ā/, *a*-consonant-*e*, tate, *t-a-t-e*. Rotate, *r-o-t-a-t-e*."

Words with both short- and long-vowel first syllables such as the following should be dictated by the teacher: *i tem, mu sic, sol id, plan et, rap id, tal ent, vo cal, bo nus, col ic, grav el, fo cus, ti rade, du plex, va cate, ban ish*, and *sec ond*. (Refer to page 86 and *TWL*, page 50.)

REVIEW

The two-syllable words listed below contain phonemes which should already have been learned. (Of course, only the teacher knows whether or not they actually have been.) Included here are short and long vowels, vowel-consonant-*e*, phonograms, and letter combinations.

lo tion	suc tion	tur moil	whee dle
blank et	par take	trink et	junk et
bri dle	whip cord	fric tion	jum ble
es cape	wob ble	clois ter	com plain
na tion	cu pid	cri sis	ar tist

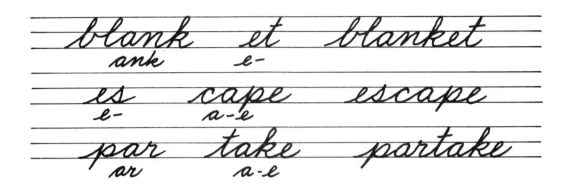

MULTISYLLABIC WORDS

The same procedures as those used with two-syllable words should be followed with multisyllabic words. However, by the time children are ready for this blending, many of the "crutches" probably will have been dropped. Concepts for spelling syllables will have been acquired as the result of the explanations and guided practice given in each day's lesson for B—Blending.

As with two-syllable words, the teacher should pronounce the word clearly and then pronounce each syllable. A child should repeat the whole word and then repeat the word syllable by syllable (sometimes drawing a line on which to write each syllable). The vowel or letter combination spelling should be written in small letters below the line before writing 1) the syllables and then, 2) the whole word.

The goal is to "think" each syllable, to spell and write each syllable, and to complete the whole word in one performance, but until that can be done *readily*, the teacher's responsibility is to provide guided practice.

The teacher should dictate the following words: *con nec tion, flam boy ant, man do lin, pre ten sion, tri um phant, ven ti late, hip po drome, con se quence, con fu sion, ad van tage, e lec tric, ev er glade, vi o lin, gen er a tion*, and *in fil trate*. (Refer to pages 77 and 86 and *TWL*, pages 36, 52, and 53.)

The teacher should give special practice with words containing the letter combinations *tion* and *sion*, and with soft *c* and soft *g*. (Refer to *TWL*, pages 52 and 56.)

As part of teaching "through the intellect," the teacher should explain to the children at elementary grade levels that vowels at the end of *unaccented syllables* usually have *modified* sounds.

The vowels *e, o,* and *u* have half-long sounds when they occur at the end of unaccented syllables, as in *pro vide', de note', re lax'*, and *u nite'*.

The vowel *i* sometimes may have a short sound when it occurs at the end of open syllables, as in *di vi sion, ve hi cle, in ves ti gate*, and *in vi ta tion*.

The vowel *a* requires special teaching. When it occurs at the end of an *unaccented syllable*, it usually has an obscure or schwa sound /ŭ/, as in *a bout', a way', a like', a side', a round', ga lore', pa rade', sa lute', a dore', al' pha bet, a bode', ca det', ca nal', ca reer'*, and *a ground'*.

NOTE: From among the words practiced in B—Blending in the daily lesson plan, the teacher should select appropriate words to practice in the C—Spelling time for functional use in phrase and sentence writing and for the addition of suffixes. Words that can be blended are of little value until they can be used functionally in writing from dictation and, eventually, in propositional writing.

C—Spelling

INTRODUCTION

C—Spelling is a conceptual approach to spelling and to the use of suffixes and prefixes. Memorizing weekly word lists is no more than rote learning and offers little help for the intelligent SLD child who must work hard to do what non-SLD children do with little conscious effort. The SLD child must group words into phrases to express fragments of thought. The phrases, when combined with one or more other phrases, form sentence units that convey complete thoughts. In succeeding years, children working in this continuum should progress from phrases to sentences, and then to paragraphs that will lead to their own propositional and, possibly, creative writing. *Learning how to spell* is necessary for this accomplishment to be realized.

Spelling is a cumulative skill that requires cognition of both phonetic and nonphonetic words. It requires knowledge of prefixes and suffixes; awareness of tense; ability to use generalizations and rules; singular, plural, and possessive forms; and ability to form contractions. All of these skills should be explained and taught to children with SLD before they begin teacher-guided practice in writing phrases and sentences. This fosters successful performances that can be improved upon and avoids unnecessary mistakes.

> NOTE: The experience of teachers trained in this multi-sensory approach has shown that children with SLD, who know the basic skills of writing, will spontaneously undertake independent, individually-inspired propositional writing for their own purposes.

Spelling involves much more than combining phonetic elements to form regularly spelled phonetic words. It becomes more difficult when words are spelled irregularly or ambiguously. Words spelled phonetically, such as those practiced in B—Blending to develop cognition for word formation, are referred to herein as Green Flag (regularly spelled) words. Examples include *strict, clasp, invent, trample*, and *goblet*. Words that must be memorized because they are not phonetic are called Red Flag (irregularly spelled) words. Some are *could, would, was, match, sign*, and *laugh*. Words that require memorization as well as grapheme discrimination (because *like sounds* may be spelled in more than one way, resulting in different meanings) are termed Yellow Flag ("caution") words. Examples are *beech* and *beach; meet, meat* and *mete*; and *slay, sley*, and *sleigh*.

Regardless of their spelling, each of these three word groupings follows the same rules when suffixes are added. Children should understand that words convey meanings (show action; name objects; describe objects; show changes in tense; and tell how, when, where, and why about something) in different ways. One of these is through the addition of suffixes which change the form of words as well as vary the meaning of root words. An explanation of the changes in word meaning conveyed by suffixes usually should precede, as well as follow, children's need for them as they write phrases and sentences.

C—Spelling is organized to assist the teacher in integrating what children already have learned with new material as soon as it is taught. New material should be introduced, practiced, and then integrated with what has been learned already. No teacher or school will be able to teach SLD children to spell all of the words that they may need over the years, but they can provide the principles that will teach them *how to learn*.

APPLYING THE MULTI-SENSORY APPROACH TO CLASSROOM SPELLING MANUALS

The teacher of SLD children should be prepared to apply multi-sensory instructional techniques to most words found in required spelling manuals at any grade level. The words should be categorized as follows into the three groups discussed above:

- phonetic or Green Flag words (remember that words are not phonetic until the phonetic elements have been learned);
- irregularly spelled or nonphonetic Red Flag words (such as *yacht, could, laugh*, or *was*; any word containing unlearned phonetic elements must be considered "Red Flag," requiring special learning and recall); and
- ambiguously spelled or Yellow Flag words (such as *brain, stream*, and *groan*).

These words, in addition to any that the teacher finds reason to include, should serve as the basic spelling list.

> NOTE: The authors of all spelling manuals undoubtedly have similar purposes — to help children learn to spell words, regardless of the order in which they are listed. By categorizing the words from spelling manuals, SLD teachers should be able to conform to school system expectations for each grade level, while, at the same time, stressing the structured multi-sensory instructional techniques.

MODALITY STRENGTHS AND WEAKNESSES

The trained SLD teacher should be sensitive to children's differences in modality strengths and weaknesses. Some children learn with greater ease through what they *see* and others, through what they *hear*.

Children with Auditory modality strengths — those who possibly possess verbal abilities — should *hear* words in association with their Kinesthetic "feel" in writing and naming them, thus strengthening perception of the weaker Visual sight-symbol units by associating them with the stronger Auditory sound-symbol counterparts. These children may have experienced no difficulties in understanding and speaking the language before or after entering school, but they do encounter difficulties when introduced to reading and, especially, to spelling. These children usually can learn phonics principles readily because their abilities to retain correctly pronounced words enable them to make a more secure association with the complementary Visual symbols for spelling. Therefore, teaching phonetic elements as outlined in A—Alphabet Cards for Auditory-Visual and for Visual-Auditory associations should not be slighted.

Children with Visual modality strengths — those who possibly do not possess verbal abilities — should see words in association with their Kinesthetic "feel" in speech and writing, thus strengthening perception of the weaker phoneme sound-symbol units by associating them with the stronger grapheme sight-symbol counterparts. *Seeing* the words as their pronunciations are *heard* strengthens recall. These children may experience difficulties with understanding and speaking the language before entering school, and also with reading and spelling after entering.

Children with various degrees of Visual modality strengths — those who possibly do not have corresponding verbal or auditory abilities — cannot always recall the correct pronunciation of words. Therefore, they cannot be expected to rely on phonics alone for spelling. Even more than children with Auditory strengths, these children require that emphasis be placed on looking at whole words at the same time they hear them while learning in association with the phonetic elements. These must be learned so that they can make correct Visual-Auditory associations of phonetic elements when checking or pronouncing words as they are being written. Therefore, the daily practice of A—Alphabet Cards for Visual-Auditory (grapheme-phoneme) and Auditory-Visual (phoneme-grapheme) associations (including the *Yellow Card Pack* from the Auditory stimulus) should not be minimized or slighted.

Sometimes the Kinesthetic modality can be adversely affected when faulty recall of the sequence of movement involved in speech or hand cannot trigger the correct voluntary motor function. Also, when the Visual appearance of letters is not perceived or recalled accurately, simultaneous association with the Kinesthetic memory of necessary movement is confused and Visual-Kinesthetic disability results.

Children with modality weaknesses should be identified and given appropriate multi-sensory instruction — both for word formation *concepts* and for spelling *usage*. Unfortunately, some children have weaknesses in two or more modalities. Multi-sensory techniques are planned to strengthen weak modalities by association with the stronger.

If perception and recall of Auditory symbols are faulty, association with the Kinesthetic memory of the "feel" for speech and hand usually is disorganized and Auditory-Kinesthetic disability results. When there is weakness in all three of the Visual-Auditory-Kinesthetic modalities, severe disability usually requires very specific multi-sensory instructional techniques to aid memory and simultaneous Visual-Auditory-Kinesthetic association.

INTEGRATING DAILY LESSON PLANS

The teacher's daily lesson plans for teaching spelling should include having the children use the letters and words taught in A—Alphabet Cards and B—Blending in a written performance. Doing so requires using words in phrases. In addition, suffixes must be used to convey the variations and shades of meaning that are needed to express the thoughts of the writer. Phrases should then be combined to form sentences. Unless these concepts are understood and practiced, learning to spell is only partly completed. Always remember that each new learning task should be integrated with previously learned material.

A daily lesson plan should include the following:

1. Words should be dictated by the teacher for the children to write in lists — sometimes in categories and sometimes in the order dictated.
2. Suffixes should be added to words selected from the lists.
   For example:
   brief + *ly, er, est,* and
   steam + *ing, er, y, ed,* and *s*.
3. Phrases including the words should be dictated for writing.
4. Phrases should be combined into sentences, dictated by the teacher, and written by the children.

NOTE: It should be pointed out to the children that no special spelling rules need be applied when suffixes are added to one-syllable root words containing vowel sounds spelled with two vowels.

SAMPLE INTEGRATED LESSON PLAN

The teacher may select a word, such as *brief*, from the words that were written in lists, either in the B—Blending or the C—Spelling time. As shown below, words should be dictated, written one word under the other, and then put into phrases and sentences. These, also, should be written one under the other to aid children in perceiving them as "units."

brief	to walk briefly
briefly	works briefly
briefer	the briefest story
briefest	briefer than before
	story is briefer

Mother has time   to walk briefly   in the park.
This story is briefer   than the other story.

After children have had guided practice under the teacher's direction, they can be asked to select a word from the list and, following the same procedure, to add several suffixes, write a phrase or two, and then a sentence.

NOTE: Children who have followed this continuum for one or more years will have acquired suffix, phrase, and sentence concepts and can be expected to understand why Green, Red, and Yellow Flag words are so labeled.

Many words have only small parts that must be recalled as "Red Flag." *Want*, in which only the *a* is irregular, is such a word. In *scream* the ambiguously spelled sound /ĕ/, must be practiced in the same way the *a* in *want* is learned. (Refer to pages 113 and 117-118.) Children entering the continuum during the third year usually respond satisfactorily to some extra instruction by the teacher combined with their observation of peer performance and the opportunity to perform as individuals, with the teacher's guidance.

OBJECTIVES FOR C—SPELLING

Learning *how to spell words* to express the writer's meaning requires more recall than does learning *how to read words* organized and spelled by someone else. The use of Visual symbols learned for decoding words in B—Unlocking of THE VISUAL APPROACH should precede their use as sound symbols in this block of time for written spelling. In addition, the teacher should select words that were learned and practiced in the time for B—Blending and integrate them into the procedures of C—Spelling where they can begin to be put to functional use. It is during this daily instruction in spelling that elementary school children should further develop more complex concepts in spelling.

At what point in scope and sequence third-year (or more advanced) children should begin depends upon:

- what year they entered this multi-sensory approach to language arts,
- what they have been taught,
- their level of achievement, and
- the training, experience, and skill of the teacher.

The following areas in spelling will guide teachers in preparing children for the demands of upper grades and adulthood.

ADDING SUFFIXES

ONE-SYLLABLE WORDS THAT REQUIRE NO RULES

Phonetic (Green Flag) words ending in two or more consonants, such as *tramp, sift, crash, link, chart, hang, pitch, pinch, part,* and *sport.*

Nonphonetic (Red Flag) words ending in two or more consonants, such as *want, walk, watch, reign, sign, build,* and *friend.*

Ambiguous (Yellow Flag) words containing two vowels and one or two final consonants, such as *leap, float, throat, sprain, screech, reach, hoist, great, roost, grouch, boost, join, fault,* and *freight.*

Words ending with *x*, which has two consonant sounds /ks/, in words such as *fix, box, tax, flax,* and *flex.*

Words ending with a phonogram having a final vowel sound — *ay* /ā/, *oy* /oi/, *aw* /au/, *ow* /ō/ — in words such as *spray, joy, draw,* and *snow.*

ONE-SYLLABLE WORDS THAT REQUIRE RULES

(Refer to pages 120-129 and to *TWL*, page 61.)

1-1-1 Rule

One-syllable words, ending with **one** consonant sound, after **one** vowel (1-1-1 Rule), usually double the final consonant when the suffix begins with a vowel.

snap — snapp *ing*		*rub* — rubb *ed*	
bus — buss *ing*		*hug* — hugg *able*	
trim — trimm *er*, but trim *ly*		*lop* — lopp *y*	
glad — gladd *er*, but *glad* — glad *ly*			

Silent-*e* Rule

Words with any number of syllables ending in silent *e* usually drop the silent *e* (unless it follows *c* or *g*) when the suffix begins with a vowel.

skate	— ska t*er* — ska t*ing*
shade	— sha d*y*, but shade *less*
stampede	— stam pe d*ing*
bubble	— bub bl*ing*, but bubble *less*
manicure	— man i cu r*ist*
bugle	— bu gl*er*
evaluate	— e val u a t*ing*
age	— a g*ing*

Words with any number of syllables ending in silent *e* after *c* or *g* usually retain the silent *e* when suffixes begin with a consonant or with the vowels *a, e,* or *u*.

trace	— trace *a ble*, but trace — tra c*ing*
grace	— grace *ful*
outrage	— out rage *ous*
age	— age *less*

The *Y* Rule

Words with any number of syllables ending in *y* after a consonant usually change the *y* to *i* and add any suffix (except those that begin with *i*).

deny	— *de* nied	but *deny*	— de ny *ing*
horrify	— hor ri fi*ed*	but *horrify*	— hor ri fy *ing*
envy	— en vi *ous*	but *envy*	— en vy *ing*
envy	— en vi*es*		

WORDS OF MORE THAN ONE SYLLABLE THAT REQUIRE A RULE

Words of two or more syllables, ending in an accented 1-1-1 syllable follow the same 1-1-1 Rule as for one-syllable 1-1-1 words.

impel' — im pel' l*ing*	*forgot* — for got' t*en*
omit' — o mit' t*ed*	*forget* — for get' t*ing*

FORMING PLURALS

(Refer to pages 148-153 and to *TWL*, pages 57-58.)

Add *s* to most nouns.

forest	— forest*s*	*building*	— building*s*
umbrella	— umbrella*s*	*airplane*	— airplane*s*
nurse	— nurse*s*	*brace*	— brace*s*
tale	— tale*s*	*horse*	— horse*s*

Add *es* to nouns ending in *s, x, z, ch,* and *sh.*

dress	— dress *es*	*fox*	— fox *es*
bus	— bus *es*	*buzz*	— buzz *es*

Add *s* to nouns ending in *y after a vowel.*

spray	— spra*ys*	*decoy*	— de co*ys*
turkey	— tur ke*ys*	*monkey*	— monk e*ys*
day	— da*ys*	*valley*	— val le*ys*

Change *y* to *i* and add *es* to nouns ending in *y after a consonant.*

*bab*y̶	— ba b*ies*	*gyps*y̶	— gyp s*ies*
*pans*y̶	— pan s*ies*	*dair*y̶	— dair *ies*
*factor*y̶	— fac to r*ies*	*myster*y̶	— mys ter *ies*

Add *s* to nouns ending in *o after a vowel.*

rodeo	— ro de *os*	*radio*	— ra d*i os*
kangaroo	— kang a r*oos*	*cameo*	— cam e *os*

Add *s* or *es* to nouns ending in *o after a consonant.*

solo	— so *los*		*tomato*	— to ma *toes*
pinto	— pin *tos*		*tornado*	— tor na *does*
burro	— bur *ros*		*potato*	— po ta *toes*
banjo	— ban *jos*	or	*banjo*	— ban *joes*

(When a child does not know the correct way to form a plural, he or she should consult the dictionary.)

Add *s* to nouns ending in *f* or *fe* and sometimes change *f* or *fe* to *ves*.

shelf	— shel*ves*		*roof*	— roof*s*
wife	— wi*ves*		*cliff*	— cliff*s*
scarf	— scar*ves*	or	*scarf*	— scarf*s*

(When the child is not sure, he or she should refer to the dictionary. When the child's memory should be "fixed," the word should be learned as a Red Flag word. Refer to pages 107-108.)

Some plurals are formed in an irregular way.

man	— men	*foot*	— feet
child	— children	*tooth*	— teeth
deer	— deer	*sheep*	— sheep

FORMING POSSESSIVES

(Refer to pages 153-157 and to *TWL*, pages 59-60.) The children should be shown how to "intellectualize" use of the apostrophe *s* (*'s*) or the apostrophe alone (') during the period of guided performance.

Singular possessive nouns:

mother — moth er*'s*		*candle* — can dle*'s*
friend — friend*'s*		*man* — man*'s*
calf — calf*'s*		*class* — class*'s*
bus — bus*'s*		*house* — house*'s*

Plural possessive nouns:

men — men*'s*		*calves* — calves'
turkeys — tur keys'		*glasses* — glass es'
boxes — box es'		*heroes* — he roes'

ADDING PREFIXES

The prefix concept should be developed with root words that have clear meanings when standing alone without prefixes or suffixes.

One-syllable root words with prefixes:

distrust	*unload*	*misjudge*	*recoil*
dis *trust*	un *load*	mis *judge*	re *coil*
dislike	*debar*	*rehire*	*untie*
dis *like*	de *bar*	re *hire*	un *tie*

One- or more-than-one-syllable root words with prefixes in which the last letter of the prefix and the first letter of the root word are the same:

disserve	reenter	unnatural	misspell
di*s serve*	re *enter*	u*n natural*	mi*s spell*

One- or more-than-one-syllable root words with prefixes to which suffixes are added without requiring rules:

unload	*disjoint*	*replay*	*unfair*
un*load*er	dis*joint*s	re*play*able	un*fair*ly
un*load*ed	dis*joint*ing	re*play*er	un*fair*ness
un*load*ing	dis*joint*ed	re*play*ing	un*fair*er
unselfish	*disenchant*		
un*selfish*ness	dis*enchant*ing		
un*selfish*ly	dis*enchant*ment		

ADVANCED CONCEPTS FOR UPPER–ELEMENTARY GRADES

NOTE: The following steps are included for teachers of upper-elementary and junior high school students who have been working within this continuum.

One- or more-than-one-syllable root words with prefixes and an accented last syllable spelled as a 1-1-1–Rule, one-syllable word. (Refer to pages 120-124.)

readmit'	recommit'
readmi*tt*ed	reco*mmitt*ing
readmi*tt*ing	reco*mmitt*ed

One- or more-than-one-syllable root words, ending in silent *e* or *y* after a consonant, with prefixes and following the same rules as words without prefixes. (Refer to pages 124-129.)

incomplete	*incomplete*	*reclassify*
incom*plet ed*	incomplete *ly*	reclassi*fied*
		reclassi*fy ing*

DERIVATIVES*

NOTE: Concepts developed for use of prefixes and suffixes (page 145) with words that can stand alone if both prefixes and suffixes are taken away, prepare the way for cognitive skill in the use of roots such as *vert, flect,* and *mit,* from which meaningful words are formed:.

revert, invert, introvert, divert, avert, convert, subvert
remit, commit, demit
emit, omit, submit, admit
reflect, deflect, inflect

Suffixes can be added to *remit, convert,* and *reflect:*

re*mit*ting	con*vert*ed	re*flect*ed
re*mit*ted	con*vert*ible	re*flect*ion
re*mit*tance	con*ver*sion	re*flect*ing
re*miss*ion	con*vert*er	re*flect*or
		re*flect*ive

*For more advanced learnings of derivatives for junior high and high school pupils, see Carol Murray and Jenny Munro, *30 Roots to Grow On,* 1989.

MATERIALS

Chart Holder and *Small Manuscript Alphabet Cards* (occasional use)
Teacher's Hand Pack for Classroom Use
Yellow Card Pack
Teacher's Word List for Reference Revised
Card Packet for Introducing Spelling Rules
Phonogram, Suffix, and Prefix Kit, 1993
Composition Paper

PROCEDURES

ADDING SUFFIXES TO ROOT WORDS TO EXTEND CONCEPTS

ROOT WORD PLUS SUFFIX

Examples will be given using short-vowel and letter combination, one-syllable words such as *crunch, length, thank*, and *husk*.

> NOTE: None of these words requires use of a rule for doubling the final consonant because they are not 1-1-1–Rule words. They end in two or more consonants. (Refer to pages 72-74.)

The children should write their names and the date at the top of lined composition paper or, possibly, on the backs of the papers on which the blended words from B—Blending were written.

> Teacher: "Write one word *under* another, not one word next to another. This way root words will stand out each time a suffix is added.* First, I will tell you a root word to write. Then I will give you the meaning to be conveyed when the right suffix is added. I will ask someone to tell us which suffix to add. . . . Crunch."
>
> Child: "Crunch, /ŭ/, *u*, crunch, *c-r-u-n-c-h*."
>
> Class: "Crunch, *c-r-u-n-c-h*," forming letters with arm swings while naming letters softly. Writes *crunch* on papers.
>
> Teacher: "Tell how to make *crunch* mean (describe) candy that crunches."
>
> Child: "Crunchy — crunchy candy."

*Refer to Slingerland, *Book Two — Basics in Scope and Sequence* for the initial introduction of suffixes, pp. 83–85.

Teacher: "What is the suffix? . . . Yes, it is *y*."
Child: "Crunchy, *c-r-u-n-c-h-y*."
Class: Repeats and writes *crunchy* under the root word.
Teacher: "Make the root word *crunch* mean what you are doing when you crunch the candy."
Child: "Crunching. Add *ing*."
Class: Repeats and writes *crunching* on the next line.
Teacher: "If you want candy that you will be *able* to crunch, it must be what?"
Child: "Crunchable. The suffix is spelled *a-b-l-e*." Repeats *crunchable* and writes, naming each letter softly as it is formed.
Teacher: "Make *crunch* mean what *one other person* (third person singular) *does* when eating crunchy candy."
Child: "Crunches. The suffix is *e-s, c-r-u-n-c-h-e-s*."
Class: Repeats and writes.

Other suffixes such as *ed* and *er* may be added. Their meanings should be made clear.

The same procedure should be followed on other days with such words as *thank* plus *ing, ed, ful*, and *less* or *husk* plus *ing, y*, and *ed*.

When a root word such as *length* is used, suffix concept can be extended with the use of more than one suffix.

Teacher: "The root word to write is *length* (not *lenth*). It is a Green Flag word. [Name], please spell it aloud."
Child: "Length, /ĕng/, *e-n-g*; length, *l-e-n-g-t-h*."
Class: Repeats the spelling and writes.
Teacher: "How is *length* pronounced to tell what is done to make something longer than it is?"
Child: "Lengthen."

If the children are unfamiliar with the suffix *en*, the teacher should explain its use and write it where all can see and refer to it during the lesson. Then it should be included on the *Suffix Chart*.

Class: Repeats and writes *lengthen* on papers.
Teacher: "What did someone do in the past, or before now, to make something longer? . . . Yes, *lengthened* and *e-d* is added, which makes two suffixes added to the word *length*, *e-n* and *e-d*."
Child: "Lengthened, *l-e-n-g-t-h-e-n-e-d*."
Class: Repeats and writes on papers.

NOTE: If a child makes a mistake in writing the root word or in spelling the suffix or omits one of the suffixes, the teacher should pronounce what the child has written. In that way the child can detect the error. Examples: If *lengthen* is written *lengten*, the teacher should say, "You have written *lengt* for *length* (or *lengthed* for *lengthened*). Did you mean to write *lengt* for *length*?"

Children should be encouraged first to cover the suffix with a finger to make sure the root word is spelled and written correctly, and then to cover the root word to see that the suffix has been spelled right.

On different days, other words can be used:

thank — thankful, thankful*ly* (*how* something is done)
        thankfulness (the *name* of what is felt)
        thankless, thanklessly
brisk — brisk*ly*, briskness
wish — wishful, wishfulness, wishfully

A day's lesson might appear as follows:

Name	Date
crunch	length
crunchy	lengthen
crunching	lengthened

PHRASE WRITING

PHONETIC AND "LEARNED" WORDS*

Spelling of root words plus suffixes should be integrated into conceptual use in phrase writing. One or two of the words blended during the previous lesson of B—Blending plus suffixes should be selected for practice in phrase writing.

> NOTE: Where possible, especially in initial lessons, paper on which the whole phrase can be written on the same line should be used to aid perception and allow the children to see a whole phrase unit. Each phrase should be written on a new line even if part of it must extend onto the next line.

> Phrase writing is the first unit of *written expression*. Up to this point, the spelling of words alone is merely *word writing* without conveying thought. Because the phrase writing concept is introduced to first-grade beginners, it can be presumed to have become well established by the time the third year of the continuum has been reached. If not, it is the teacher's responsibility to give special instructions where concepts and practice are needed.

*For initial lessons in phrase writing, refer to Slingerland, *Book Two — Basics in Scope and Sequence*, pp. 85–87.

Assuming that the word *crunch* is to be used, the teacher could introduce the phrase writing by saying, "Let's write phrases with the word *crunch*. Remember, unless a phrase is the first one in a sentence, it does not begin with a capital letter. Do not use capitals unless I tell you the phrase is supposed to introduce a sentence."

Sample lesson for phrase writing

Teacher: "The phrase will tell what someone is doing: *is eating crunchy candy*. How many words are in the phrase? . . . Yes, four words. What one word tells what someone is doing? . . . Yes, *eating*. Be sure to think of the root word before writing *eating*. What one word describes, or tells, the kind of candy it was? . . . Yes, *crunchy*. What is the suffix? . . . You are right; it is *y*. Before beginning to write, someone spell *candy*."

Child: "Candy, can-dy, *c-a-n-d-y*." (If help is needed on the last syllable, the teacher should tell the child that the sound /ē/ is spelled *y* in this instance.)

Class: Repeats *candy* and spells orally, "*C-a-n-d-y*," using arm swings.

Teacher: "Now write *is eating crunchy candy*."

Class: Writes the phrase (leaving one or two finger spaces between words).

While the teacher circulates to check performances, the children should check their own spelling by covering root words and then suffixes with their fingers as explained previously.

Teacher: "What one little word tells how many were eating candy? . . . Yes, the word *is*. What does that one person (third person, singular) do to the candy when eating it?"

Child: "Crunches. I must add the suffix *e-s*. *C-r-u-n-c-h-e-s*."

Teacher: "Write *crunches all of the good candy*. How many words in the phrase? . . . Yes, six words."

Class: Repeats the phrase orally and then writes on papers.

The teacher and the children check their work. Continue in the same way but with less analysis of the dictated phrases. The children should begin to do this for themselves, following the introductory procedure to get them started.

crunching peanut butter candy
crunched with the back teeth

The teacher should continue to circulate among the children, giving assistance where needed.

RED FLAG WORDS

Red Flag words* often can be introduced, or reviewed, in phrase writing where their use is meaningful. Rather than allow a review word to be unnecessarily misspelled as the phrases are being written, the teacher should have a child spell the word orally, followed by the class'

*Refer to Slingerland, *Book Two — Basics in Scope and Sequence*, pp. 104–106.

repeating and spelling the word aloud, forming letters with arm swings as they are named. A Red Flag word to be learned should be written by the teacher where all can see to copy it. After a phrase including the word has been written by the children, the word should be studied as a Red Flag word.

The child's procedure for studying a Red Flag word is as follows: 1) pronounce the word, 2) trace over the pattern, naming each letter as it is traced, 3) repeat the tracing practice until the word can be written from memory, and 4) write it from memory on a separate paper. If the hand falters in writing from memory, that should indicate to the child that more practice is required until the word can be written without hesitation.

Sample phrases using the word *length*:

> the length of the r*oa*d
> lengthening the cou*ntry* road
> *could* be lengthened by spring

(*Road* is a Yellow Flag word. *Country* is a Red Flag word. *Could* is a Red Flag review word.)

SENTENCE WRITING

Sentence concept, as in the sentence, *The older boy ran   the length of the country road   before resting*, should be developed as suggested below.

Teacher:	Says the sentence for all to hear. *"The older boy ran the length of the country road before resting.* Who is the sentence about? . . . Yes, *the older boy.* What one word tells what he did? . . . *Ran* is the right word."* Repeats the whole sentence and asks, "How far did he run? . . . Yes, *the length of the country road.* When did he run?"
Child:	"Before resting."
Teacher:	"I will dictate the sentence, phrase by phrase, for you to write. Remember how sentences begin and end. *The older boy ran.* Think how many words are in the phrase."
Class:	Repeats and writes the phrase.
Teacher:	"*The length of the country road.*"
Class:	Repeats and writes.
Teacher:	"*Before resting.* Do not forget to show that the sentence is ended."
Class:	Repeats and writes.

The teacher should circulate about the room checking performances and guiding or helping. The children should check their own work as explained above.

Other sentences that could be used are as follows:

Every day we *watch*   the *workers*   lengthening the country road. (Dictate in three phrases. *Every* is a review word. *Watch* is a Red Flag word. *Workers* is a review word or, possibly, a Red Flag word.)

If they keep working   we think   it could be lengthened   by spring. (Dictate in four phrases.)

The teacher should know which words, such as *watch, workers*, and *country*, must be copied and learned, and which should be reviewed by naming each letter as it is traced in study.

At the conclusion of sentence writing, and after the words that were copied have been approved by the teacher, each child should study according to individual need. (Refer to page 108.)

The teacher should plan future lessons to include studied words as an aid to "fixing" memory with repeated use.

ADDING SUFFIXES AND WRITING PHRASES AND SENTENCES

The same procedure should be followed with 1) words ending in *x*, which has two consonant sounds, or 2) words ending with two or more letters that have *one vowel sound* and no consonant sound at the end of the word, such as those ending with *aw* /au/, *ay* /ā/, *oy* /oi/, *eigh* /ā/, and *igh* /ī/.

WORDS ENDING IN *x*

With Suffixes

fix	*wax*
fix*es* (third person singular)	waxing
fixed	wax*es*
fixable	waxy
	waxless
	waxable

(No rule is involved because the words end in two consonant sounds; therefore, they are not l-l-l–Rule words.)

In Phrases

fixing the box
fixing *every* box (*Every* is a review word.)
too old to be fixable (Discuss *too* as meaning "more than enough.")
when *Mother* fixes lunch (Before the phrase writing begins, explain that *Mother* should be capitalized because it is used as a proper name. Also point out that *fixes* indicates third person singular, with the word *Mother* representing that one person.)
will use the *large* waxer (*Large* should be copied and learned or reviewed with practice.)
was not waxy *enough* (*Enough* should be learned as a Red Flag word or practiced for review.)

In Sentences

Mother fixed the box   before filling it   with fixable old toys.
The floor   should not be made   too waxy.
If the floor   is too waxy,   *people might* slip. (*People* is a Red Flag word.
     Might is a phonetic Yellow Flag word.)

Spelling List

The teacher should select words from the above guided study for the children to practice remembering. The words should be used in subsequent phrase and sentence writing as *review words*.

every	mother	large
enough	was	people
one	use (verb)	might
ma*k*e	floor	too (the meaning should be given)
ma*d*e	before	

WORDS ENDING IN *aw*

With Suffixes

paw	*saw*
pawing	sawed
pawed	sawing
paws (third person singular)	saws (third person singular)

In Phrases

pawing the gro*und* (*Ground* is a Yellow Flag word.)
pawed with its *front feet* (*Front* should be copied and learned. *Feet* is a Yellow Flag word.)

In Sentences

A big deer   paws through the snow   to find grass.
Several big deer   paw through the snow   to find grass. (*Several* should be learned.)

NOTE: The teacher must judge whether children have the cognitive ability to understand the difference between third person singular (suffixes *s* or *es*) and third person plural (no suffix) with nouns having identical singular and plural forms, such as *deer, sheep*, and *moose*.

WORDS ENDING IN *ay*

With Suffixes

> *stray*
> strayed
> straying
> strays
> strayer

In Phrases

> strayed *away from* us (*Away* and *from* should be learned or reviewed with the usual
> practice.)
> straying into the *woods* (*Woods* is a Yellow Flag word.)

In Sentences

> The little *child*   strays *away*   if not *watch*ed by us.
> We strayed too far away   from the others   and got lost.

Spelling List

> (Each word should be traced and named, written from memory, and checked.)

ground	one	feet	away	lost	shook
found	mother	street	from	several	brook
front	other	deer	far	through	stood
find	brother	sheep	once	forest	woods

WORDS ENDING IN *oy*

With Suffixes

> *joy* (the *name* of a *feeling*)   joyful
> joyous   joyfully
> joyless   joyfulness

In Phrases

> a joyful time
> joyfully th*ey* went (*Joyfully* tells *how* they went. Two suffixes are used.)
> a sad, joyless feeling

In Sentences

The children had	a joyful time	at the *carnival*.
(Who?)	(What?)	(Where?)

The day became	a joyless time	because it did not stop storming.
(What about?)	(What?)	(Why?)

WORDS ENDING IN *eigh*

With Suffixes

weigh   *weight*
weighing   weighty
weigher   weightless
weighs
weight

In Phrases

weighed every *bale*
weighing *more* and more
    (*Bale* and *more* require review of vowel-consonant-*e*.)

In Sentences

My brother   weighs more than   I weighed   when I was ten.

NOTE: When children have consistently had help within this continuum, the sentences should be made more difficult.
    In outer space   the men were weightless.
    The books were   a weighty load,   too *heavy* for me.

WORDS ENDING IN *igh*

With Suffixes

sigh
sighed
sighing
sighs (third person singular)

In Phrases

sighed with thankfulness
sighing *sound* of the tree (*Sound* is a Yellow Flag word.)

In Sentences

We could *hear* him   sighing with sadness.
Mother and we *heard*   the sighing sound   of the tree.

SUFFIXES *er* AND *est* WITH THE COMPARATIVE AND SUPERLATIVE DEGREES

high, high*er* (comparative degree)
high, high*est* (superlative degree)

flew higher than the other one
went the highest of all *others*

The oak tree   is higher than   the apple tree.
The new building   is the highest one   in the *city*.

YELLOW FLAG WORDS SPELLED WITH PHONOGRAMS

By the time children have been following the continuum for two or more years, all of the phonograms shown on the *Phonogram Chart* (page 74) should be "fixed" in memory if teachers have followed the procedures in B—Blending and B—Unlocking. Practice with the *Yellow Card Pack* enables the children to recall the various ways of spelling a given sound to assist in generalizing spelling or in using the dictionary to determine the correct spelling. (Refer to A—Alphabet Cards, pages 60–61.) Children must remember which phonogram to use for automatic spelling. To develop that memory, children should write words from the teacher's dictation as explained in B—Blending and from guided practice with words commonly needed. This practice should include suffixes and phrase and sentence writing as shown in this section on C—Spelling.

GENERALIZING AND INTEGRATING

ai AND *ay* WORDS

After the papers are headed as shown below, a child should be asked to 1) listen for placement of the vowel sound within the word named by the teacher, 2) tell if the vowel sound occurs at the end of the word or if it is followed by a consonant sound, 3) name the letters that spell the vowel sound (phonogram), and 4) spell the word orally. Then the class should spell the word orally before writing the word in the correct column.

> NOTE: Sometimes it helps children to have each heading show vowel sound at the end (v/), and vowel sound followed by a consonant (v-), as shown below.

Name	Date
ai (v-)	ay (v/)
grain	clay
trail	slay
brain	sway

Teacher: "Grain."
Child: "Grain, /ā/ followed by a consonant sound, *a-i*. Grain, *g-r-a-i-n*. Write it in the *vowel-consonant* column."
Class: Spells orally and then writes *grain* in the correct column.
Teacher: "Clay."
Child: "Clay, /ā/ at the end, *a-y*. Clay, *c-l-a-y*. Write it in the *vowel-at-the-end* column."
Class: Spells orally and writes *clay* in the correct column.

Examples

trail	brain	sway	drain	*waist* (discuss meaning)
slay	faint	quaint	jay	Fay

(Refer to *TWL*, page 24.)

When all of the words have been written, the lesson should be summarized by noting that *ay* is used to spell the sound /ā/ when it occurs at the end of a word and *ai* is used when the sound /ā/ is followed by a consonant.

To extend and integrate meaningful spelling tasks, the teacher should select one or more of the words from those just written by the children to use functionally.

With Suffixes

(No spelling rules are needed in adding suffixes to *ai* or *ay* words because they either contain two vowels or end in *y* after a vowel.)

> Teacher: "Write *quaint*." After the children do so, point out that *quaint* is a describing word and discuss its meaning. "If a child is quaint, name the way he or she behaves."

Child: "Quaintly, and we must add *ly, q-u-a-i-n-t-l-y*."
Class: Repeats oral spelling and writes *quaintly* under the word *quaint*.
Teacher: "If no other child was as quaint as one particular child in a group, that child
            would be the _____ one. . . . Yes, the *quaintest* one."
Child: "Quaintest, *q-u-a-i-n-t-e-s-t*. The suffix was *est, e-s-t*."
Class: Repeats oral spelling and writes *quaintest* under *quaintly*.

In Phrases

Teacher: Write this phrase, *does behave quaintly*, and think how many words are in
            the phrase before you begin writing."
Class: Writes *does behave quaintly*.

NOTE: If the word *behave* is new and if the children have been learning to spell
two-syllable words in which the first syllable ends with a vowel (*TWL*, page 50),
a child should be asked to spell it orally for the class to repeat before using
behave in writing the phrase. This helps prevent mistakes. It should be studied
while the teacher circulates to check performances.

In Sentences

Teacher: "Listen for the number of phrases you hear in the sentence I will dictate:
            To us   the little child   seems to behave quaintly."
Class: Writes each phrase as it is dictated.

Again, the children should study any word to be memorized while the teacher checks
children's performances.

oi AND *oy* WORDS

Words to write in columns:

coy	joy	coin	en joy
toil	join	moist	em ploy
spoil	hoist	joint	de stroy

In summarizing what has been written by the children, it should be noted that, as with
the *ai* and *ay* words, *oi* is followed by a *consonant* and *oy* comes at the end of words.

oi Words with Suffixes

(No rules are required for adding suffixes because the words contain two vowels or end
in *y* after a vowel.)

join   (An *action* word that tells what someone can do.)

joining
joiner
joined
joins
joint   (By adding *t*, *join* becomes the *name* of something.)
joint + ly (Tells how something or someone performs.)

In Phrases

joined the club   are not joinable parts
will join them   joining them *together*

In Sentences

I will try to mend the joint before you go.
We shared the work jointly.
The rods must be joined to be strong.

oy Words with Suffixes

joy   (The name of a feeling.)
joyful
joyous (Describe.)

enjoy (Two-syllable word with prefix *en* becomes an action word that tells what we do.)

enjoying
enjoyed
enjoyable
enjoys

In Phrases

a joyous feeling   many joyful times
enjoyed our trip   joyfully they went

In Sentences

They *thought* of many things to make our trip enjoyable.
We enjoyed *every* day of our trip to the *ocean*.

A spelling list to study and to write from dictation:

before	want	thought	together
begin	wanting	thoughtful	togetherness
beside	wanted	thoughtfully	joyously
between	does	thoughtfulness	joyfully

/ou/ SPELLED *ou* OR *ow* AND /au/ SPELLED *au* OR *aw*

After the children write words in lists as shown below, it should be noted that *ou* and *au* are followed by consonants but *ow* and *aw* are usually used when the sounds /ou/ and /au/ end a word. However, *ow* and *aw* are sometimes followed by a consonant.

Words to write in columns

ou	ow	au	aw
ouch	plow	Paul	paw
pouch	how	haul	jaw
ground	howl	fault	straw
mouth	brown	daunt	shawl
bound	cow	vault	crawl
boun*ce*	town	taunt	law
troun*ce*	crowd	haunt	caw
sprout	growl	cause	
slouch	drown		

(Refer to *TWL*, pages 27 and 31.)

The teacher should select words for use in adding suffixes, and in writing phrases and sentences. For writing phrases and sentences, other words to be learned or reviewed must be included for study. The same procedures should be followed as the children advance in elementary grade levels.

Only the teacher can determine how fast the class can advance. Daily lessons should be challenging — not too difficult, but not too easy. Refer to standard spelling manuals as an overall guide to grade level expectations and make adaptations to the children's needs if necessary.

WORDS WITH VOWEL SOUNDS SPELLED WITH PHONOGRAMS

(Refer to *Phonogram Chart*, page 74 and to *TWL*, pages 21-33.)

Another procedure that the children enjoy is using the *Yellow Card Pack* to learn the various ways of spelling given sounds as explained on pages 61-62. One child at a time should be called upon to stand at the front of the class with his or her back to the class. The teacher should name the word and hold up the Yellow Card that shows the various vowel spellings for all but the performing child to see. The teacher should keep a finger by the correct spelling, which would be *ea* for the sound /ē/ if the word named was *streak*.

Teacher: "Spell *streak*."
Child: "Streak, /ē/." If unsure of the correct vowel spelling, "Do I use *e-e*?"

The class, but not the performing child, will be able to see the teacher's finger pointing to the correct spelling, *ea*.

Teacher: "*E-e* spells /ē/ but is not the right spelling for the word *streak*."
Child: "Is it *i-e*?"

Teacher: "No, it is not *i-e*."
Child: "Is it *e-a*?"
Teacher: "Yes, it is *e-a*."

The child should immediately turn to look at the Yellow Card and the class usually joins in with expressions of corroboration.

Child: Repeats *streak* and spells orally.
Class: Repeats, and writes *streak* in the correct column.

Examples of Vowel Sound /ē/ Spelled ee, ea, ie

fleet	thief	cheek	stream	three
shriek	chief	clean	cheep	beef
dream	bleed	sheep	beep	jeep
need*	heal*	seem*	steal*	
knead*	heel*	seam*	steel*	

(Refer to *TWL*, pages 23, 32, and 28.)
The children should head their papers as shown below:

NOTE: Using the same composition papers on different days to continue adding to the dictated lists provides an opportunity to note a generalization: more words have the /ē/ sound spelled with *ee* or *ea* than with *ie*. Knowing this should help in the future when reference is made to the dictionary.

The *homonym concept* should be introduced and explained.

Other examples of vowel sounds spelled with phonograms having like sounds are:

/ō/	— ow, oa	/ou/	— ou, ow
/au/	— au, aw	/o͞o/	— oo, ou
/ûr/	— er, ir, ur	/ā/	— ai, ay, eigh, ey
/ī/	— igh, ie		

NOTE: Children taught by this multi-sensory approach can be expected to have learned to use all of the phonograms shown on the *Phonogram Chart* (page 74) by or before the middle of the third year depending upon the consistency of the instruction they have been given.

---

*The teacher should discuss with the children the meanings of these homonyms.

REVIEWING DISCRIMINATION OF VOWEL SOUNDS
SPELLED WITH PHONOGRAMS

To review discrimination of vowel sounds, a list, such as the one shown below, should be prepared by the teacher. Only words with previously taught phonograms should be included. They should be written in columns, one word under another.

poach	sheen	sleet	crowd	groan
thorn	skirt	whirl	spoil	sprout
spray	moist	throw	drown	smart
sleigh	stood	bread	mew	scarf
proof	quail	quoit	queer	squeak

Sometimes the dictated lists should contain a mixture of words with vowel sounds spelled with phonograms and others with short vowels, as shown below.

slush	spurt	squaw	spend	chart
sneeze	crest	pond	broom	print

At times, writing words in lists should be integrated with adding suffixes, usually following this procedure: After the children write a root word, such as *roast*, the teacher should say, "Write the word that tells what your mother is doing when she roasts a turkey." A child would say, "Roasting." The class should write *roasting* under the word *roast*. Continuing in the same way:

Teacher: "What do we call the cooking utensil into which the turkey is put?"
Child: "Roaster."
Class: Repeats and writes the word *roaster* under the word *roasting*.

The same procedure for adding different suffixes should be followed with any other word the teacher may wish to have the children practice.

STRUCTURED STEPS FOR TEACHING SPELLING RULES*

NOTE: At any grade level, not all of the steps shown below should be included in the lesson introducing a rule. Possibly only the first two steps should be used in the initial lesson. Other steps should be added in succeeding lessons under the teacher's guidance. When, in the teacher's judgment, the children are ready to apply the rule functionally, the procedures explained previously for root word plus suffixes, and phrase and sentence writing should be followed. (Refer to *TWL*, pages 61-73.)

*Preferably the *Card Packet for Introducing Spelling Rules* should be used when rules are being introduced.

1-1-1 RULE

Words of *one* syllable, ending in *one* consonant, after *one* vowel (e.g., *sad*), *double* the final consonant if the suffix begins with a vowel (*sadder*) but do *not* double the final consonant if the suffix begins with a consonant (*sadly*). (Refer to *TWL*, pages 65-67.)

> NOTE: To memorize, or try to memorize, such a rule unless it is understood and can be applied to actual spelling needs is of little use to children with SLD who must "learn *how* to learn to spell." Therefore, the teacher should point out the reasons for doubling or not doubling the final consonant in words of one syllable when the children are learning to add suffixes.

With words such as *flash, quench,* and *sprint,* the teacher should tell the children that when one-syllable words end in more than one consonant, any suffix can be added without doubling before adding the suffix. When words such as *read, coil,* and *spout* require suffixes, no doubling is necessary because there are two vowels used to spell the vowel sound. When one-syllable words end in more than one consonant and contain two vowels, such as *paint, feast,* and *point,* no doubling is required, whether the suffix does or does not begin with a vowel. The children should be helped to recognize that doubling the final consonant is necessary *only* when the word has one syllable and ends in one consonant, after one vowel, as in *snap, dig,* or *trim,* and then, *only* if the suffix begins with a vowel.

Step One: The goal is to teach children how to use the 1-1-1 Rule. Therefore, the words to which suffixes are to be added should be phonetic and easy to spell until "rule concept" is reasonably secure. Then "learned," or Red Flag, words can be used.

The teacher should explain the rule and use a consistent verbal format for each step, demonstrating with cards on the Chart Holder or writing each word on the chalkboard and pointing out the reasons we do or do not double the final consonant. The children should watch, listen, and question without being expected to perform. It should be a time of input both for conceptual and performance purposes.

A word such as *dim* should be formed with cards from the card packet on the Chart Holder or written by the teacher on the chalkboard. A suffix such as *ing* should be placed to the right of the word.

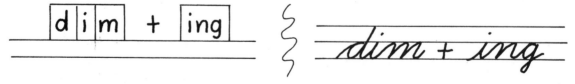

Teacher: "Let's check to see if *dim* is a one-syllable word to which the 1-1-1 Rule applies." Points to *dim* and says, "*Dim* is a word of one syllable," and places a *1* card in the margin or above the word. Points to the letter *m* and says, "It ends in one consonant," and adds another *1*: 1-1. Points to the vowel *i* and says, "*Dim* contains one vowel," and adds the third *1*: 1-1-1. "*Dim* is a 1-1-1 word."

Summarizes by saying, "*Dim* is a word of *one* syllable, ending in *one* consonant (pointing), after *one* vowel (pointing). I must check the suffix to see if it begins with a vowel." Points to the vowel *i* in the suffix *ing*, and says, "Because the suffix begins with the vowel *i*, I must double the final consonant in *dim*."

If using the Chart Holder, the teacher should remove the + card and place another *m* card after the *m* in *dim*. Then the suffix card should be joined to the root word *dim* to form *dimming*.

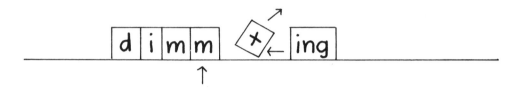

If using the chalkboard, the teacher should write the word *dim* in the second column and, on the same line, add the second *m* and the suffix *ing*.

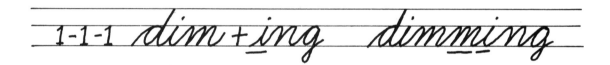

To make sure the children understand, the teacher should demonstrate with several more 1-1-1 words that require doubling, such as:

hop	+ ed	mud	+ y
flop	+ ing	big	+ est

When the children can recognize 1-1-1 words, identify suffixes beginning with vowels, and understand when to double or not to double the final consonant, suffixes beginning with consonants should be used to teach the children where doubling is not necessary. Suggested words to use are:

sun	+ less	sin	+ ful
glad	+ ness	spot	+ less

No doubling is required with words containing two vowels:

sleep	+ ing (1-1-2)	shout	+ ed (1-1-2)
sleep	+ less (1-1-2)	stain	+ able (1-1-2)

Other words that require no doubling are:

mash	+ er (1-2-1)	quilt	+ ed (1-2-1)
coast	+ ing (1-2-2)	foam	+ less (1-1-2)

The teacher should help the children recognize that doubling is not required, regardless of how the suffix begins, because the words are not 1-1-1 words.

NOTE: In words such as *claw* and *play*, the *w* and the *y* are a part of the vowel sound and are not final consonants; therefore, the words are not 1-1-1 words and require no doubling regardless of how the suffix begins (1-0-2). In words ending in *x*, such as *fix* and *tax*, the *x* has two consonant sounds /ks/ and therefore requires no doubling (1-2-1).

This introduction should be summarized by encouraging the children to recognize that the rule to double the final consonant applies only to 1-1-1 words, and only when the suffix begins with a vowel.

NOTE (to teachers of older children): Not until the rule can be conceptualized and applied functionally with one-syllable words should any attempt be made to apply it to words of more than one syllable in which accent on the final 1-1-1 syllable determines doubling the final consonant. Therefore, upper-grade and secondary level children should not be expected to learn and to use the rule for words of more than one syllable until they can spell and recognize accent in such words as *per mit'*, *con trol'*, *re gret'*, and *for bid'*.*

Step Two: Children should take turns performing the same procedure demonstrated by the teacher in Step One — verbalizing and pointing to the particular part of the word that must be noted when applying the rule. The teacher should guide the children's verbalizations. SLD children often require much help in verbalizing Auditory-motor performances. Therefore, children should use the cards on the Chart Holder before being required to perform the double task of applying the conceptualized spelling rule and writing the word at the same time.

Step Three: This step provides experience in applying the rule in written form. A root word plus the suffix, e.g., *fit + ing*, should be shown with cards or written on the chalkboard. The children should copy the word on their papers.

A child at the Chart Holder or the chalkboard should follow the same procedure learned in Step Two, pointing and verbalizing for the class to see and hear. *The class* should repeat the word and write it in the air, naming each letter as it is formed. The word should be covered or erased before the children write it on their papers. *The teacher* should check each child's written spelling for accuracy before the child traces over the written word to "fix" it in memory.

Step Four: The teacher should place a list of root words plus suffixes where they can be copied by the children. After a word plus the suffix to be added is copied, the child should immediately indicate if the word is a 1-1-1, a 1-2-2, or a 1-1-2 word, as shown on page 123, and write the word on the other half of the paper, always *noting in the left margin the rule that applies*. The teacher should move about to give help and guidance as needed.

Step Five: Procedures are the same as for Step 4, but the children should work independently while the teacher helps another group of children, possibly a reading group.

---

*1-1-1 Rule for words of more than one syllable: Words of *more* than one syllable, ending in one consonant, after one vowel, double the final consonant before a suffix beginning with a vowel *only* if the accent is on the last syllable: *re gret'*, *regrettable;* not *gar' den*, *gardening.*

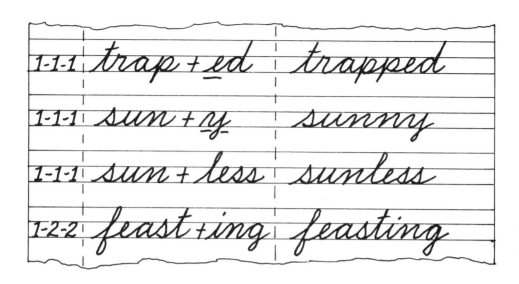

1-1-1	trap + ed	trapped
1-1-1	sun + y	sunny
1-1-1	sun + less	sunless
1-2-2	feast + ing	feasting

Applying the 1-1-1 Rule Functionally

Root Word Plus Suffixes

The teacher should dictate a one-syllable word that may or may not require the final consonant to be doubled when a suffix is added. After the word has been written correctly, the teacher should follow the procedure for having the children add suffixes. The meaning of the word with the suffix should be given and the children should write the word. Other suffixes should be used with the same root word — some requiring, and some not requiring, doubling of the final consonant.

Examples

star (a 1-1-1 word)
starry
starless

cool (a 1-1-2 word)
cooling
coolness
cooled
cooler
coolish

snap (a 1-1-1 word)
snapping
snapped
snapless
snappy
snapper

boast (a 1-2-2 word)
boasting
boastful
boasted
boaster

Phrases

a starry night
a dark, starless sky
starred with gold stars

felt a coolish wind
cool and snappy breeze
cooling the food

Sentences

We looked   at the starry sky   and felt glad.
The lid of the box   snapped wide open.

Independent Use

When the children use propositional writing for their own purposes, they should under-stand that if they use a word with a suffix, such as *clapping*, they must think first of the root word, *clap*, and how it is spelled. Then they can determine whether or not a rule must be applied when adding the suffix. This can be discussed before they begin writing.

To give practice, the teacher should say, "If you were to write, *The moth flitted around the light*, in which word do you hear a suffix?" A child should answer, "Flitted."

> Teacher: "Think of the root word, name, and spell it. Now think if it requires a rule before adding the suffix."
>
> Child: "Flit, *f-l-i-t* (or flit, /ĭ/, i, flit, *f-l-i-t*). *Flit* is a 1-1-1 word and the suffix *ed* begins with a vowel. I must double the *t, f-l-i-t-t-e-d*."

If the phrase to be written is *flashed the bright light*, the child should say:

> "Flashed, flash, *f-l-a-s-h. Flash* is a 1-2-1 word because it ends in two con-sonants. That means no rule is needed. Flashed, *f-l-a-s-h-e-d*."

SILENT-*e* RULE

Words ending in silent *e* usually drop the silent *e* before adding a suffix beginning with a vowel but do not drop the silent *e* if the suffix begins with a consonant. (Refer to *TWL*, page 69.)

> NOTE: Although the teaching of rules begins in the latter part of the third year of the continuum, the initial *concept* for using rules probably will have been introduced to second-year children. At that time, they usually are shown when to drop, and when not to drop, the silent *e* before adding suffixes.* This is done both for encoding and decoding words, such as:

*pin*ning	pin͎ing	*plan*ned	plan͎ed
*din*ning	din͎ing	*purr*ing	pur͎est
*tap*ping	tap͎ing	*stir*ring	cur͎able

The children should be shown that there are a few exceptions to the rule (examples: *true* and *truly, awe* and *awful, whole* and *wholly*) and that such words should be learned as Red Flag words.**

*Refer to Slingerland, *Book Two — Basics in Scope and Sequence*, pp. 106–111.

**Copy* and *trace*, naming each letter as it is formed, until the word can be *recalled* and *written* from memory, and put to functional use in propositional writing.

NOTE: After upper-grade children have learned to apply this rule, they usually are able to understand why silent *e* must be retained when it follows *c* or *g* and the suffix begins with the vowels *a, o,* or *u* — to preserve the soft sound of the *c* or *g,* as in *traceable* and *outrageous*. The teacher should not require this double task in thinking until the basic rule (a single unit) is thoroughly understood and can be applied with reasonable ease.

Step One:* The goals are to teach the children how to use the Silent-*e* Rule and to apply it to independent propositional writing. Phonetic words should be used to teach the rule before nonphonetic words are introduced.

The teacher should explain that the silent *e* is not needed when a suffix that begins with a *vowel* is to be used. The suffix adds another syllable and a new syllable division. This places the first vowel at the end of a syllable where it no longer needs the help of the silent *e* to make it have its long sound.

Examples

make	*ma* k*e̸*ing	es cape	es *ca* p*e̸ing*
crate	*cra* t*e̸*ed	ex plode	ex *plo* d*e̸*ed

Suffixes beginning with a consonant add another syllable but syllable division does not change and the silent *e* must be retained to preserve the long-vowel sound in both one-syllable and multisyllabic silent-*e* words.

The format used for introducing children to the 1-1-1 Rule can be adapted for teaching the Silent-*e* Rule. A vowel-consonant-*e* word (v-*e*) should be formed with cards** on the Chart Holder, or written on the chalkboard, and followed with the symbol + and a suffix beginning with a vowel.

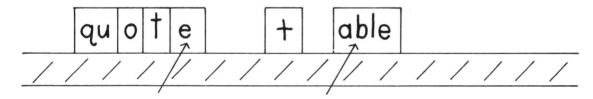

Teacher: "This is a vowel-consonant-*e* word." Points to the v-*e*. "Before adding the suffix, we must drop the silent *e* *if* the suffix begins with a vowel." Points to the *a* in *able*. "The suffix does begin with a vowel. I will drop the silent *e*."

The silent-*e* card should be removed and placed somewhere above the word and the suffix card(s) should be pushed over to join the root word, making sure that the *plus* card is either covered or removed.

*Refer to the procedures in Steps One through Five and Independent Use for the 1-1-1 Rule on pages 120-124.
**Slingerland, *Card Packet for Introducing Spelling Rules.*

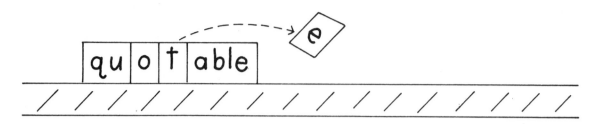

On the chalkboard, the vowel at the beginning of the suffix should be underlined and the silent *e* crossed out, as shown below. The word should be written correctly on the same line to the right.

The teacher should introduce the rule with the children watching and listening while each part of the performance is verbalized — a conceptual-Auditory-Visual *intake* for them. Other words should be used to illustrate the rule. Two-syllable, as well as one-syllable words, should be used by the teacher to show that the rule applies to both.

The introduction should be summarized by noting that the silent *e* is dropped only when the suffix begins with a vowel. Therefore, the children should train themselves to think how the suffixes begin. If the suffix does not begin with a vowel, then it is added without dropping the silent *e*.*

Step Two: Individuals should take turns applying the rule to a word prepared by the teacher on the Chart Holder or on the chalkboard. Each step should be verbalized by the child while the class watches and listens and the teacher provides direction and guidance if needed to prevent mistakes or misconceptions.

Step Three: For this step, the rule should be applied to words written on composition paper. Each child should 1) copy the word plus the suffix, e.g., *chime + ing*, 2) apply the rule by underlining the vowel in the suffix and crossing out the silent *e* in the root word — *chimé + ing*, and then, 3) write the word to the right of the same line — *chiming*.

The same procedure should be followed with other words, and the teacher should continue to observe and guide individual performances.

Step Four: In Step Four, a list of vowel-consonant-*e* words, plus suffixes, should be written on the chalkboard. The children should 1) copy the first word with the suffix, 2) indicate with markings whether the Silent-*e* Rule needs to be applied, and 3) write the word correctly to the right of the same line. The same procedure should be followed with other words, but each child should be expected to progress from word to word at his or her own rate of performance. The teacher should continue to circulate among the children to ensure that they understand and work correctly.

> NOTE: It is more beneficial to a child to complete all the steps with a few words than to copy every word without having time left to write them with the added suffixes before the work period ends.

*Retaining the silent *e* to soften the preceding *c* or *g* is a special learning. Refer to pp. 85–86, the note on p. 125, and to Slingerland and Murray, *Teacher's Word Lists Revised*, pp. 55, 56.

Step Five: The teacher should place a list of v-*e* words and suffixes on the chalkboard for independent work while he or she helps another group of children, possibly a reading group. However, this step should not be used until the children can securely apply the rule independently, as determined in Step Four performances.

Applying the Silent-*e* Rule Functionally

The teacher should dictate silent-*e* words for children to spell orally. The class should repeat the spelling and then write on their papers, placing one word under the other.

Teacher: "Spell the vowel-consonant-*e* word, *sprite.*"
Child: "Sprite, /ī/, *i*-consonant-*e*, sprite, *s-p-r-i-t-e.*"
Class: "Sprite, *s-p-r-i-t-e.*" Writes on papers.
Teacher: "Now write *spritely* — meaning *how* someone moves" [in a spritely way].
Child: "I'll add *ly*. I need not drop the silent *e* because *ly* begins with a consonant. *S-p-r-i-t-e-l-y.*"
Class: Spells orally and writes *spritely* on the line below *sprite.*

The same procedure should be followed with other words, as shown below:

glaze	froze	spine
glaz*ed*	froz*en*	spine*less*
glaz*ing*		
blame	pride	shine
blam*ing*	pride*ful*	shin*ing*
blame*less*	prid*ed*	shin*y*

Some of the words should be written in phrases and sentences as dictated by the teacher. (Refer to page 123 for the procedure.)

Independent Use

Sometimes the teacher should dictate phrases which contain silent-*e* words with suffixes. The children should listen for these words and *think* of the root words. They should name the root word and spell it to determine if it requires use of a rule before adding the suffix. When practicing the Silent-*e* Rule, only silent-*e* words should be used — a single unit performance. (Refer to page 124.)

Phrases

is *pruning* the trees	each dug one *spadeful* of dirt
sang many *tuneful* songs together	*chasing* the goats through the gate
took a long and *tiring* hike	found a *homeless* little pup
played *scary* kinds of games	will be *naming* the pup

(Refer to pages 107-108 for Red Flag word study. Refer to *TWL*, page 38, for *u-e* words.)

NOTE: Eventually, the children who are more advanced and who have learned more than one rule should be given practice in 1) listening for root words, 2) spelling the root words, and 3) determining which rule, if any, to apply — a performance requiring "more than a single unit."

THE *Y* RULE

Words of one or more syllables ending in *y* after a consonant change the *y* to *i* before adding a suffix unless the suffix begins with *i*; then the *y* does not change. Words ending in *y* after a vowel do not change the *y* to *i* but simply add the suffix. (Refer to *TWL*, pages 70-71.)

Step One: Preferably the rule should be introduced with cards* on the Chart Holder as shown below.

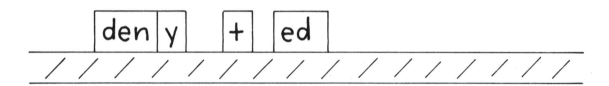

The teacher should explain that 1) a word such as *deny* ends in *y* after a consonant; therefore, the *y* must be changed to *i*; 2) the *y* card should be turned over — not removed — to expose the *i* on the reverse side and placed in the same position; 3) the *plus* card should be removed or covered by the *suffix* card as it is joined with the root word to form *denied*.

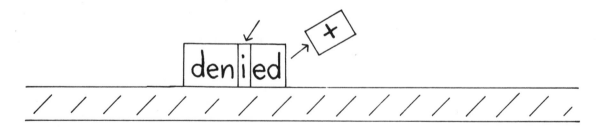

If cards are not available, the teacher should write the words on the chalkboard. When the *y* must be changed, it should be erased and the *i* immediately written in its place.

The same procedure should be followed with other suffixes, such as *es* and *able*. With the suffix *ing*, demonstrate and explain that *y* is not changed when the suffix begins with *i*; two *i*'s together usually do not occur in words of English origin.**

When children understand the concept for adding suffixes to words ending in *y* reasonably well, demonstrate with the cards that any suffix can be added to words ending in *y* after a vowel without application of any rule.

---

*Slingerland and Murray, *Teacher's Word Lists Revised*, p. 33.

**The word *ski* comes from Norwegian. Its ending in *i* necessitates putting two *i*'s together when *ing* is added to form *skiing*.

Words ending in *y* after a vowel:

spray	+ ing, ed, er, less, able
joy	+ ful, less, ous
en joy	+ ing, able, ed, s
re pay	+ ing, ed, ment, s, able

Demonstration and discussion will help the children understand that it is only when words 1) end in *y* after a consonant and 2) the suffix does *not* begin with an *i* that the *y* must be changed to *i* before adding the suffix.

Steps Two, Three, Four, and Five should follow the same structure used with the 1-1-1 and Silent-*e* Rules.

Words ending in *y*:

pray	+ ing, er, ed, s
try	+ ed, es, ing
lucky	+ er, est, ly, ness
em ploy	+ s, er, ing, ment, able
rainy	+ er, est, ness
glory	+ ous, ing, ed, fy
envy	+ ed, ing, es, ous, able

The teacher should give the variation in meaning of the word and the children should decide what suffix to use before spelling the word.

Teacher: "The root word is *glory*. What kind of a sight was it?"
Child: "Glorious."
Teacher: "How was something wonderful performed?"
Child: "Gloriously."
Teacher: "What was someone *doing* while feeling the glory of something?"
Child: "Glorying."
Teacher: "What would something without any glory be?"
Child: "Gloriless."

If the suffix needed is unknown to the children, an opportunity is provided to discuss and learn that new suffix. The teacher should name other words containing the same suffix for the children to hear and comprehend (without spelling).

Succeeding lessons should include phrase and sentence writing requiring application of the *Y* Rule in preparation for self-reliant use in propositional writing.

TWO-SYLLABLE WORDS

Procedures for teaching and practicing two-syllable words are the same as those for one-syllable words. (Refer to pages 69-86. Refer to *TWL*, pages 47-57, to find organized word lists.) Appropriate words should be selected from among those containing syllables with vowel spellings that have been taught, such as short vowels (*ham-let*), letter combinations (*trink-et*), vowel-consonant-*e* (ath-*lete*), or phonograms (*saw*-dust). If a phonogram or letter combination has not been taught, it should not be used in phrase and sentence writing until after it has been introduced and practiced in words dictated by the teacher in B—Blending time.

NOTE: Children who have been following this continuum before reaching the third- or fourth-year level probably will have been introduced to the spelling of two-syllable, Green Flag (phonetic) and Yellow Flag (sometimes ambiguous) words.* For learning to blend such words, refer to pages 87-93.

The teacher should select words from those given during lessons in B—Blending to integrate into teacher-dictated phrase and sentence writing in C—Spelling. Examples are shown below.

WORDS WITH SHORT-VOWEL SYLLABLES (PHONETIC)

napkin	cactus	ladder	polish
goblet	zipper	letter	rumpus
sampan	hammer	muffin	pepper

Phrases (not all necessarily to be used in one lesson)

put the napkin and the goblet
cactus with sharp thorns
the zipper on the skirt
a small boat or sampan
a good, big muffin

Sentences

A sampan is a small boat   that the Japanese use.
Put a napkin and a goblet   at each *place*   on the table.
My mother placed   a good, big muffin   by my place at the table.
A cactus with sharp thorns   got caught   on the zipper of my skirt.

NOTE: In learning to spell *caught* as a Red Flag word, emphasis should be placed on remembering the *gh* or the *augh* because all other sounds can be heard clearly. The teacher of more advanced children must select words of appropriate difficulty — depending entirely on how many years the children have been following this multi-sensory approach, the degree of disabilities, and the level of achievement. The structure of presentation and practice is basic for any grade level and depends upon the teacher's training, experience, and ability to make proper adaptations.

*Refer to Slingerland, *Book Two — Basics in Scope and Sequence*, pp. 75-81.

WORDS WITH SILENT-*e* SYLLABLES

dazzle	saddle	snuggle	apple
rumble	giggle	dwindle	handle
kettle	feeble	turtle	gargle

(Refer to pages 90-91 and *TWL*, page 47.)

Phrases

can crawl faster   than a turtle (can be dictated in one or two phrases)
put the new saddle on his horse
heard a feeble rumble
likes to snuggle close
the lights will dwindle away

Sentences

They heard a feeble rumble   as the sounds of thunder   moved far away.
Robert could hardly* wait   to put the new saddle on his horse   this
    morning.**
The little kitten   likes to snuggle close   and purr loudly.

WORDS WITH A VOWEL-CONSONANT-*e* SYLLABLE

trom*bone*	em*brace*	cas*cade*	trape*ze*
en*dure*	com*pete*	in*vite*	dis*pute*
stam*pede*	dic*tate*	um*pire*	ship*shape*

The teacher should dictate phrases and sentences containing words selected from those above, sometimes requiring the use of the v-*e* Rule.

WORDS WITH A PHONOGRAM SYLLABLE

ex *ploit*	*law yer*	*road* ster	*ther* mos
mar mot	*gar* den	*car* pet	pon *toon*
plat *form*	*or* phan	*saun* ter	*Nor* man
oat meal	*art* ist	*mar* ket	*Jor* dan

Follow the same procedures for phrase and sentence writing as explained above. Two types of words take suffixes without a rule: 1) ones in which the last syllable is not a 1-1-1 syllable, or 2) ones in which the last syllable *is* a 1-1-1 syllable but is unaccented.

---

*Hard + ly — makes it tell *how* or means *barely* or *with difficulty*.
**Morn + ing — makes another name or noun.

INTRODUCTION TO ACCENT

It is in the third year of the continuum that awareness of accent should begin to be developed through discussion and practice in *listening to* and *feeling* the accented taps made by the teacher on an object or on children's shoulders. The presence of rhythm in all phases of life should be discussed — in night and day, the seasons, tides, music, sounds of voices, events in a story, growing up, even in the happenings each day at home or at school. The teacher should demonstrate how uninteresting speech would be if spoken in the same tone of voice without accent. This idea should be discussed in conjunction with the effect accent has on the pronunciation of words and on word meaning. (Refer to pages 142-143.)

The teacher should explain that the dictionary uses accent marks to show which syllable is accented. Because perception of accent often is difficult for children (and many adults), the teacher should overemphasize the accented syllable when the words are pronounced for spelling. The children should be shown where to place the accent mark as the word is written.

Examples

lum' ber	cos' tume	den' tal	pow' der
fun' nel	ad' verb	splen' did	let' ter
suc' tion	junk' et	frac' tion	fric' tion
cat' tle	bub' ble	tab' loid	cac' tus
hor' net	Al' pine	ton' sil	blank' et
com pel'	sub mit'	dis miss'	ex plode'
in sist'	pas tel'	in vade'	con fuse'
sur vive'	sub ject'	com pose'	dis tort'
un til'	un less'	in vent'	

As explained previously, words should be selected by the teacher to use in dictating phrases and sentences for the children to write. (Refer to *TWL*, pages 49, 50, 52 for additional words.)

NOTE: Children should be taught how to make accent marks* correctly — slightly slanted little lines — and where to place them.

As stated earlier, the teacher should not dictate any word that requires use of a rule (as with *compel* and *submit*) until after the rule has been taught and practice for its functional use has been given. Such words should be copied or "learned."

Syllables Ending in Vowels: Open Syllables

The children should be told that syllables ending in long-vowel sounds that are spelled with single vowels at the end of the syllables usually are accented.

ba' con	vo' ter	va' cate	si' lent
fra' cus	to' paz	de' mon	in vi ta' tion

*The difference between primary and secondary accent should not be taught until the children reach more advanced levels and have had some experience in dictionary usage.

ta′ ble	po′ tion	ri′ fle	pro mo′ tion
bo′ rax	bu′ gle	cu′ bi cle	trans por ta′ tion
na′ tion	sta′ tion	re la′ tion	

When unaccented, the vowels *e, o,* and *u* have half-long sounds as in:

se dan′	*e* late′	*pro* pel′	*re* peat′
u nite′	*re* lax′	*re* gard′	*u* surp′
hu mane′	*pro* pose′	*pro* tect′	*pre* tend′

The unaccented vowel *i* usually has its short sound in words such as:

di rect′	*di* vine′	in *vi* ta′ tion
ev′ *i* dent	*di* lute′	*ti* mid′ *i* ty
Ti bet′	*di* lu′ tion	his tor′ *i* cal

NOTE: The vowel *i* has its short sound when it is followed by a consonant or is at the end of an unaccented syllable. (Refer to pages 86-95, noting pages 86 and 92 especially.)

The vowel *a* has its obscure or schwa sound in unaccented syllables:

pa rade′	*ga* lore′	*a* like′	*Da* ko′ *ta*
sa lute′	*a* round′	*a* shore′	*ca* bal′
a lone′	*a* bout′	*a* way′	*ba* nan′ *a*
ca nard′	da′ *ta*	*ca* det′	*ca* boo′ dle

NOTE: The suffix *able* is pronounced /ə b'l/ but the word *able* is pronounced /ā′ b'l/ owing to accent.

For integration, the teacher should dictate phrases and sentences containing words selected from the list written from dictation.

Examples

direct the children	watch the parade
salute the flag	saluting the flag (Silent-*e* Rule)

We will direct the children   to the parade.
Each cadet   will salute the flag   as it passes by.

THE SUFFIX *ed*

Children usually understand the concept of suffixes by the time they reach the third or fourth year of this program. An appropriate time to explain the three sounds of the suffix *ed* — /ed/, /d/, and /t/ — is after syllable division and accent have been introduced and understood.

When the suffix *ed* is added to root words ending in *d* or *t*, such as *plant, round*, and *lift*, another *d* or *t* sound could not be formed comfortably in speech nor would the sound be pleasant to the ear. Therefore, the *ed* is pronounced /ĕd/, adding another syllable with the *e* providing the necessary vowel sound — short, because it is followed by a consonant. When the suffix *ed* is added to words ending in other consonants, such as *ask, limp, buzz, bloom,* and *join,* the suffix is pronounced /d/ or /t/ without adding another syllable, and the *e* in *ed* is silent.

For practice, the children should be given composition paper and instructed to fold it into three columns. Columns should be headed /ed/, /d/, and /t/. The teacher should dictate short-vowel (*twist*), letter combination (*wink*), and phonogram (*count, claim*) words that do not require the use of a rule when adding the suffix *ed.* The children should write the words in the correct column.

Teacher:	"Crush, showing action *right now* or the present time. Make *crush* show action *before now* or in time already gone by."
Child:	"Crushed (/crusht/); I will write *crushed* in the third column because the suffix has the sound /t/. Crushed. *C-r-u-s-h-e-d.*"
Class:	Writes *crushed* in the appropriate column, under /t/, after writing the word with arm swings.

The same procedure should be followed with other words.

NOTE: When the children are able to perceive the final sound independently, lists of words should be written on the chalkboard by the teacher for them to copy and place in the correct column as independent work while the teacher is giving help to other children (in a reading group, for instance).

Examples

1. lunch	7. shout	13. hand	19. watch
2. plow	8. hump	14. want	20. chill
3. act	9. pick	15. last	21. stump
4. pound	10. yell	16. team	22. wheel
5. wash (Red Flag)	11. roam	17. kneel	23. pout
6. bless	12. leap	18. dream	24. toil

Sample performance

/ed/	/d/	/t/
3 acted	2 plowed	1 lunched
4 pounded	10. yelled	5 washed
7 shouted	11 roamed	6 blessed

1-1-1 Rule

The same learning and practice procedures should be followed with word lists containing some words that require the 1-1-1 Rule. (Refer to pages 120-124.)

> NOTE: When children no longer use paper with spaces between the writing lines, they should be taught to use every third line for the writing line to prevent letters that go below the line from touching two-space letters.

Other words to add to the list could be:

1. drop	4. pet	7. mint	10. fix
2. pad	5. slam	8. hunt	11. camp
3. shift	6. crawl	9. float	12. trot

Silent-*e* Rule

It should be pointed out to the children that when the silent *e* in root words, such as *blame, dive,* and *poke,* is dropped and the suffix *ed* does not add another syllable sound, the *e* in *ed* serves to preserve the long-vowel sound in the root word — bl*a*me*d,* d*i*ve*d,* and p*o*ke*d.*

When the suffix *ed* adds another syllable sound in words such as *note, fade,* and *quote,* the syllable division changes — *no' ted, fa' ded, quo' ted* — and the long-vowel sound of the first syllable is preserved because it occurs at the end of the first accented syllable.

Examples

fade	hope	blame
phrase	scare	blaze
wade	whine	pride
hike	like	glide

The *Y* Rule

Words ending in *y* after a consonant (*defy*) must follow the Y Rule before adding the past time suffix *ed*. Therefore, such words should not be used until the rule has been taught and is understood and reasonably functional. By then, children should recognize the three sounds of the suffix *ed* and be ready to integrate this knowledge with the Y Rule, although they may not be ready for this until they are well along in upper-elementary grades.

The teacher first must understand the underlying concepts before his or her judgment can determine when the children are ready for this next step in teaching "through the intellect."

Examples for adding ed to Y-Rule words

cloudy	glory	hor ri fy
envy	copy	sig ni fy
muddy	im ply	beau ti fy
pity	stead y	i den′ ti fy

For older, more advanced children, words that require no rules should be mixed with those that do, for practice adding the suffix *ed*.

Examples — 1-1-1 Rule and no rule

pre vent′	(no rule)	ac quit′	(rule)
re treat′	(no rule)	ex cel′	(rule)
re cur′	(rule)	sug gest′	(no rule)
gar′ den	(no rule)	gath′ er	(no rule)
pro pel′	(rule)	mar′ ket	(no rule)
com plain′	(no rule)	re gret′	(rule)
re frain′	(no rule)	de mand′	(no rule)
re spect′	(no rule)	re mount′	(no rule)
ad mit′	(rule)	de liv′ er	(no rule)
dis cov′ er	(no rule)	trans mit′	(rule)

(Refer to pages 120-124.)

Examples — Silent-e Rule

in volve′	(/d/)	cre ate′	(/ed/)
dec′ o rate	(/ed/)	ca′ ble	(/d/)
dis like′	(/t/)	de bate′	(/ed/)
lo′ cate	(/ed/)	hum′ ble	(/d/)
ex plode′	(/ed/)	re voke′	(/t/)

Examples — Y Rule and no rule

car ry	(/d/—rule)	jus ti fy	(/d/—rule)
em ploy	(/d/—no rule)	in lay	(/d/—no rule)
dis play	(/d/—no rule)	mul ti ply	(/d/—rule)
im ply	(/d/—rule)	for ti fy	(/d/—rule)
dis may	(/d/—no rule)	sal a ry	(/d/—rule)

The goal is for children to recognize when rules are or are not needed in propositional writing. Teaching "through the intellect" and giving supervised practice in writing dictated phrases and sentences that require thought when adding suffixes to known root words helps develop the skills necessary for independent written expression.

AMBIGUOUSLY SPELLED WORDS

More recall is necessary for ambiguously spelled words than for phonetically or irregularly spelled words. Children with strong Visual modalities, but with possible weakness in Auditory perception and/or recall, are apt to remember words for spelling if they can be *seen* correctly written, and *felt* in forming the letters while practicing and pronouncing them. Children with strong Auditory modalities, but with possible weaknesses in Visual perception and/or recall, may find their Visual memory less trustworthy than their hearing of the word as it is pronounced or inwardly proposed by themselves. For them, *hearing* correctly sequenced sounds of the word in association with Visual *appearance* and Kinesthetic *feel* in writing aids memory of the sequential letter arrangement.

Because of the above modality strengths and weaknesses in children, the teacher should conscientiously give supervised practice with emphasis on the particular part of the word that has ambiguously spelled sounds. Learning to spell such words is not enough; those that are most commonly used should be repeatedly included in phrase and sentence writing.

For example, the children must make a real effort to remember whether *j* or *g* is used when the sound /j/ is followed by the vowel sounds of *e, i,* or *y.* Such words should be practiced in the same way Red Flag words are learned. (Refer to pages 107-108 for spelling of Red Flag words.)

Examples

gem	gib′ let	jel′ ly	jeep
gyp′ sy	gi′ ant	jerk	jeer
gym	gy′ ro stat	jim′ my	jibe
gin′ ger	gym na′ si um	jew′ el	jet′ ty
gym′ nast	gen′ tle	jes′ ter	jest
gy′ ro	gi gan′ tic	jig′ saw	jib
gist	ge og′ ra phy	jit′ ney	jig′ gle
gi r*affe′*	gy′ rate	jit′ ters	jinx
germ	gen′ er ous		
Ger′ man	gen′ er al		

When the hard sound of *g* is followed by the vowel sound *e, i,* or *y,* there is no other letter to use in place of the *g* (as there is for the hard sound of *c* where *k* serves the need). The *g* must be used to spell *give, get, gift, gig, gilt,* and *geese.*

Similarly, the children may have difficulty remembering whether the sound /s/ followed by the vowel sound of *e, i,* or *y* is spelled with *s* or *c.*

Examples

cent (discuss meaning)	cir′ cle	cy′ press	cy′ clone
cen′ ter	cir′ cus	cyn′ ic	ci′ der
ci′ pher	cell (discuss meaning)	cyl′ in der	cy′ cle

sylph	as sist'	si' lent	sell (discuss meaning)
sigh	as sign'	sec' tion	sig' ni fy
syr' up	syn' drome	sys' tem	syl' la ble
sil' ver	si' lage		

A Suggested Procedure

After pointing out the ambiguities as shown above, the teacher should dictate one of the lists (e.g., the words in which *c* is the correct spelling) for the children to spell orally and then to write in the usual way when working together. In another lesson, the words beginning with *s* should be dictated. After each list of words is written, those words most commonly used should be dictated in phrases and sentences and then studied. When both groups of words have been practiced, a mixed list made up of the more commonly used words that contain the ambiguously spelled /s/ sound should be dictated and followed by phrase and sentence writing.

If a child is not sure whether to use *c* or *s*, he or she should be encouraged to ask, "Should I use *c* or *s*?" or, "I would look in the dictionary under *c* (or *s*) but if *c* is not right, I would look under *s*." The teacher, serving as the "dictionary," should tell which letter is the right one, and the word should be spelled orally and then written. The same practice should be followed when phrases and sentences are dictated.

With more advanced children who understand the suffix concept, the teacher should be sure to use words that require addition of suffixes.

> NOTE: Children should be helped to recognize that the more syllables there are in a word, the more apt they are to be spelled phonetically and that usually ambiguous spelling requiring special memory occurs when there are no more than one or two letters in any given word or syllable.

As another example, these children should learn words ending in the sound /j/, usually spelled *ge* or *dge*. Judging which spelling to use will be easier when it is known that words containing a *short vowel* and ending in the /j/ sound usually are spelled with *dge* (*pledge*). Words that have long-vowel sounds (*page*), have vowel sounds followed by consonant sounds (*plunge*), or contain a phonogram (*gouge*) usually are spelled with *ge*.

Until children in early-elementary grades are ready to distinguish between *ge* and *dge*, they should be expected to do no more than practice a needed word by tracing and naming and by having the word dictated in phrases and sentences, a procedure already explained and familiar to them.

Examples of /j/ spelled dge

bridge	lodge	dredge	dis lodge'
nudge	trudge	hedge	be grudge'
wedge	budge	fudge	a bridge'
Madge	smudge	sledge	be smudge'

Examples of /j/ spelled ge

w*age*	barge	man' age	ad van' tage
stage	cringe	out' age	un hinge'
lu*nge*	huge	re venge'	dis charge'
urge	range	ex change'	in fringe'
g*ou*ge	stooge	in dulge'	di vulge'
flange	surge	en gage'	ex punge'

NOTE: Whenever there is doubt about the correct spelling, children should be encouraged to look in the dictionary or ask the teacher to determine which of the two spellings is correct.

Phrases and sentences

the long, low bridge	stayed at the lodge
bridging the river	found ample lodging

Review the Silent-*e* Rule before suffixes are added to *ge* and *dge* words.

All of the pe*o*ple trudged	across the bridge.		
We stayed	at the lodge	where ample lodging	was available.

Phonograms That Spell /ûr/ and /ẽr/

Words containing the sound /ûr/ as in *fern, first, hurt, earth* and *(w)ork*, are good examples of Yellow Flag or ambiguously spelled words. Those words that are commonly used should be used frequently in phrases and sentences dictated by the teacher to strengthen memory. Learning the several ways of spelling /ûr/ and /ẽr/ will make it possible for children to refer to the dictionary. These procedures can be applied to other ambiguous spellings.

/ûr/ Spelled *er, ir, ur*

Children enjoy the group participation activity explained on pages 61-62 in which one child stands with his or her back to the class while the teacher:

1. exposes the Yellow Card on which various ways of spelling /ûr/ are listed for the class, but not the performing child, to see;
2. names a word to be spelled, e.g., *churn*; and
3. places a finger by the correct spelling of /ûr/, which would be *u-r*, for the class, but not the performing child, to see.

The child having the turn should give the vowel sound, /ûr/; if the correct spelling is known, spell the sound *u-r*; and then repeat and spell *churn*.

If the correct spelling of /ûr/ is not known, the child should name the various ways of spelling /ûr/ and the teacher should indicate which one is correct. When the correct spelling is given by the teacher, the child should turn to *see* where the teacher's finger is pointing; this will provide an Auditory-Visual association. The word should be spelled orally and then written on the chalkboard or on the children's papers. By voicing and writing the word, a complete Auditory-Visual-Kinesthetic association is experienced.

Other children should be called upon to spell the word with a suffix, e.g., to show past time (*churned*), what someone is doing (*churning*), or what a churner does (*churns*).

Sometimes, children's composition papers should be folded into a given number of columns, each headed with one of the ways to spell /ûr/. After a chosen child spells a word named by the teacher — applying what has been learned previously to determine correct /ûr/ spelling — the children should write the word in the appropriate column.

Some of the words can be written with various suffixes. Also, words from the lists should be selected to use in phrase and sentence writing and then dictated by the teacher. For independent work, children can follow the same procedure, proposing for themselves the phrases and sentences to write while the teacher is occupied with other children.

Examples of one-syllable /ûr/ words

stern	squirt	shirt	birch
serf	church	burst	merge
surf	thirst	stern	third
chirp	verb	nerve	swerve
twirl	curt	term	curve

NOTE: As the children advance into upper-elementary levels, words of more than one syllable should be used.

Examples of more-than-one-syllable /ûr/ words

con cern′	in ter′ nal	re ver′ sal	ser′ pent
con fer′	ter′ mite	her′ mit	ster′ ling
gur′ gle	tur′ ban	pre fer′	di vert′
con verge′	*ker*′ nel	re turn′	sir′ loin
con firm′	gir′ dle	cir′ cus	cir′ cle
squir′ rel	re vert′	skir′ mish	dis turb′
Thurs′ day	ser′ vant	fur′ nish	hur′ dle

NOTE: If a word requires that children recall a rule before adding a suffix, the teacher should not dictate that word unless he or she has taught the rule and given practice for its functional use. If such a word is needed before the children have learned the rule, the teacher should tell them what to do, explaining that they will be taught the rule when they are more ready for it.

/ûr/ Spelled *ear*

In a relatively few words, the sound /ûr/ is spelled *ear*.

earth	learn	earn	earnest
earthly	learned	pearl	earnestly
early	learn′ ed	pearly	earnestness
earlier	earl	yearn	search
earliest	Earl	dearth	heard

/ûr/ Spelled *(w)or*

When /ûr/ is preceded by the sound /w/, the spelling usually is *wor* as in the frequently used words:

work	worst	world	worth
word	wor′ sted	worldly	wor′ thy
worm	worse	world′ wide	wor′ ship

Some of the above words are often combined with other words to form compound or hyphenated words.

workbench	work′ a day	wormseed	worldly-wise
workbook	workman	wormroot	worldly-minded
workbox	workmen	wormwood	worldwide
workday	worktable	wormhole	worm-eaten
workout	workmanship	budworm	wormy

/ẽr/ Spelled *er, or*

The spelling of /ẽr/ as a suffix is *er* and *or*. Children in the primary levels learn to use *er*, and as they advance to higher levels *or* is included. Practice for memorization must be relied upon, with repetition of the more commonly used words in phrase and sentence writing.

Examples

learn er	north′ ern er	ac′ tor	ed u ca′ tor
jok′ er	west′ ern er	ed′ i tor	ven′ ti la tor
train′ er	south′ ern er	vis′ i tor	con duc′ tor
teach′ er	east′ ern er	in ven′ tor	ob jec′ tor
join′ er	con sum′ er	cre a′ tor	am bas′ sa dor
dream′ er	pro pel′ ler	vi′ bra tor	el′ e va tor
sing′ er	re charg′ er	sen′ a tor	in ves′ ti ga tor
tramp′ er	dis turb′ er		

/ẽr/ Spelled *ar, or**

As the last syllable in a word, the ambiguous spelling of /ẽr/ usually is *ar* or *or*.

po′ lar	cal′ en dar	mus′ tard	doc′ tor
so′ lar	mus′ cu lar	cus′ tard	o′ dor
col′ lar	pop′ u lar	haz′ ard	par′ lor
ce′ dar	cir′ cu lar	wiz′ ard	va′ por
ped′ lar	gran′ u lar	liz′ ard	val′ or
cel′ lar	vas′ cu lar	cow′ ard	col′ or
gram′ mar	or′ ac u lar	stan′ dard	splen′ dor
		or′ chard	har′ bor

*When early-elementary children need such words as *dollar, collar,* or *calendar,* they should learn them as Red Flag words. Refer to pp. 107-108. *Or* can be a noun suffix as in *educator, dictator,* etc., just as *er* in *stamper, camper, baker,* etc. *Or* is usually used with words of Latin origin and *er* with words of English origin. If in doubt, refer to the dictionary.

ACCENT (continued)

As children progress through the elementary levels, they should become aware of accent on some syllables, consciously listen for it, and learn its use both for spelling and for conveying meaning in words.

For spelling, the 1-1-1 Rule for adding suffixes to one-syllable words is applicable to words of more than one syllable if the last syllable is *accented* and ends in one consonant after one vowel. In such cases, the final consonant is doubled before adding suffixes that begin with vowels but is not if the suffixes begin with consonants — just as with suffixes added to one-syllable words. (Refer to 1. the Note on page 122, 2. pages 120-123, and 3. *TWL*, pages 65-67.)

Examples for spelling without doubling

In the words listed below, the accent is *not* on the last syllable or, if it is, the syllable ends in more than one consonant or contains more than one vowel. Therefore, no rule is required before adding suffixes.

trans po*rt'*	de ma*nd'*	be*n'* e fit	nu*m'* ber
re pe*nt'*	con t*ain'*	de li*v'* er	ga*r'* den
con c*eal'*	sub tra*ct'*	de ve*l'* op	e*n'* ter
blu*n'* der	in ve*nt'*	re me*m'* ber	qua*r'* rel
re str*ain'*	ap p*ear'*	dis m*ount'*	com pl*ain'*
plu*n'* der	sla*n'* der	ma*r'* ket	in ha*b'* it
po*w'* der	tru*m'* pet	l*a'* bor	di*f'* fer
per fo*rm'*	ac qu*aint'*	ex pl*oit'*	dis co*v'* er

Examples for spelling where doubling is required

oc cu*r'*	trans mi*t'*	pro pe*l'*	for ge*t'*
be gi*n'*	for go*t'*	ac qui*t'*	for bi*d'*
ad mi*t'*	re gre*t'*	re cu*r'*	re mi*t'*
sub mi*t'*	con tro*l'*	ex ce*l'*	oc cu*r'*
com pe*l'*	con cu*r'*	de mi*t'*	o mi*t'*

NOTE: During practice and with use, upper-elementary children should be led to observe that relatively few words require use of the 1-1-1 Rule for final accented syllables.

The meaning of words that are spelled alike can be changed by accent. For example, when the first syllable is accented in a word such as *per' mit*, it is a noun (the name of something) and when the last syllable is accented, *per mit'*, the word is a verb (showing action).

Examples

Nouns	Verbs	Nouns	Verbs
con' tract	con tract'	re' ject	re ject'
im' port	im port'	con' vict	con vict'
con' vert	con vert'	ref' use	re fuse'

Nouns	*Verbs*	*Nouns*	*Verbs*
re′ peat	re peat′	con′ serve	con serve′
sus′ pect	sus pect′	pres′ ent	pre sent′
ex′ ploit	ex ploit′	proj′ ect	pro ject′
in′ cline	in cline′	com′ bat	com bat′

Words in the above lists should be blended, spelled orally, and written. From the written lists, words should be written with suffixes. The teacher should select words for phrase writing using suffixes. Sentences containing some of the practiced words should be dictated by the teacher.

Intellectual Outgrowth

Intellectual outgrowth occurs when children begin to realize that both verbal and written language depend upon suffixes to convey necessary shades and variations of meaning. Such knowledge should increase children's reading comprehension.

PREFIXES

Prefixes should be introduced within the same framework used for suffixes, with immediate follow-up in usage, usually at the second- or third-year levels.

The process begins with a "single unit" performance — familiar root words that require no reading or spelling but only listening and understanding should be spoken by the teacher. A conceptually simple prefix, such as *re*, meaning "again, to do over," should be used with root words. The teacher should pronounce the root words and then repeat them using the prefix *re*, e.g., *take—retake, count—recount, name—rename, multiply—remultiply, capture—recapture,* and *build—rebuild.* The meaning of each root word and the change or modification in meaning when used with the prefix should be elicited from the children until they comprehend the prefix concept. (Refer to *TWL*, pages 43, 44.)

Written Practice

The prefix *re* should be written where it can be seen by all. Composition papers should be folded into two columns and headed as shown below:

The teacher should name a root word, e.g., *take*, and a child should blend the word orally in the usual way: 1) repeat the word, 2) give the vowel sound /ā/, 3) spell the vowel sound (*a*-consonant-*e*), 4) repeat *take*, and 5) spell orally, *t-a-k-e*. The class should repeat the word and spell it orally, using arm swings before writing on papers under the column headed "*root.*" The teacher should say, "Make the word tell that you *do something over* or *again.*"

Another child should say, *"Retake,"* and the class should write the word in the second column.

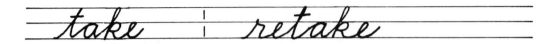

Other words should be dictated by the teacher who, as the children are learning, should keep in mind the goal, which is the conception of prefixes. Avoid using words which are difficult to spell because that could detract from the desired focus on comprehending the use of prefixes.

> NOTE: When the teacher dictates words that the children know how to spell orally, the "crutch" shown above should be eliminated, and the chosen child should do no more than repeat the word and spell it orally for the class to hear before writing it on their papers.

Examples

re (again, to do over)

re count	re seed
re do	re cook
re line	re chart
re blend	re draw
re write*	re sig nal
re name	re pol ish
re join	re fo cus
re string	re set tle
re print	re stretch
re read	re paint
re think	re dic tate
re use	re an nex
re word	re fun nel
re loan	re strug gle

un (not, reversed action)

un tie	un bro ken
un like	un faith ful
un lace	un faith ful ly
un do	un in formed
un hitch	un buc kle
un hook	un val ued (rule)
un lock	un dress
un bend	un coil
un bolt	un mask
un pack	un e ven
un cap	un im pressed
un clasp	un clamp

mis (wrong, wrongly)

mis use
mis spell
mis judge
mis fit
mis fed
mis quote
mis la bel
mis send

dis (reversed, away from)

dis like
dis taste
dis loy al
dis con tent
dis please
dis trust
dis trust ful
dis lodge

*Lines are drawn under those parts of words to be learned as "wholes," if not already known.

mis (wrong, wrongly)

   mis lo cate

   mis val ue

   mis read

   mis treat

   mis un der stand

dis (reversed, away from)

   dis a gree

   dis ap pear

   dis <u>hon</u> est

   dis <u>hon</u> est ly

   dis o <u>bey</u>

As soon as the use of prefixes for spelling is understood, show the children that prefixes can be added to root words in the same way that root words are combined with suffixes.

Examples

plant	— replant	+ed, ing, s, able, er
use	— misuse	+ed, ing, er (Silent-*e* Rule)
		+s (Silent-*e* Rule not required)
trust	— distrust	+ful, ed, ing, s (third person singular)
k<u>ind</u>	— unkind	+ly, ness, er, est
co<u>py</u>	— recopy	+ed, s, ing, er (Y Rule)
snap	— unsnap	+ed, ing, s (1-1-1 Rule)
spell	— misspell	+er, ed, ing, s
truth	— untruth	+ful, <u>ful ness</u>, <u>ful ly</u>
quote	— misquote	+er, ing, ed, able (Silent-*e* Rule)
		+s (no change required because the suffix *s* is a consonant)
unite	— disunite	+s, ed, ing (Silent-*e* Rule)

New concepts always should be put to functional use in writing phrases and sentences, thereby enabling children to gain independence for their own propositional writing.

Phrases and sentences

will rejoin my grandmother

should not disobey

to repaint the house

was very trustful

After we reswam the river, we were *ready* to eat.

I will rejoin my grandmother when the game is over.

My father plans to repaint the house this summer.

Intellectual Outgrowths

- *Suffixes* do not change the meaning of the root words to which they are added but they do give variations or shades of the same meaning or idea.
- *Prefixes* modify the meaning of the root words to which they are added at the beginning of the words.
- *Root words* with prefixes can add suffixes, and they require the same rules as they did before the prefixes were added.

As children progress into more advanced levels, they should note that when the last letter of the prefix is the same as the first letter of the root word, neither letter is dropped.

misspell	disserve	unnerve	reenter
misstep	dissatisfy	unnatural	reenlist
misshape	dissolve	unnumbered	reemerge

"Prefix concept" leads easily into the "derivative concept" at more advanced levels, as shown below.

ject (to throw)	*vert* (turn aside)	*mit* (to send)
inject	divert	remit
subject	convert	commit
reject	subvert	demit
object	invert	intermit
interject	introvert	submit

CONTRACTIONS

When helping children understand contractions, teachers can use the same procedure as that used for introducing rules, as explained on pages 125-127 and in *TWL*, page 62. Only in the first lesson is it necessary for the teacher to give a complete explanation of how contractions are formed for speech. He or she should use examples in speech only — there should be no reading or spelling at this point — e.g., "*Is not* can be shortened to *isn't, has not* to *hasn't,* and *does not* to *doesn't*, without changing meanings. I will name a phrase and call upon one of you to form a contraction by making one word out of two." (The teacher should write *contraction* where it can be seen by all of the children.)

Teacher: "How can *Did not travel* be shortened?"
Child: "Didn't travel."
Class: "Did not travel — didn't travel."
Teacher: "Has not climbed."
Child: "Hasn't climbed."
Class: "Has not climbed — hasn't climbed."
Teacher: "He is not here."
Child: "He's not here."
Class: "He is not here — he's not here."

The same procedure should be followed in forming other contractions orally before written practice is given as shown below.

Step One: The teacher should write on the chalkboard several examples of words that can be formed into contractions: *was not, could not, is not*, and *cannot*. Each contracted form should be pronounced and written to enable children to note the omitted *sounds* and corresponding *symbols*. The teacher should 1) cross out the omitted symbols, 2) in their places, put apostrophes, and 3) write the contractions as shown:

Step Two: Individuals should be given turns at the chalkboard 1) writing the two words named by the teacher, 2) pronouncing the contracted form and marking out the letters to be dropped, and 3) writing the shortened form as a contraction.

Children should note that, with only a few exceptions, the first word does not change in either its pronunciation or its spelling. It is the second word in which the change occurs.

Examples

is nøt	isn't	they ⱥre	they're
does nøt	doesn't	we ⱥre	we're
has nøt	hasn't	you ⱥre	you're
was nøt	wasn't	you wįll	you'll
had nøt	hadn't	I wįll	I'll
he ɩs	he's	I ⱥm	I'm
she ɩs	she's	cannøt	can't
it ɩs	it's	they wįll	they'll
that ɩs	that's	she wįll	she'll
Mother ɩs	Mother's	it wįll	it'll

Exceptions to be learned as Red Flag words

w<u>il</u>l nøt	won't
sh<u>al</u>l nøt	shan't
do nøt	don't (pronunciation only)

Step Three: Words to be contracted should be written on the chalkboard. Individuals should be called upon to follow the procedure explained in Steps One and Two while the class watches. After this has been done several times, the class should copy additional words from the list and perform independently, as individuals. The teacher should circulate among the children to ensure that each is performing correctly and understands what he or she is doing.

After the papers are completed, the teacher should dictate phrases and sentences for the children to write, thus providing an exercise in conceptual use of contractions and how to spell them.

Phrases

isn't in his room	don't shut the door
they'll run faster	tell me which way I'm to go
I'll try harder	this can't be right
couldn't find our way	doesn't want to travel far

Mother is cooking — Mother's cooking
the letter is unsealed — the letter's unsealed
you are to have all of it — you're to have all of it

Sentences

My brother isn't in his room   just now.
We couldn't find   our way to the park.
You are taller than Bob,   but you're not as tall as Tom.

Step Four: A list of words to be copied and rewritten as contractions should be placed on the chalkboard by the teacher. At other times, the *contractions* should be written by the teacher for the children to copy and rewrite as two words. Sometimes the teacher should dictate the list for the children to spell independently and then rewrite as contractions. Before allowing the lists to be rewritten, the teacher should check each child's paper, thereby preventing unnecessary mistakes. The children should frequently propose phrases to be written independently.

Step Five: For independent work, the children should copy simple sentences containing words that can be written as contractions and rewrite the sentences with those same words *written as contractions*. For example, *I will try to be on time* would be rewritten *I'll try to be on time*.

One of the goals is to avoid confusion in concept between such words as *your* and *its* (showing ownership) and *you're* and *it's* (showing a state of being).

SINGULAR-PLURAL

The concept of singular ("just one") and plural ("more than one") helps children spell "through the intellect." This concept must be taught before children will understand singular-plural ownership (possessives). Similarly, teaching the spelling of singular-plural words is necessary before introducing spelling of words showing singular-plural ownership. The two concepts should not be taught at the same time.

Forming plurals should be taught as a "single unit" performance that will form the basis for teaching singular-plural ownership. Integrated, the two will form a more comprehensive concept. Teacher-directed practice should be given in spelling plurals so that the desired meanings will be conveyed when phrases and sentences are written.

The purpose is for children to use written language independently for expression of their own ideas. Children with Specific Language Disability do not necessarily acquire these skills on their own — it is necessary for trained teachers to *show them how*. The children furnish the creativity, ideas, imagination, and their own special interests and motivation. The teacher helps them learn how to use language skills which will serve their needs throughout life.

The teacher should instruct and provide learning experiences within the structured steps previously explained.

Step One: Teacher explains and demonstrates (a time of Auditory-Visual *input* for the children).

Step Two: Children are given turns for individual performance at the chalkboard with the teacher's guidance while the class watches (A-V-K *output* for the performing child, and A-V *input* for the class).

Step Three: Two or three individuals perform (A-V-K) while the class watches before each child writes on his or her paper, under supervision of the teacher (*input* while watching and *output* while performing).

Step Four: Each child copies a list, or writes a list from the teacher's dictation (spelling), and then performs as an individual, working at his or her own tempo under some supervision (A-V-K *output* with limited supervision).

Step Five: Following the same procedures, the class copies and performs without supervision before completed performances are checked (independent *output*).

Unless children can put the spelling of singular-plural words into functional use in phrases, sentences, and paragraphs, no more than word writing is accomplished and the purpose of learning to spell (to convey meaning or thought) is lost.

Regular (Plus *s* or *es*) Plurals

By the time primary children reach the third year of the continuum, they probably will have had an introduction to the singular-plural concept.* The spelling experience suggested in this multi-sensory approach is with singular words that form plurals in the regular way, by adding *s* or *es*. *Es* is added to words ending in *s, x, z, ch,* and *sh*.**

The procedure for learning phonetic or nonphonetic nouns should be:

1. Copy singular words in a column headed *Singular* and write them to mean *more than one* in a second column headed *Plural*.
2. Write the words, after study, from dictation in singular forms and then, after the teacher checks them for correct spelling, rewrite them independently in the plural.
3. Copy words in plural form and rewrite them as singular words.

Special explanation and practice should be given in forming singular words from plurals where the singulars end in *e* (*horses, houses, reserves*) and vowel-consonant-*e* (*lakes, faces, wishbones*). Children tend to confuse the plural-forming *s* for an *es* when used with words ending in *s, x, z, ch,* and *sh*, such as *dresses, boxes,* and *wishes*. They make the mistake of dropping the *es* to form the singular, e.g., *horses–hors* or *lakes–lak*.

Examples for copying or writing from dictation

Singular	Plural	Singular	Plural
Singular	Plural	flash	flashes
clamp	clamps	mandolin	mandolins

*Slingerland, *Book Two—Basics in Scope and Sequence*, pp. 111–116.
**Slingerland and Murray, *Teacher's Word Lists Revised*, p. 57.

train	trains		class	classes
fox	foxes		lunch	lunches
plan	plans		napkin	napkins
doll	dolls		human	humans
buzz	buzzes		nation	nations

The first column should be copied or written from dictation and the second column written independently.

Plural	*Singular*	*Plural*	*Singular*
axes	*ax*	*horses*	*horse*
craters	*crater*	*bridles*	*bridle*

wishes	museums
votes	saddles
thimbles	kites
peaches	insects
axes	macaroons
infants	orphans

The children should draw the lines under the singular form of the words copied in the first column before writing the singular form in the second column, as shown above.

Words taken from the lists that were studied for memory should be learned in the usual way — tracing and naming each letter as it is formed and writing from memory.

Phrase Writing

The teacher should say a phrase and ask a child to fill in the missing singular or plural form of a given "learned" noun. After the child says the complete phrase, the class members should repeat and *write the phrase* on their papers.

Examples

vote

counted my one _____ (vote)
counted all the _____ (votes)
was given two _____
just one _____

mu se' um

went to a _____
a little _____
to visit several _____
saw many _____

peach

pick that _____
eat those _____
take this _____
several big _____

sad' dle

my new _____
gave us this _____
a number of _____
so many good _____

Sentence Writing

Sometimes the teacher should dictate sentences for the children to write, and at other times, the children should propose their own sentences that contain phrases taken from those written for phrase writing.

Irregular Plurals

The children should be shown that some commonly used singular nouns form their plurals in irregular ways and must be "learned" as Red Flag words. A few other nouns have singular and plural forms that are alike.

Examples

Irregular		*Alike*	
child	children	deer	deer
man	men	moose	moose
woman	women	sheep	sheep
tooth	teeth		
foot	feet		
mouse	mice		

Words Ending in *y*

When giving the introduction, Step One, the teacher should tell the children that the same procedure used for adding suffixes to words ending in *y* is used with singular words to show the plural. (Refer to pages 128-129.) Nouns ending in *y* after a consonant change the *y* to *i* and add *es*. Nouns ending in *y* after a vowel add *s* without making any change. The procedures for learning and practice explained on page 149 should be used.

Examples

Singular	Plural

babi *babies*

fl*y*	fl*ies*	ar*my*	arm*ies*
la*dy*	lad*ies*	ci*ty*	cit*ies*
puppy	puppies	story	stories
party	parties	cherry	cherries
penny	pennies	gypsy	gypsies
candy	candies	berry	berries

d*ay*	days	bo*dy*	bod*ies*
donk*ey*	donkeys	t*oy*	toys
monk*ey*	monkeys	vall*ey*	valleys
spr*ay*	sprays	s*py*	spies
turk*ey*	turkeys	myst*ery*	mysteries
rel*ay*	relays		

Plural	*Singular*
pup*pies*	pup*py*
libra*ries*	libra*ry*
rub*ies*	ru*by*
lil*ies*	li*ly*
bab*ies*	ba*by*

Sentence Writing

We ran many relays   while at the picnic.
I read a mystery story   because I enjoy mysteries.
At our party   we had a berry pie   made of the berries   that we picked.

More Advanced Concepts

By the time children reach higher levels of elementary school, their concept of singular-plural should have attained the level needed for both verbal and written skills. They should have little difficulty in learning how to form the plurals of singular nouns ending in *o* and *f* or *fe*.

- Nouns ending in *o* after a consonant add *s* or *es*; the right ending must be learned for recall.
- Nouns ending in *o* after a vowel add *s*, just as do nouns ending in *y* after a vowel, both without making any change in singular spelling.
- Most nouns ending in *f* or *fe* add *s* to form the plural.
- Some nouns ending in *f* or *fe* change the final *f* or *fe* to *ves*. Such plural forms must be memorized and repeated in phrase and sentence writing to strengthen memory.

(Refer to *TWL*, pages 57 and 58.)

Words Ending in *o*

o after a vowel (add *s*)   *o* after a consonant (add *s*)

Singular	*Plural*	*Singular*	*Plural*
rod*e*o	rodeos	piano	pianos
cam*e*o	cameos	rancho	ranchos
stud*i*o	studios	soprano	sopranos
shamp*oo*	shampoos	dynamo	dynamos
rad*i*o	radios	kimono	kimonos
kangar*oo*	kangaroos		

o after a consonant (add *es*)

tomato   tomatoes
potato   potatoes
torpedo   torpedoes
hero   heroes
mosquito   mosquitoes

Some words ending in *o* after a consonant add either *s* or *es*.

s or *es*	*Preferred*	*Accepted*
domino	dominoes	dominos
cargo	cargoes	cargos
hobo	hoboes	hobos
banjo	banjos	banjoes
motto	mottoes	mottos
halo	halos	haloes
pinto	pintos	pintoes

The children should note that the singular form does not change its spelling when *s* or *es* is added to form the plural.

Words Ending in *f* or *fe*

add *s* to form the plural		change *f* or *fe* to *ves*	
Singular	*Plural*	*Singular*	*Plural*
roof	roofs	elf	elves
fife	fifes	loaf	loaves
reef	reefs	life	lives
waif	waifs	knife	knives
dwarf	dwarfs	shelf	shelves
staff	staffs	calf	calves
cliff	cliffs	self	selves
		wife	wives
		thief	thieves
		scarf	scarves (sometimes scarfs)

Children should learn to think first of the singular spelling of a word, and from that, determine plural spelling. If they do not know the singular spelling, they may ask or use the dictionary.

SINGULAR-PLURAL OWNERSHIP

The concept of ownership (possession) usually develops long before children learn to read or write. It begins verbally in the preschool years of phenomenal language development. When it is needed for spelling, the teacher should begin with discussion.

Children should be shown that an apostrophe followed by *s* ('s) or simply an apostrophe (') added to the name of a person, place, or thing indicates that something is owned. It should be pointed out that the sound /s/ is heard at the end of words showing ownership and that these words are followed by the name(s) of whatever is owned.*

Bring out in discussion that sometimes just *one* person owns something — *Bob's* nose, the *boy's* mother — and sometimes more than one person has a share in owning the same thing — *the three boys'* mother (which does not mean the same as *the three boys'* mother*s*). The absurdity of a phrase such as *the three boys' nose* should be discussed. These kinds of examples prepare children to understand that both *spelling and punctuation* must be thought about rather than learned by rote or memorized from word lists in order to pass weekly spelling tests. Children with SLD will promptly forget words learned in such a way. Correct spelling and punctuation enable the reader and writer to have a common understanding.

Singular Ownership

Singular ownership should be taught first. The children should learn that singular ownership is shown by spelling the word that means *one* of something before adding the punctuation that shows possession — an apostrophe and *s* to indicate ownership of the item(s) or object(s) named by the word(s) that follow(s). Introduction and practice leading to independent use should follow the steps explained on pages 120-124 or 148-152.

Examples of singular ownership of one thing

Singular	Ownership	Usage
cup	cup's	one cup's handle
kit' ten	kitten's	the kitten's paw
flow' er	flower's	this flower's petal
lem' on	lemon's	that lemon's color
shoe (Red Flag)	shoe's	this one shoe's strap
horse	horse's	her horse's long mane
chick' en	chicken's	the little chicken's leg
car	car's	the old car's wheel
side' walk	sidewalk's	the sidewalk's crack
night	night's	each night's darkness
Jane	Jane's	Jane's new dress
bus	bus's	the bus's flag

Practice procedure

cup   cup's

one cup's handle

*Implied ownership should not be taught until children have had experience in using possessive forms in writing phrases and sentences — probably not until sixth- or seventh-year levels, depending upon previous teaching and learnings.

Examples of singular ownership of more-than-one thing

Singular	Ownership	Usage
mother	mother's	my mother's dresses
Mrs. Brown	Mrs. Brown's	Mrs. Brown's children
river	river's	one river's banks
wagon	wagon's	big wagon's sides
earth	earth's	our earth's lakes
star	star's	that star's bright twinkles
landslide	landslide's	that landslide's dangers
bobolink	bobolink's	bobolink's nest and babies
goblin	goblin's	a goblin's hideouts
clock	clock's	any clock's hands
davenport	davenport's	the davenport's pillows
nation	nation's	our nation's *people*
child	child's	your child's toys

Phrases and sentences

one big elephant's baby
one old plant's roots
my grandfather's crutches
Daddy's new shirts
your dad's black coat
sitting in the driver's seat
the hospital's *patients* (Red Flag)

My plans are to travel in Ted's car.
Put the food in that family's truck.
One potato's skin was burned.
This story's ending is a happy one.
Our school's rooms are large.
That bus's driver will wait for us.

Plural Ownership

After singular ownership is understood and can be used correctly, *plural ownership* should be explained. If more than one person, place, or thing owns something, its name should be spelled in its plural form *before showing ownership*. If it ends with the sound /s/ (*socks, dresses*), usually no more than the apostrophe need be added to show possession (*socks', dresses'*).

Examples

Plural	Ownership	Usage
nails	nails'	the nails' big box
bags	bags'	six bags' contents
poodles	poodles'	all of the poodles' trainers
planes	planes'	several planes' landing gear
chairs	chairs'	these chairs' legs
guides	guides'	two guides' horses
roosters	roosters'	the roosters' tails
magazines	magazines'	weekly magazines' stories
foxes	foxes'	the foxes' dens
children	children's	the children's mother
men	men's	the men's children

Sentences

All of the best peaches' pits   were dumped   into one can.
Five boxes' ribbons   can be used again   to tie them.
All of the coaches' drivers   are ready to go.
The dogs' tails   got caught   in the fence.
The boys' friend   joined them   to play ball.
Everyone enjoyed   the new people's songs.

Practice with the teacher's guidance should establish "thought patterns" that will assist children in:

- showing singular possession by spelling the word that names one owner of something before adding explanatory punctuation, usually an apostrophe and *s* (*'s*).
- showing plural possession by spelling the word that names the "more-than-one" owners of something before adding the punctuation, usually an apostrophe (*'*), unless the plural word does not end in the sound /s/; if it does not, the punctuation should be an apostrophe and *s* (*men's, children's*).

More Advanced Concepts

With adequate preparation, children should understand the singular-plural ownership concept and procedures for its written expression when the plurals are formed regularly. They should then be ready to apply the same "thought patterns" to plural words formed less regularly from singulars ending in:

- *y* after a vowel or consonant,
- *o* after a vowel or a consonant, or
- *f* or *fe*.

(Refer to pages 149-153 for spelling plural words and to *TWL*, pages 57-60, for singular-plural and possessive spellings.)

Examples

Singular	Singular Possessive	Plural	Plural Possessive
desk	desk's	desks	desks'
lake	lake's	lakes	lakes'
bench	bench's	benches	benches'
horse	horse's	horses	horses'
tree	tree's	trees	trees'
orange	orange's	oranges	oranges'
season	season's	seasons	seasons'
shelf	shelf's	shelves	shelves'
American	American's	Americans	Americans'
company	company's	companies	companies'
table	table's	tables	tables'
mouse	mouse's	mice	mice's
dinner	dinner's	dinners	dinners'

Singular	Singular Possessive	Plural	Plural Possessive
diner	diner's	diners	diners'
buffalo	buffalo's	buffaloes	buffaloes'
valley	valley's	valleys	valleys'
radio	radio's	radios	radios'
atlas	atlas's	atlases	atlases'
child	child's	children	children's
bus	bus's	buses	buses'

Learning to spell and use the words in C—Spelling in phrases and sentences will enable the children to make progress in another basic skill, writing paragraphs, which will be explained in the next section.

D—Dictation

INTRODUCTION

The children should be given an opportunity to express paragraph structure verbally while cursive writing is being learned. (Refer to pages 21-49.) Verbalizing a paragraph and learning cursive penmanship are each "single unit" performances that, combined, form a larger, more complex unit of language performance. Children should already have developed cognitive abilities to think of phrases as fragments of thoughts and sentences as complete thoughts. Learning to write a single, simple paragraph should have begun in the second year of the continuum* if children entered SLD classes at the first-year level. The earlier experience should have prepared third- and fourth-year children for paragraph enrichment.

Written work for children at third-year levels should be minimized until letter forms can be automatically recalled and written correctly. This is one reason for emphasizing the learning of cursive writing at the beginning of the third year, and not spreading it out over weeks or months or neglecting it in the belief that children will "pick it up" for themselves. As soon as cursive handwriting begins to become a "tool" or basic skill, there need be no delay in introducing paragraph writing.

Teaching children the different spelling and punctuation requirements to write a given paragraph should enable them to follow the teacher's dictation of each sentence without having to concentrate on penmanship. Attention can then be focused on the correct spelling and punctuation of thoughts to be expressed. In that way, the train of thought need not be interrupted by unsure recall of letter formation.

The teacher should remember that successful performances can be achieved by preventive instruction and preparation for writing a dictated paragraph. This will elicit self-confidence and self-motivation for future tasks. Therefore, verbalizing paragraphs should precede attempts at writing paragraphs.

*Teachers are advised to read Slingerland, *Book Two — Basics in Scope and Sequence*, pp. 116–144 before moving ahead into advancing forms of written expression.

PROCEDURE FOR VERBALIZING PARAGRAPHS

When a paragraph is to be constructed orally, either the teacher or a child should propose an introductory sentence that expresses an idea or subject which can be enlarged upon with additional sentences. The teacher or child should not hesitate to suggest rewording or enrichment that improves the thought or structure of the introductory sentence.

The teacher should tell the children to think ahead for ideas that add to or relate to whatever thought was expressed in the beginning sentence. By asking leading questions or making suggestions, the teacher should elicit one, two, or three good sentences to form the body of the paragraph. Because this is an oral exercise, spelling and punctuation need not be considered. Each time a sentence is added, a child should repeat the introductory sentence as well as those in the body. A concluding sentence should complete the overall thought expressed in the paragraph. (The teacher should write the paragraph for his or her own reference.)

Sample paragraph

I wish I were a pilot of an airplane. I could see out in many directions. I could look out into the sky and onto the earth below. Sometimes clouds might hide the earth. I would be in a world all by myself.

As the paragraph is being built, different children should take turns repeating as much of it as possible. Each child should state the introductory sentence, each following sentence, and then the concluding sentence. Recalling exact wording is difficult for almost anyone; the sequence of thoughts may be recalled more easily than the exact words. Perfect quotation of introductory or final sentences may be helped by the teacher's giving the first phrase and asking a question that stimulates recall of the succeeding phrase. For example, the final sentence in the paragraph above may be prompted as follows:

Teacher: "I would be where?"
Child: "In a world."
Teacher: "In what way?"
Child: "All by myself."
Teacher: "Now repeat the whole sentence beginning with 'I would.'"
Child: "I would be   in a world   all by myself."

Children should be encouraged to 1) retain the sequence of ideas given in the body, 2) detect and delete extraneous ideas when they occur, 3) recall exact wording of the introductory and final sentences, and as much of the body as possible with the help of questioning by the teacher to stimulate recall.

NOTE: Children who experience difficulty in recalling exact wording from auditory stimuli that leave no points of reference to aid recall should understand the desirability of putting what is to be remembered into the visual stimuli of written words that serve as constant points of reference. Therefore, children come to understand that learning to put into writing what we wish to say enables us to record and recall the exact wording for others and ourselves to read and reread.

The practice gained from verbalizing paragraphs and then from writing paragraphs will enable each child to propose wording that expresses individual thoughts and to write them for future reference — a performance referred to as *propositional writing.*

The lessons which follow are meant to show how all of the components of The Daily Format are integrated for propositional writing. Children should write from dictation in preparation for the propositional writing expected of them not only as they advance into higher grade levels but also throughout life.

PLANNING FOR DICTATION LESSONS

It is advisable for the teacher to compose the paragraphs for dictation before they are presented to the children for study. They should be worded according to children's current learning abilities and previous instruction and experience in writing studied paragraphs. The teacher should know which words:

- conform to concepts previously learned, such as two-syllable, short-vowel words, e.g., *ton-sil*;
- have been learned as Red Flag words, e.g., *laugh*;
- contain suffixes that require no spelling rules, e.g., *laughable, conforming*;
- require use of a rule that has been learned, e.g., *baking* (*bake*);
- require special teaching and practice because they have not yet been learned, e.g., *cringe*;
- are to be learned as Red Flag words, e.g., *jour-ney*;
- are to be left as a constant point of reference for copying, e.g., *thoroughly, courageous* (unlearned rule).

The same criteria apply to marks of punctuation.

OBJECTIVES FOR D—DICTATION

The overall objective is to enlarge the "paragraph unit" concept begun in the second year of the continuum,* first, by having paragraphs verbalized, and then by having paragraphs studied and written from dictation.

LOWER-ELEMENTARY GRADES

Use simple "paragraph units" composed of sentences related to a single thought or idea with:

- an introductory sentence to convey the idea of what is to be expressed;
- sentences for the body to enrich the subject or idea; and
- a concluding sentence to convey completion or an ending to the "idea unit."

*It is recommended that the teacher read D—Dictation in Slingerland, *Book Two — Basics in Scope and Sequence*, pp. 117-144, as a foundation for this section.

UPPER-ELEMENTARY GRADES

Following the same organization (introduction, body, and conclusion) used for short paragraphs, students will learn to develop longer paragraphs and essay-type "units" or themes.

VERBALIZING

- Verbalize an introductory paragraph of one or two sentences to introduce the theme or subject.
- Verbalize paragraphs to develop and enrich the theme or body.
- Explain why the last sentence in each paragraph should give an idea of what is to follow in the succeeding paragraph.
- Verbalize a concluding paragraph of one or two sentences.

WRITING

The following activities are appropriate for children in upper-elementary grades:
- Follow the procedures for verbalizing a paragraph, but for writing, paragraphs should be kept short and to the point.
- Lesson plans of A—Alphabet Cards, B—Blending, and C—Spelling should include teaching and practicing new learnings required for writing a paragraph from dictation.
- From verbalized themes, select one of the paragraphs for study before having it written from dictation.
- Use a teacher-composed paragraph containing new learnings or needed review.

FUNCTIONAL USE OF PUNCTUATION

Explanation of and practice with punctuation marks to convey specific meanings should be included for:
- periods for various purposes,
- commas for various purposes,
- quotation marks,
- dashes,
- exclamation points, and
- other marks required to convey the meaning of what is to be written.

OUTLINING

Show how introductory sentences in each paragraph point the way to *outlining* when one is planning for required propositional writing assignments and for independent needs.

PROCEDURES

COPYING

During the third year of the continuum (while the children are gaining experience in cursive writing as an automatic skill), the teacher should use well-formed cursive letters — not manuscript — to write the paragraph on the chalkboard while the children watch. Later, he or she should make a copy on twenty-four-by-thirty-six-inch lined paper (butcher paper) that can be hung on the wall and discarded when the lessons are over. The copy should be left where it can be seen easily by the children during the several days of study. It *must be removed* before the paragraph is dictated on the last day of the dictation lessons.

The teacher should follow structured steps such as those listed below in preparing the children to write the paragraph, thereby ensuring integration of different concepts.

- The paragraph should be presented by the teacher, who should write it on the chalkboard while the children observe. During this time, teacher and children should discuss spelling, punctuation, organization, first sentence indentation, margin alignment, etc. Sentences for introduction, body, and conclusion should be noted.
- Words that are not expected to be spelled from memory should be doubly underlined to indicate that they will be available for copying and need not be learned.
- New words, including Red Flag words, to be learned for spelling should be underlined once. (Younger children enjoy drawing a red flag over Red Flag words. Third-year children can place red crayon lines under the part of the word that requires special memory, e.g., *jour ney*.)
- Children should be helped to realize that it is their responsibility to study, as shown on page 162, all of the words for independent recall except those that will be available for copying.

The paragraph written on the chalkboard should be copied by the children on lined paper while the teacher circulates and gives guidance as needed. In the course of time, children should be able to copy without supervision, but until that stage is reached, the teacher's guidance and supervision *should not be withdrawn*.

> NOTE: In upper-grade levels (fourth, fifth, and sixth) the teacher sometimes should write the paragraph in manuscript for the children to copy in cursive — to make sure recall of cursive letter forms is securely established.

As soon as a child completes the copying, the teacher should check the paper for accuracy before placing a mark to indicate that the child is ready to begin individual, independent study of the words. The pre-study check-up should prevent the study of incorrectly copied words. Any word, except those to be made available for copying, whether underlined or not, should be studied for instant recall.

Children should understand that their copied papers are "study papers" and must be turned in to the teacher after each day's study time and not left in their desks.

INDIVIDUAL STUDY

To study a word, each child should:

1. Pronounce the word and trace lightly over each letter, naming it as it is traced until he or she can remember it.
2. Write the word with an arm swing to check memory, keeping eyes closed while doing so.
3. Write the word on paper and compare it with the one on the study paper. If it is correct, the next word should be learned or reviewed. If it is incorrect, more study is indicated. Words already securely remembered need not be studied.

Punctuation marks should be noted with the reason for their different uses. (Refer to pages 233-236.)

INTEGRATED LESSON PLANNING

From the dictation lesson, the teacher should select words to place in the different divisions of The Daily Format for review practice or learning. Doing so provides an opportunity to review what already has been taught and to introduce new concepts. The intent is to foster children's realization of the way in which each component must be combined, or integrated, with others to create the complete or "whole performance" necessary to accomplish the primary purpose — writing a paragraph that embodies a particular thought.

SAMPLE PARAGRAPH FOR INTEGRATIVE STUDY*

who? did what?

All of us enjoyed our

how?

vacations in different ways.

who? did what?

Some of us stayed home.

who? did what?

Some children went on

*The small words written above phrases are not to be written on the copy made by the teacher. They are written on the above example for the teacher who is becoming familiar with these teaching techniques.

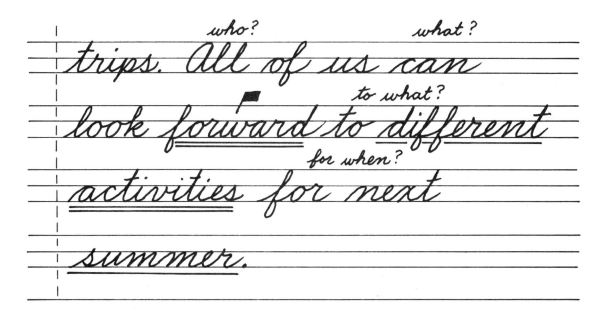

A LESSON PLAN FOR DAY ONE

The paragraph to be used for study should be read to the children by the teacher, and together they should note the introduction, the body, and the concluding sentence. They also should state the main idea given in the paragraph — something about *vacations*.

The teacher should write the paragraph on the chalkboard while the children watch and take part by telling the teacher how to spell, and how to organize, capitalize, and punctuate by pointing out that:

- the first sentence should be indented to show that it is the beginning of a paragraph;
- the sentence should begin with a capital;
- when moving from one line to the next, the writer should return to the margin line because the paragraph is not ended; and
- the correct mark of punctuation should be used to show when each sentence ends — periods for the sentences above, which make statements and do not ask questions or show exclamations about something.

The teacher should show children how to divide into syllables a more-than-one-syllable word when there is room to write only part of it at the end of a line. Use of a hyphen to indicate the division of the word should be explained. One-syllable words that would have to be crowded onto the line always should be placed on the succeeding line.

EXAMPLES OF TEACHER-CHILDREN INTERACTION

While writing the paragraph, the teacher should encourage participation from the children as suggested below.

With the word *enjoyed*

Teacher: "We go on vacations, hoping to *enjoy* ourselves. How many syllables do you hear? . . . Yes, two. Someone spell the word for me to write."

Child: "En joy, en, /ĕ/, e (or e-consonant) *e-n*; joy, /oi/, *o-y, j-o-y*; enjoy, *e-n-j-o-y*."

Teacher: 'When we say *all of us enjoyed*, are we talking about right now or a time in the past?"

Child: "In the past. We must add the suffix *ed*."

With the word *vacations*

Teacher: "Va-ca-tions. How many syllables? . . . Yes, three. What vowel sound do you hear in the first two syllables and what is it? . . . Spell the syllables."

Child: "I hear /ā/ at the end. Va, *a, v-a*; ca, *a, c-a*; vaca, *v-a-c-a*."

Teacher: "What letter combination do you hear in the last syllable?"

Child: "/shŭn/, *t-i-o-n*."

Teacher: As each syllable is spelled, the teacher should write it. "Vacation*s*. Why must I add the *s*? . . . Yes, to make vacations mean *more than one* vacation."

With the word *children*

A child who can do so should spell the singular word *child* and then the irregular plural. If necessary, the teacher may explain how to form the plural before completing the written word.

With the word *forward*

Forward should be taught as a Red Flag word. Have the children recognize that the first syllable is phonetic and easy to spell, but the last syllable, *ward*, /wĕrd/, must be studied and remembered. (Refer to page 141.)

With the word *activities*

If a word is to be made available to be copied when the paragraph is dictated, the teacher should inform the children and should write it, naming each syllable as it is written, e.g., "Activities, ac, *a-c*, tiv, *t-i-v*, /ĭ/, *i*, ties, *t-i-e-s*."

NOTE: The children at the third-year level probably have learned how to form the plural of *activity*. There are other concepts that should be learned prior to the children's spelling the word. The presence of several syllables and the necessity of using the rule for words ending in *y* after a consonant make it difficult for some children to spell. (Refer to pages 151-152.)

The same procedure should be continued until the paragraph is completed.

NOTE: From the teacher's writing of the paragraph, both Visual and Auditory modalities are stimulated. Those who have stronger Visual sensory channels are helped by *seeing* in association with hearing. Those with stronger Auditory sensory channels are benefited by *hearing* in association with seeing. When children copy the paragraph, the Kinesthetic sensory channel is added to the "three-fold language pattern."*

COPYING

Children should head 3/8-inch spaced, lined composition paper as shown below.

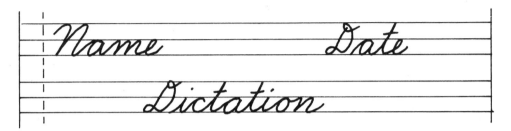

The teacher should circulate among the children to give assistance or guidance as needed.

STUDY OF WORDS TO BE LEARNED

As soon as each child finishes copying, his or her paper should be checked for accuracy before individual study begins, as explained on page 161. If some children — possibly those with more pronounced difficulties in writing or Visual perception and discrimination — cannot complete the copying, they can do so during the next lesson. (By then, the teacher's copy made on butcher paper should be displayed.)

Study of the words does not necessarily begin at the same moment for each child but does begin for each child when the copying and teacher check-up have been completed. Then, each child works independently.

A LESSON PLAN FOR DAY TWO

Refer to the paragraph on pages 162-163.

LEARNING TO WRITE

- Teach, or review if already taught, the capitals *a* and *s*. (Refer to pages 24, 26.)
- Dictate, "Capital *a* and small *a*. Capital *s* and small *s*." (Refer to page 40.)
- Dictate capitals *a* and *s* connected with other letters. (Refer to pages 42-43.)
- Dictate, "Write capital *A* and small *l*, connecting the letters."

The children should continue tracing until the next letters are named by the teacher.

*Gillingham and Stillman, *Remedial Training for Children*, p. 40.

Examples

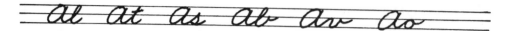

Each day, time should be provided for children to study the words on their copies of the paragraph.

A—ALPHABET CARDS (AUDITORY APPROACH)

Select phonograms that appear in words in the paragraph to include with others to practice for instant recall.

Sample Teacher's Hand Pack

(Refer to pages 57-60.)

ou, ov, er, o-e, i-e, u, a, e, y, oi, oo, ay, or, b, ai

Procedure: Expose no card until the child spells the sound given by the teacher. If the sound is correctly spelled, show the card to complete the *Auditory-Visual association*, which is linked to the Kinesthetic mode by speech and arm swings.

Teacher: "Spell (or "name the letters that spell") what says /ā/ as in *baby*."
Child: "*A*, baby, /ā/." Looks at card from the Hand Pack when it is exposed.
Class: Repeats, using arm swings.
Teacher: "/Oi/, as in *boy*."
Child: "*O-y*, boy, /oi/," and class repeats.
Teacher: "Tell different ways to spell /ē/."
Child: "*E* at the end of a syllable, secret, /ē/; *e*-consonant-*e*, these, /ē/; *e-e*, feet, /ē/; *e-a*, eat, /ē/; *i-e*, chief, /ē/; *y*, candy, /ē/."
Teacher: Shows the appropriate card from the *Yellow Card Pack*.

NOTE: The same procedure should be followed with the other sound symbols given by the teacher, who may need to use both the Teacher's Hand Pack and the *Yellow Card Pack*.

B—BLENDING (ENCODING)

Dictate a word from the paragraph for the children to write. In a word such as *our*, note the vowel sound /ou/. Dictate other words containing the same vowel spelling for children to write, one word under the other, after each word is spelled orally by a child.

Teacher: "Shout."
Child: "Shout, /ou/, *o-u*, shout, *s-h-o-u-t*."
Class: Writes with arm swings before writing on papers.

Teacher: "Mound."
Child: "Mound, /ou/, *o-u, m-o-u-n-d*."
Class: "Mound, *m-o-u-n-d*," forming each letter with arm swings before writing on paper (or until the arm writing "crutch" can be dropped).

Follow the same procedure with other words, such as:

shout	mouth	mouse	ouch
mound	south	loud	stout
scout	grouse	grouch	proud

NOTE: Sometimes the teacher should request that a variety of suffixes be added to one of the words after it has been written, e.g., *loud, loudly, loudest, louder, loudness.*

C—SPELLING

Continuing from Blending into Spelling, dictate a word such as *joy* — from the word *enjoy* (*joy*, /oi/, *o-y, j-o-y*).

NOTE: It should be noted that the word *joy* is the name of a feeling people experience. When the suffixes *ful, less*, and *ous* (the children may need to see *ous* in writing) are added, they make *joy* into descriptive words, e.g., *joyful, joyless*, and *joyous*. When the suffix *ly* is added to descriptive words, the words *joyfully, joylessly*, and *joyously* express *how* something was performed. Each word should be dictated by the teacher for children to write — one word under another to aid perception, with the root word *joy* remaining clearly visible and unchanged.

The teacher should explain that when the prefix *en* is attached to the word *joy*, the feeling of joy has been put into a person. Following the procedures explained above, the teacher should dictate the words: *enjoy, enjoying, enjoyed, enjoyable*, and *enjoys*. When the suffix *ment* is added to *enjoy, enjoyment* is the name of that feeling.

Dictate phrases composed of some of the words used in C—Spelling and from the paragraph:

our joyful shouts	enjoyed our trips
all of us went joyfully	an enjoyable vacation
enjoy looking at it	some of us are enjoying
enjoyed looking at it	for our enjoyment

D—DICTATION

Dictate a sentence so that children will have experience writing a complete thought with its appropriate punctuation:

We will enjoy   our trip to the beach.
Our enjoyment began   when we climbed   onto the raft.
We hope our vacation   will be a joyful time.

NOTE: Because most of the words are phonetic and fit previously learned concepts, the children should be prepared to use known skills with independence. If some word is too difficult for children to tackle independently, it should be written where it can be seen for copying.

A LESSON PLAN FOR DAY THREE

LEARNING TO WRITE

Identify the letter *o* as one of four (*b, o, v,* and *w*) that end at the midline and require attention when they are connected with other letters. For purposeful practice, dictate letters to be written and traced until succeeding letters are named by the teacher. Penmanship is used functionally when the paragraph is written from dictation.

Examples

A—ALPHABET CARDS

(Refer to pages 62-65.) Give the sound and its key word for the children to spell and write, e.g., "What says /ŭ/ as in *umbrella*?" The child who is called upon says, "*U*, umbrella, /ŭ/." The children repeat and write on their papers.

NOTE: Sometimes each grapheme should be written in a column. If written on the same line, children should be taught how to separate them with well-made commas ("periods with tails") or with dashes.

Examples

/oi/ as in *boy*	/ôr/ as in *corn*	/ā/ as in *play*	/ō/ as in *home*
/o͝o/ as in *book*	/ẽr/ as in *her*	/ī/ as in *pine*	/ē/ as in *candy*

or

B—BLENDING

Blend two-syllable words for the children, syllable by syllable. (Refer to footnote on page 89.) Have children blend one syllable at a time and then spell the entire word orally. Have the class pronounce the word and spell it orally, forming each letter with arm swings before writing on paper.

Examples

sum′ mer	thun′ der	chil′ dren
riv′ er	lum′ ber	for′ est

Pronounce, syllable by syllable, the three-syllable words that occur in the paragraph and have children write them, e.g., *dif′ fer ent* and *va ca′ tion.*

C—SPELLING

Have the Red Flag word *forward* written syllable by syllable. The first syllable, being phonetic, is possible for children to work out independently, e.g., *for,* /or/, *o-r, f-o-r.* The second Red Flag syllable, *ward,* probably learned in one of the study times, should be spelled orally (not blended) and written on papers.

Teach (or review) how to write words that end in the suffix *ward* (which indicates direction) and have the children write such words as:

in′ ward	back′ ward	south′ ward
out′ ward	side′ ward	north′ ward
up′ ward	home′ ward	west′ ward
down′ ward	for′ ward	east′ ward

(Children should not show the syllable division when writing the word.)

NOTE: After this "conceptual spelling," children should have a better understanding of the spelling of *toward* (*to ward*), and the basic principle of teaching "through the intellect" has been served.

Dictate phrases composed of words selected from those above:

all of us look forward	went on downward
going homeward to our home	a step backward
some are looking outward	toward our vacation

D—DICTATION

We look forward   to vacation trips,   but we enjoy   going homeward.

A LESSON PLAN FOR DAY FOUR

LEARNING TO WRITE

Teach, reteach, or review writing the letter *x*. (Refer to page 45.)

First stroke   Completed

B—BLENDING

Teach, reteach, or review words containing long-vowel sounds at the end of accented syllables spelled with vowels. (Refer to pages 132-133 and *TWL*, pages 47, 50, 52.)

Examples (from which to select words)

na′ tion	mo′ tion	no′ ble
lo′ tion	e mo′ tion	bu′ gle
no′ tion	si′ lent	ma′ ple
sta′ tion	to′ tem	tri′ fle

Dictate short-vowel words containing *x*, such as: *hex, tax, fix, wax, mix*, and *next*.

NOTE: Remind or tell children that *x* makes two sounds /ks/; therefore, words with three letters have four sounds and words with four letters have five sounds.

Use words ending in *x* in C—Spelling for further practice in use (integration).

C—SPELLING

First dictate the word *fix* and then have the children add suffixes to change the meaning.

NOTE: Because *fix* ends in *two* sounds, it is a 1-2-1 word that requires *no* rule before adding a suffix.

Teacher: "Write *fix* to show what someone is doing. . . . Yes, you add *ing*.
"*Fix* to show past time. . . . Yes, *fixed* by adding *ed*.
"Make *fix* into the name of one who fixes something. . . . Yes, *fixer*.
"Spell *fix* in the way that it describes something that can be fixed. Something would be _____. . . . Yes, *fixable*."

Dictate phrases to be written, such as:

will fix this next one
for our next vacation

D—DICTATION

Next time,   all of us   will enjoy staying   with you.

A LESSON PLAN FOR DAY FIVE — DICTATING THE PARAGRAPH

After several days of study and "integrative" practice, the paragraph should be dictated. (Refer to pages 162-163.) Have the children head their lined composition papers as shown on page 165.

Have children:

1. clear their desks or tables of all but the composition papers and pencils;
2. sit correctly with feet together on the floor;
3. place composition papers in correct positions (Refer to page 33);
4. hold pencils with thumb and first two fingers, away from the points and where the colored part begins — not on the sharpened part of the pencil;
5. place brackets around a word on which they know a mistake has been made before rewriting the word (to avoid making any erasures and smearing up the paper).

DICTATION

Dictate the paragraph phrase by phrase and sentence by sentence.

Example of procedure

Teacher: "The sentence, *All of us enjoyed our vacations in different ways*, the first one of the paragraph, begins in a certain place. . . . Yes, it is indented. Write *All of us*."

The children should write the phrase while the teacher moves about to observe (but not to give help as was done on previous days).

"Next phrase: *enjoyed our vacations*. Remember, if there is not plenty of room to write a one-syllable word at the end of the line, put it on the next line. Divide other words by syllables, always returning to the margin when beginning a new line.

"*In different ways* — Be sure to show that the sentence is ended.

"Continue the next sentence on the same line if there is room. If not, go to the next line. *Some of us stayed home*. Write *Some of us*.

"*Stayed home*.

"The next sentence is *Some of us   went on trips*. Write *Some of us*.
"*Went on trips*.
"The last sentence is *All of us   can look forward   to different activities   for next summer*. Remember that *activities* is on the board for you to copy.
"*All of us*.
"*Can look forward*.
"*To different activities*.
"*For next summer*.
"Look over your papers to make sure you have all of the words spelled correctly and have put punctuation marks where they belong."

The papers should be collected and corrected *by the teacher* at a later time. Then they should be returned to the children for discussion and correction of errors after they understand why they made mistakes.

CORRECTION OF PAPERS BY THE TEACHER

Scoring

Allow one point for:
1. each spelled word, including copied words,
2. each mark of punctuation,
3. each capital letter, and
4. indenting the first sentence.

In addition, allow points for:
1. return to margin lines,
2. not crowding words at the ends of lines,
3. not having to bracket and rewrite more than one or two mistakes, and
4. overall organization and neatness.

The total score for the dictated paragraph (pages 162-163), is as follows:

Written Performance

| | Punctuation | | | | |
	Capitals	Periods	Indenting	Spelling	Totals
First sentence	1	1	1	9	12
Second sentence	1	1	0	5	7
Third sentence	1	1	0	5	7
Fourth sentence	1	1	0	12	14
				Total	40

Overall Performance

Organization and neatness	Margin lines	Not crowding	Not more than two brackets	Totals
4	2	2	2	<u>10</u>
			Possible Total	50

Marking Papers

Place a mark, such as an *x* or ✓, where mistakes occur.

Count up errors on *Written Performance* and subtract from total score: 40 on the above example.

Determine score on *Overall Performance* (10) and combine the two scores.

Place child's total score over possible total which, in the above dictation example, would be 50.

If child's written and overall performances are without errors, write the score as 50/50.

If 4 errors occur in spelling alone, write the score as 46/50.

If a total of 9 errors occur in spelling and in overall performances, write the score as 41/50.

> NOTE: The children should be encouraged to note where errors are made — in spelling, punctuation, etc., or in overall performance.

Quartiling

The performance scores of the class, when quartiled, show the teacher:

1. how each child rates within the group;
2. how each child rates when measured against himself or herself from one performance to the next;
3. that if all of the children make nearly perfect scores, the paragraph may be too easy and without challenge in building study habits and techniques; and
4. that if one-third of the children make many errors, the paragraph may be too difficult or instruction and practice may have been insufficient for some individuals.

PLANNING PARAGRAPHS FOR DICTATION

With experience, a teacher becomes skillful in planning paragraphs for dictation lessons. They should contain new learnings, a review of skills that already have been taught during the periods devoted to B—Blending and C—Spelling, and/or reteaching to ensure security in functional use.

Paragraphs for dictation lessons should be proposed by the teacher and may be about any subject of interest. After several days of guided study, and when the children are prepared to write the paragraph from dictation, the teacher's copy on the wall should be removed. It should not be saved for use from year to year.

Paragraphs should be pertinent to each school year's children, whose particular needs and abilities should determine the words and form of expression to be used. Paragraphs should be adapted to the children; children should not be expected to adapt to paragraphs that were suitable for different purposes and different children.

When paragraphs are introduced, they should be written by the teacher as children watch and share in the procedure. (Refer to page 163.) Time should be arranged, either before or after the teacher-directed lessons, for the children individually to study the words of the paragraph by lightly tracing and naming the letters. (Refer to pages 107-108 and 162.)

SAMPLE PARAGRAPH FOR INTEGRATING STUDY AND PRACTICE

> *Fish that are called flying fish really do not fly. They whip their tails back and forth until they gain enough speed to push themselves out of the ocean. They glide for a few seconds before they*

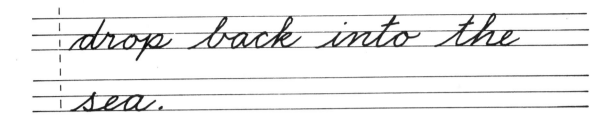

SAMPLE DAILY FORMAT FOR DAY ONE

The paragraph should be introduced and then copied by the children. (Refer to pages 163-165.) Children who are unable to complete the copying within the given time should be allowed extra time, or they may be allowed to finish on the following day. As soon as any child completes the copying and the paper is okayed by the teacher, his or her individual study should begin.

Any word in the paragraph that is already known should be noted at the time children watch the paragraph being written on the chalkboard. Ways to make mnemonic associations should be pointed out, as with *sea* (Yellow Flag) and *ocean* (Red Flag), which have similar meanings and contain the vowels *e-a*. Another example is *they* and *their* which both begin with *t-h-e*.

Words that may need to be learned, such as *push, ocean, enough*, etc., should be underlined. (Refer to page 161.) The word *themselves* should be underlined twice to designate it as a word that will be placed where it can be copied at the time the paragraph is dictated.

> NOTE: The singular-plural spelling of words ending in *self* or *selves* may not have been taught and the teacher may not wish to give instruction on this at this particular time. Therefore, any such word can be a word to *copy* or to *learn* as a Red Flag word. If, however, the children are ready, instruction and practice, including phrase and sentence writing, may take place during lessons of C—Spelling. (Refer to page 153.)

Singular	*Plural*
herself	
himself }	themselves
itself	
myself	ourselves
yourself	yourselves

Usually, in an SLD classroom there are a few children who are able to learn all of the words that are required more readily than can the majority. They should be encouraged to learn any of the words left for copying. The other children, working at their functional levels, *should not be pressured* to do so, but, instead, encouraged to do well with whatever they are expected to accomplish.

SAMPLE DAILY FORMAT FOR DAY TWO

Learning to Write

Review (or teach) capitals *f* and *t*.

Practice: Capital and small *f*; capital and small *t*; capital and small *f* connected with other letters.

A—Alphabet Cards

Teacher's Hand Pack (Refer to pages 57-60.)

NOTE: Unless children respond automatically and correctly, "they have not attained instant A-V-K association"* necessary for functional use.

The teacher should give the *sound*, and the children should make the Auditory-Visual-Kinesthetic association.

/y/ as in *yellow*	y	/ôr/ as in *corn*	or
/ē/ as in *eat*	ea	/ou/ as in *ouch*	ou
/ĭ/ as in *gym*	y	/ū/ as in *few*	ew
/ā/ as in *play*	ay	/ŏ/ as in *olives*	o
/ā/ as in *rain*	ai	/ō/ as in *pony*	o
/ō/ as in *home*	o-e	/ŭ/ as in *honey*	o

NOTE: If *o*, having the sound /ŭ/, has not been taught, but appears in a word such as *second*, it may be introduced when it is needed as one of the words in the paragraph. It should not be used in Alphabet Card practice until it has been introduced elsewhere. The word *second* should be underlined for *study* as a Red Flag word, or underlined twice as a word to be copied.

Yellow Card Pack (Refer to pages 60-62.)

/ō/	all the ways that are known should be named
/ŭ/	*u* as in *umbrella* and *o* as in *honey* (if known) (Refer to page 54.)
/ā/	all known ways
/ē/	all known ways
/ĭ/	*i* as in *inch* and *y* as in *gym* (Refer to page 54.)

B—Blending

Blend and write words with vowel sound /ĭ/ spelled with *y*: *fly, try, spry, dry, fry, sky, shy, why,* and *by*.

*Gillingham, personal communication to the author.

NOTE: When the children have not been taught the rule for words ending in *y*, they should be told that *suffixes beginning with i*, such as *ing*, can be added to any verb ending in *y*.

Dictate the following words for written blending: *trying, flying, drying, crying, frying, playing, replaying, saying*, and *enjoying*.

C—Spelling and D—Dictation

In order to learn words that are underlined once on their copied paragraphs (*enough, ocean, sea, seconds, they*, and *really*), the children should practice in the usual way.
Dictate: *glide, gliding, glider, glided*, and *glides*.

enough to glide	had enough speed
trying to glide	speedy enough for flying
to slide and glide	trying to get enough fish

We may see   some flying fish   on our trip   over the ocean.

SAMPLE DAILY FORMAT FOR DAY THREE

Learning to Write

Review or teach capital *h*.
Practice capital and small *h*.
Practice capital *h* connected with other letters:

Practice lowercase *h* connected with other letters:

A—Alphabet Cards

Teacher's Hand Pack

/ē/ as in *eat*	ea	/ū/ as in *few*	ew
/ī/ as in *sky*	y	/ū/ as in *mule*	u-e
/ŭ/ as in *honey*	o	/ûr/ as in *her*	er
/ī/ as in *pine*	i-e	/shŭn/ as in *nation*	tion
/ō/ as in *home*	o-e	/o͝o/ as in *book*	oo

Yellow Card Pack

The children should spell all sounds that have been taught and can be remembered. (Refer to pages 51 and 60-62.)

/ĕ/	/ĭ/
/ū/	/k/
/oi/	/ă/

B—Blending and C—Spelling

Practice writing vowel-consonant-*e* words, and if the Silent-*e* Rule has been taught, dictate words such as:

chore	slide	glide	hope
more	sliding	glides	hoping
core	chime	gliding	hopeful
before	sprite	glider	hopeless

Teach the word *real* as a descriptive word meaning *actually*.

a real orange	a real treat
a real, live duck	some real animals
real ships	a real mother

Add the suffix *ly* to form *really*, making it describe *how* something actually is.

really big enough	really flying
really a shooting star	really happy to go

Dictate phrases such as:

saw real fish	not really flying fish
are really gliding fish	birds really fly

Dictate a sentence such as:

They look like flying fish   when they glide,   but they really are not.

NOTE: The above sentence provides an opportunity to instruct the children in forming contractions. If they already know how to do so, they can use their learning functionally and write the final phrase *but they really aren't*. (Refer to pages 146-148.)

A Written Spelling Lesson

Select from the paragraph words that the children have been expected to learn in independent study time, as well as other words that may have been learned in previous dictation lessons. Cover the paragraph on the wall and collect the individually copied paragraphs before dictating the words.

Examples

flying	them	speed	before
fish	their	speedy	out
called	gain	speeding	ocean
calling	until	push	isn't
caller	enough	pushing	wasn't
they	forth	think	aren't

Uncover the paragraph on the wall. Return the individually copied paragraphs. The teacher and children should check papers to determine individual need for clarification and further study.

SAMPLE DAILY FORMAT FOR DAY FOUR

Learning to Write and A—Alphabet Cards

Have the children practice capital *g*, which begins with the same stroke as capital *s*.

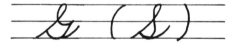

Tell the children to "Write the letter that says /g/ as in the girl's name, *Gail*," if they already have been taught capitalization for proper names.

/s/ as in a boy's name, *Sam*	S
/ā/ as in *play*	ay
/t̶h̶/ as in *this*	th
Write it again with a capital letter at the beginning	Th
/ôr/ as in *corn*	or
/ou/ as in *ouch*	ou
/ū/ as in *few*	ew
/t/ as in a boy's name, *Ted*	T
/f/ as in a boy's name, *Fred*	F
/h/ as in a girl's name, *Heidi*	H

B—Blending

Blend orally and write words containing vowel sound /ū/ spelled *ew: few, mew, stew, new, dew,* and *chew.* (Refer to *TWL,* page 33.)

After two-syllable words containing a "phonogram syllable" have been taught (pages 92-93, dictate words for the children to write, such as: *pew' ter, sin' ew, neph' ew, re new', re-newed', re new' ing, re new' a ble,* and *re news'.*

Blend and write words containing the vowel sound /ŭ/ spelled with *o*, words that the children need to learn as Yellow Flag words with the difficult parts *remembered: s*o*me, h*o*n' ey, sec' *o*nd, c*o*me, m*o*n' ey,* and *M*o*n' day.*

C—Spelling and D—Dictation (Integrated)

Practice singular-plural of words found in the paragraph. Have the children fold composition paper into two columns and head it: *Singular* and *Plural*.

Dictate, using phrases for comprehension, nouns to be written in the correct column.

Examples

their tails	tails
a large ocean	ocean
in just one second	second
crossed both oceans	oceans
a sea near China	sea
in ten seconds	seconds
many rough seas	seas
a short tail	tail

The completed papers should have words arranged as follows:

Singular	*Plural*
ocean	tails
second	oceans
sea	seconds
tail	seas

NOTE: Depending upon past instruction and cognitive readiness, this might be the time to explain singular-plural spelling of the word *fish*: When speaking of *one* kind of fish, such as cod *or* halibut *or* salmon, the plural is *fish*. When speaking of *several* kinds of fish, such as cod *and* halibut *and* salmon, the plural is *fishes*.

In discussion with the children, show how the same principle is applied to the word *people* when showing singular and plural.

Suggestions for phrase and sentence writing

just seconds away	really try hard
back and forth in seconds	not really hard to do
to push out	
to push outward (if *ward* has been taught — page 141)	
to fish in the ocean	looking at many flying fish

He saw many flying fish   one day.
One flying fish   glided to the deck   of the ship.

SAMPLE DAILY FORMAT FOR DAY FIVE

Remove all points of reference to the paragraph by taking the paragraph from the wall and keeping children's copies. Have the children head their composition papers as shown on page 165. Refer to page 171 for an example of the procedure to adopt in dictating the paragraph for the children to write.

Suggested phrasing

Fish that are called   flying fish   really do not fly.   They whip their tails   back and forth   until they gain   enough speed   to push *themselves*   out of the ocean.   They glide   for a few seconds   before they drop back   into the sea.

The word *themselves* should be made available for copying. Remind the children to look over their papers for their own final check. Collect the papers and check them at a later time (48 points plus 10 or 12 for a total of 58 or 60 depending on what points are allowed for each item).

The teacher should check the papers and keep records of each child's progress as explained on pages 172-173. At a later time, papers should be returned to the children for them to see, for discussion of organization, placement of words, punctuation, etc., and for notation of which words may require more practice during individual free time. The teacher should save the papers for future display, reference, placement in individual folders, or other purposes. Children's performances serve to direct the teacher's planning for progressive instruction and integration of new with past learnings.

PARAGRAPHS FOR PLANNING: EXAMPLE ONE

This paragraph and the one on page 183 are samples for a teacher to study in preparation for planning The Daily Format:

Seals are great swimmers. Many from the far north swim thousands of miles each year. They swim south to avoid the cold winters of the north.

Learning to Write

Letter connections such as the following may be practiced: *mm, ou, voi, or, we, om, the, ol, Th,* and *ey*.

Teach and/or review capital and lowercase letters *s*, *m*, and *t*.

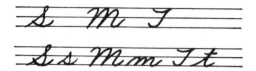

A—Alphabet Cards

Teacher's Hand Pack

Practice all of the Auditory symbols the children may need, plus:

/ā/ as in *steak*	ea
/är/ as in *star*	ar
/ī/ as in *pine*	i-e
/oi/ as in *oil*	oi
/ī/ as in *sky*	y
/ā/ as in *they*	ey

Yellow Card Pack

Review the cards needed for over-practice, plus:

/ĕ/	e ea
/ī/	all known ways
/ĭ/	i y
/ā/	all known ways

B—Blending

Blend and write words with /ā/ spelled *ey*: *they, whey, prey,* and *o bey'* plus the suffixes *ed, s,* and *ing.*

> NOTE: If the symbol sound /ā/, spelled *ey* has not been taught, the word *they* should be learned as a Red Flag word in lessons planned for C—Spelling, and the above blending should be omitted.

Blend and write, for review, words containing v-*e, ar, ou, ea* /ĕ/, *or,* and *oi.* (Refer to *TWL*, pages 21-33, 38.)

C—Spelling

Use two-syllable words from the paragraph plus others, for example: *win' ter, swim' mer, a void'* plus *ing, ed, s,* and *ance, thou' sand,* and *great* (as a two-syllable word after adding the suffixes *ly, er, est,* and *ness*).

Use singular-plural words: *seal, thousand* (if not used for copying only), *mile, year,* and *winter.* (Refer to pages 148-153 and *TWL*, pages 57-58.)

Review the 1-1-1 Rule for practice (or over-teaching if the rule has been taught); if not, it may be the time to introduce the rule. (Refer to pages 120-124 and *TWL*, page 67.)

swim　　+ er, ing, s
step　　+ er, ing, s, ed
snap　　+ ed, y, less, er, ing, s

Use selected words from the paragraph for phrase and sentence dictation.

PARAGRAPHS FOR PLANNING: EXAMPLE TWO

Bob's *brothers* want to *kn*ow about *nature* in the woods. The best way to learn *would* be to li*v*e or camp there. They would see and hear birds, insects, *animals*, and even plants. They would *discover differences* by day and night in the woods.

Learning to Write

Letter combinations: *ob, oth, ow, ou, oo, ov, ous, oul, eve,* and *ve.*

A—Alphabet Cards

Arrange both the Teacher's Hand Pack and the Yellow Cards to make use of the grapheme-phoneme associations found in the paragraph, such as *ow, ou, u-e, ear, ir, ee, ea, igh, ay, oo, ey,* and *er.*

B—Blending

Blend and write words containing:

/ûr/ spelled *ear*

earn	ear' nest	earnestly	earth	earthly
Earl	learn	learning	yearn	early

/ŏŏ/ spelled *oo*

shook	brook	hook	fishhook	crook
stood	woods	foot	cook	book

/ō/ spelled *ow*

snow	throw	thrown	grow
growth	know	known	knowing
knows	blow	blown	grown

/ī/ spelled *igh*

night	sight	right	high
knight	blight	fight	fright
flight	might	light	bright

C—Spelling

Red Flag words to learn and to use in dictated phrase and sentence writing: *want, could, would, should, mother, there, live, view, animal,* and *brother.*

NOTE: When the sound /ŭ/ spelled *o* has been learned, the words *mother, brother,* and *other* become Yellow Flag words.

Words of two or more syllables to use: *na' ture, cul' ture, fu' ture, lec' ture, fix' ture, e' ven, dif' fer, in' sect, an' i mal,* and *dis cov' er.*

Singular-plural — use singular nouns from the paragraph to form regular plural nouns. (Refer to pages 149-151.)

brother	brothers	insect	insects
way	ways	plant	plants
camp	camps	animal	animals
bird	birds	day	days
woods*	woods	night	nights

Singular ownership — use singular nouns to show ownership (or possession) formed regularly. (Refer to pages 153-157.)

day	day's trip	brother	brother's pack
bird	bird's nest	animal	animal's den
Bob	Bob's boots	insect	insect's head
plant	plant's stem	night	night's sounds

Dictate phrases and sentences for practice using words from the paragraph.

birds and insects
at Bob's camp
want to know the way
would know how to camp

could learn about the woods
would learn about nature
wants to camp there
will see birds, insects, animals, and more

We want to learn   about nature.
I wish I could   discover an animal's den.
Do you know   the way to the camp   in the woods?

INTRODUCING COMMAS FOR WORDS IN A SERIES

The teacher should explain that commas are used to replace the word *and* in separating a series of words all related to the same idea in the sentence. Using the word *and* repeatedly does not sound pleasant to the ear. By putting a comma in place of *and*, the word *and* need not be repeated. The comma and all punctuation marks (periods, question marks, dashes, quotation

Woods is usually used for both singular and plural. Explain this irregular spelling to the children.

marks, etc.) serve a particular purpose — to convey the meaning the writer intends and to make it easier for readers to understand that meaning.

Demonstrate with a phrase by erasing each unnecessary *and* and placing a comma in its place. Show how the last *and* is retained to bring the series to a conclusion. After the demonstration, let children take turns performing using phrases written by the teacher. Teach children how to form commas — periods with little tails, not carelessly made slashes.

> NOTE: Instructions for and practice with any punctuation mark should be given in the periods allotted to C—Spelling. The same procedure — explaining, demonstrating, and practicing under the teacher's guidance — should be applied when introducing other new punctuation marks. The teacher is the best judge of when children are ready cognitively and need a skill for use in writing from dictation or for propositional writing.

Below is an example of a phrase as it should appear for children to see before and after elimination of the words *and*.

saw birds a̶n̶d̶ animals a̶n̶d̶ insects a̶n̶d̶ snakes a̶n̶d̶ worms and flies

saw birds, animals, insects, snakes, worms, and flies

First the phrase should be read aloud, including each one of the *and*'s. Each *and* to be eliminated should be crossed out and the phrase reread. The crossed-out words should be erased and commas inserted before reading the phrase a final time.

Examples (before erasures and comma insertions)

took ham and bacon and bread and doughnuts and eggs and apples
hiked in dirt and puddles and grass and rocks and sand
bought toys and books and clothes and socks and boots
saw flowers and plants and trees and bushes and berries
will see lions and bears and monkeys and elephants and giraffes and tigers

Phrases always should be reread after the commas are inserted to replace the *and*'s. After the explanation and controlled practice, phrases should be dictated for children to write. For instance: *Get some ham, butter, meat, and apples.*

PARAGRAPH CONCEPTS FOR DICTATION IN UPPER-ELEMENTARY GRADES

The procedures shown on previous pages should be followed as children advance to higher levels of language use. As the need for them arises, various forms of punctuation and capitalization should be explained and included in paragraphs planned for dictation study. These needs include use of quotation marks; dashes (—) to separate enriching or explanatory phrases from the rest of the sentence; commas with words of direct address, words in a series, words in apposition, and phrases to be separated from others within a sentence; hyphens for dividing words; and any other punctuation required to clarify the thought being conveyed in the paragraph for dictation study.

Paragraphs sometimes should be worded to include a particular kind of punctuation or spelling which children are *ready to learn*. At other times, the teacher may deem it appropriate to teach a particular form of punctuation or spelling that *is required* in writing the paragraph. In order to present appropriate language learnings, the teacher must know the overall goals and the children's readiness and cognitive abilities.

The teacher's purpose at this point is to show how to organize and write the sentences in paragraph form and that spelling and punctuation are necessary tools. The teacher's task is to help children acquire and use these tools for their writing needs (usually propositional, but sometimes creative).

As children progress into higher elementary levels, they can understand how complete ideas can be expressed within single paragraphs: introduction, body, and conclusion. Through discussion and relating what has been read (THE VISUAL APPROACH) to the same organization used for written expression, the children can be made aware of the numerous types of paragraphs required for various kinds of purposeful writing. They should be led to understand that the same organization is applied to reading material as to written expression.

INTEGRATING VERBALIZATION INTO WRITTEN FORM

The teacher and children should select some topic of interest. An introductory paragraph — with one, two, or three body sentences — should be constructed orally, beginning with a sentence that gives an idea of what the overall topic is and ending with a sentence that tells what to expect in the succeeding paragraph. Each succeeding paragraph should begin with a "subject sentence" as part of the body and conclude with a final sentence leading into the subject of the next paragraph.

The use of long and involved sentences or paragraphs should be discouraged. Preferably, emphasis should be placed on organization and adherence to the topic as indicated in the introductory paragraph or in the first sentences of succeeding paragraphs. A concluding paragraph should be verbalized by following the same procedures.

> NOTE: Children can apply these basic principles to verbalizing an application for a job, reporting a sports event, making an announcement of coming events, describing a vacation or special trip, writing a letter to someone, writing reports, etc. (Refer to pages 158-159.)

If a topic, such as "Cold Regions," is to be verbalized, the teacher should occasionally write the first sentence of each paragraph as it is introduced where it can be seen by all — one way of developing the *outline* concept.

Example

Two of the coldest places on Earth, our planet, are in the Arctic and Antarctic regions . . . .
. . . .
Explorers were the first people to venture into these cold regions . . . .
. . . .
. . . .

Scientists have lived in these cold regions for limited times to learn about these freezing zones . . . .
. . . .

Today, people from all over the globe meet there to study and assemble information but not to stay as settlers . . . .
. . . .

Obviously, writing each of the paragraphs completely for children to copy would be impractical and would defeat the purpose (teaching spelling needs and writing procedures). It would overload and drag out the time that should be devoted to the daily dictation study. Therefore, only one paragraph should be selected to complete and to use for that study. The teacher should make the final judgment as to sentence wording, new spelling words, and punctuation rules to be taught or reviewed through usage in this study paragraph.

Sample introductory paragraph

Two of the coldest places on Earth, our planet, are in the Arctic and Antarctic regions. The Arctic region — frozen ocean — encircles (refer to page 167 for prefix *en*) the North Pole. The Antarctic region — frozen mountains — encircles the South Pole. Both regions are among the last places into which people have ventured.

SUGGESTED LEARNINGS FOR PLANNING LESSONS WITHIN THE DAILY FORMAT

Learning to Write

Capitals: *a, n, p, t,* and *b.*
Letter Connections: Capitals *r, l,* and *j* with vowels and consonants.

A—Alphabet Cards

/j/	*j, dge,* soft *g* (*ge, gi, gy*) (Refer to pages 85–86.)
/är/	*ar*
/ou/	*ou*
/ō/ as in *home*	*o-e*
/ō/	all ways
/ē/	all ways
/ĕ/	*e* and *ea*
/ŭ/	*u* and *o*
/s/	*s* and soft *c* (*ce, ci, cy*)
/ûr/ as in *earth*	*ear* (Refer to page 82.)

B—Blending

Words with vowel-consonant-*e,* such as *pole, froze, ven' ture, struc' ture, cul' ture,* and *com pose'.*

Silent-*e* syllable words such as *hurdle, circle, bundle, bubble*, and *humble*.

Soft *c* and *g* words such as *circle, circus, cycle, center, cellar, gem, gym, region* (re/jŭn), *gentle, gesture*, and *urge*.

Explain that *o* followed by one or more consonants sometimes (as an exception) says /ō/, and dictate for blending such words as *old, bold, hold, told, sold, mold, molding, cold, coldness, coldest, fold, enfold, host, hostess, most*, and *post*.

Explain also that any suffix may be added without changing the spelling of the words because they end in two consonants, and do not end in either silent *e* or *y* after a consonant.

C—Spelling

Add suffixes and prefixes to the action words (verbs), and apply rules where needed in such words as:

venture	+ ing, ed, er, s, ous, some
*ad*venture	+ ing, ed, er, s, ous, some
freeze	+ing, s, er, able
froze	+ en
fold	+ ed, ing, able
*en*fold	+ ing, ed, s
circle	+ ing, ed, s, er

(Refer to pages 124-127 and to *TWL*, pages 55-56.)

Explain "words in apposition," using the phrase from the dictation paragraph — *on Earth, our planet* — and then discuss and dictate such examples as *gave gold, a fine metal, to him* and *saw Bob, my younger brother, and then my older brothers*.

Teach, if not already taught, that the sound /ĭn/ in the word *mountain* and other words, is spelled *ain*. For example: *curtain, fountain, bargain*, and *certain*. Dictate these words and use them in phrase writing.

Give experience in singular-plural spelling with nouns from the paragraph such as *venture, adventure, place, region, mountain, ocean, globe, man*, and *planet*.

Sample spelling test

mountain	region	Arctic	circle
encircle	south	north	east
west	globe	pole	North Pole
South Pole	among	both	mountainous*

Suggested phrase and sentence writing

a mountainous region	the planets, Earth and Venus, in space
mountains of our earth	Mars, the smallest planet
to the South Pole	encircles a region

---

*At an opportune moment, explain that the suffix sound /ŭs/, used to form descriptive words, is spelled *ous* but when the sound /ŭs/ is part of a word itself, as in the nouns *campus, lotus*, and *crocus*, it usually is spelled *us*.

One very cold region,   the North Pole,   is north of us.
It took brave men   to venture   into *unknown* regions   of this earth.
Other adventurers *climb*   mountainous regions.

NOTE: To increase spelling abilities of children in advanced levels of the continuum, words such as *explorers* and *scientists* can be selected from the overall topic and used for spelling many words, as shown below. Children and teacher, working together, can write the words where all can see and learn that root words (to which prefixes and suffixes are added in somewhat regular ways) make learning how to spell easier. Children are learning "through their intellects."

explore	scien*tist*—scientists
explor*er*	scien*ce*—sciences
explor*ing*	scien*tific*
explor*ed*	scien*tifical*
explore*s*	scien*tifically*
explor*ation*	scien*tial* (studies)
explor*able*	*un*scien*tific*
explor*ative*	*un*scien*tifically*
explor*atory*	*un*scien*tial* studies
*un*explor*ed*	
*un*explor*able*	
*re*explore + ing, s, ed	

It is hoped that guidance from the teacher will enable children with Specific Language Disability (as well as other children) to acquire the skills needed for using written language for individual purposes in either propositional or creative writing.

E—Propositional and Creative Writing

INTRODUCTION

After learning some of the basics in sentence and paragraph writing in the lessons planned within the divisions of The Daily Format, many children begin to write spontaneously. Now the children express themselves in sentences of their own composition, rather than write dictated sentences in which another person proposes the wording.

To foster independent written expression, there should be a discussion of the reasons individuals need to use language skills with independence:

- to write letters,
- to write answers to questions,
- to write reports in school and, someday, for one's job or for college, and
- to use for other reasons (suggested by the children).

Depending upon cognitive maturities and abilities, language skills are used for different purposes in propositional and creative writing. The skills are needed by almost everyone in daily life for writing letters, reports or orders, or for taking notes and answering questions. Only a few people write creatively to express their own thoughts or ideas or to compose stories about real or imagined events, adventures, or people. In either performance, however, the writer uses words of his or her own choosing arranged in correct sentence and paragraph form.

PROCEDURES

Practice for propositional writing can be provided by:

- placing written questions in the same place on the chalkboard or wall each day for the children to *copy* and answer in *writing* in a complete sentence that contains a subject and something about it;
- suggesting a topic about which children write three sentences using introductory, body, and concluding sentences;
- having children propose their own wording for an invitation to some event;
- having the children write a letter to someone, either named by the teacher or chosen by each child;
- having children write applications for the jobs they think they will want in the future; and
- having children write a paragraph with information about a particular topic chosen by the teacher or by each child, such as "Horses," "Our School Yard," "What about Sports?"

NOTE: For each purpose an opportunity is provided for the teacher to discuss and show the children the recognized form to use for letter writing, applications for jobs, invitations, etc. Sometimes such needs can be used for study in a lesson of D—Dictation.

In a lesson for constructing several oral paragraphs about a subject such as "Cold Regions," as explained on pages 186-187 (and from which the first introductory paragraph was used for D—Dictation study), the children could be grouped according to the number of paragraphs for which only an introductory sentence was written.

Each child in a group, such as the one writing about explorers, should write his or her own paragraph. The teacher should collect the papers and, after checking each one, integrate the lessons for D—Dictation and E—Propositional Writing into one lesson during which corrections can be made with the teacher's guidance, and better understanding for future propositional writing can be fostered.

To show children that the same topic can be written about in different ways, one child from each group should be selected to read his or her paragraph in sequence to form an entire "article." Other groups should be arranged to follow the same procedure, thereby giving all of the children an opportunity to read their paragraphs aloud. The children should judge which paragraphs go together best for expressing the overall ideas about "Cold Regions" and the teacher or a child should read that group of paragraphs aloud for all to hear.

Daily classroom activities and interests expressed by the children should provide worthwhile suggestions for propositional writing.

CREATIVE WRITING

No special time should be planned for "creative" writing. When children feel an urge to express their inner thoughts or imaginative stories or happenings in writing, they frequently do so in their free time or at home, bringing the papers to the teacher to read.

Classroom discussions lead some children to write what they feel, as did one twelve-year-old about to enter junior high: "I can't tell you how I feel but I could write it." This boy's voluntary creative writing brought out his fears and apprehensions about facing the new situation and revealed an unsuspected side to his nature.

Propositional and creative writing should be regarded as different forms of communication. The language skills acquired from the teacher's instruction and guidance afford freedom for each child to use whichever form of written expression is required, or desired, for individual purposes. The skills are *not learned phenomenally* and *must be taught*, but their use depends upon individual needs and individual abilities to spell and write what they want to say. Therefore, the teacher's task is to teach, to structure and integrate step-by-step advancement, to provide practice for functional use, to guide, and, if possible, to inspire.

Written expression begins from a Conceptual-Auditory approach with an expectation that what is written will be read. Reading begins from a Visual approach that, ideally, results in comprehension of what is read. As with writing, reading is a skill which must be taught. How to help SLD children succeed in learning to read is explained on the following pages.

Part 4

TEACHING PROCEDURES FOR LEARNING TO COPY AND THE VISUAL APPROACH TO READING

Copying

INTRODUCTION

Copying originates from Visual stimuli. Handwriting, however, begins with inner Auditory stimuli. Children should not be expected to copy until they can readily recall written letter forms. Attention needs to be focused on letter and word sequencing, not on forming letters. Inability to copy is one cause of failure. Teachers should keep in mind that writing of any kind is not a phenomenal learning. Some children require structured guidance while learning to copy. The different purposes for which copying is required should be discussed — copying lists of words, directions, dictation lessons, homework assignments, and, sometimes, passages from a book. Copying, unlike propositional writing, can be done without knowing how to spell or read the words, but, when most of the words can be spelled or read, copying becomes much easier.

Handwriting, which makes thoughts visible on paper, is initiated from inner, simultaneous Auditory-Visual-Kinesthetic association of the symbols that represent the thought. Copying, initiated from Visual perception of a possibly confusing figure-ground sequencing of written symbols, requires retention of organized and correctly sequenced words for transcription to a blank page. Helping children approach copying as a skill should begin with the smallest unit of sight-sound-feel (single letters) and advance step by step to increase ability to perceive and recall groups of letters, words, and even phrases without repeated reference to the model.

The teacher should present the entire model to be copied before the children's copying begins. If a model is to be copied in cursive writing, it should be written in cursive by the teacher. This practice should be followed until the children have learned *how to copy* and are prepared to transcribe various kinds of manuscript writing into cursive handwriting.

Kinesthetic reinforcement is necessary for some children, who should name and form the letters while perceiving them, before they write from memory — Visual-Auditory-Kinesthetic association.

Each child should work at his or her own rate of speed. Faster performance develops when attention can be focused on *what* to copy rather than *how* to copy.

OBJECTIVES FOR COPYING

Objectives for learning to copy should follow three procedures:
1. Copying letter units in groups.
2. Copying words, phrases, and sentences.
3. Copying words, phrases, sentences, and paragraphs functionally.

With a teacher's guidance, children should be able to copy:
- groups of letters in correct sequence without having to look back and forth at each individual letter before writing;
- three- or four-letter words in one operation without looking again to recall each letter;
- three- or four-letter words ending in suffixes by focusing on the root word and then adding the familiar suffix;
- letter groups within polysyllabic words;
- a preposition or article with the words that follow to form phrases;
- word groups of phrases in sentences and paragraphs that require figure-ground discrimination; and
- words written in manuscript or any print in cursive handwriting.

PROCEDURES

PROCEDURE ONE

COPYING LETTERS ARRANGED VERTICALLY

Introductory lessons should begin by showing children how to copy single letters written one under the other. Lined paper folded in columns by the children (if they have learned to do so) should be used. Sample models to copy should be written on the chalkboard.

t	g	c	x	t	c
l	a	e	b	k	g
f	h	n	v	u	l
j	o	i	j	r	qu
m	r	p	m	z	y
d	b	s	d	w	w
s	h	t	s	a	m
v	w	z	v	f	r

Teacher: "Sometimes lists of letters, numbers, or words need to be copied. Our practice will help each person's memory hold a certain number of these letters (pointing) while writing without having to look back at them until writing is completed. Let's begin with the letters in this first column (pointing)."

"Look at the first two letters, *t* and *l*. Name them to yourself to help you remember without having to look again until you finish. When finished, look at the next two letters, name them to yourself, and then write them without looking back until finished. Continue in the same way until all of the letters in this first column are written." Observes children's independent performances.

"In this second column, try to hold three letters, *g a h*, in memory without having to look back. If you do forget, you must look back and name them to yourself again to help your memory hold them while you write.

"Continue in the same way with letters in these next two columns. Don't hurry; try to remember as you write without looking back."

When the children are ready to copy the last three columns, encourage those who have no difficulty remembering three letters to try *four letters*. The others should be encouraged to continue their practice with only three letters because it is the "patterning" of their "computer systems" that is important. All children work together but at their own rates of speed.

The teacher should observe performances and give help where needed. Good letter formation should be expected of each child. Lessons should not be long and should be given at whatever time fits best into the day's program. After capital letters have been learned, lists including uppercase letters for copying should be presented by the teacher.

Letter groupings should be extended to include lists such as the following:

2-letter groupings		*3-letter groupings*	
p s	m s	s t r	i g h
f r	v e	t c h	a n g
g h	d r	i f f	t l e
g l	h t	s c r	a n k
h z	w h	s h r	o f t
f c	k s	p i l	qu i n

Real words should not be used until the children have had practice in *recalling* groups of letters that convey no meaning and thus require perception and memory alone. Words that can be recalled as *already-learned spelling words* do not require the same concentrated "patterning" for perception and recall as do the nonsense letter arrangements. However, it is advisable to use letter groupings that appear in real words.

Children should be helped to understand that only they can train their eyes to span the number of letters they can "hold" in memory without having to look again until they have finished writing. Over-stretching the eye span, if it leads to errors, should be discouraged. Practice with what can be held in memory leads to accurate copying and, possibly, eventually to lengthened eye span.

4-letter groupings   *5-letter groupings*

ough	*Stra*	*aists*	*sprin*
udge	*Ible*	*anter*	*stroy*
Orch	*atch*	*unded*	*Squand*
igns	*inst*	*Squint*	*Flail*
ouch	*Stra*	*udges*	*Bland*
		schoo	*strai*

COPYING LETTERS ARRANGED HORIZONTALLY

Although words sometimes must be copied from, and in, columns, more often copying needs to be done from horizontal lines necessitating a considerable amount of figure-ground discrimination. Letter groupings should be clearly spaced or separated with commas or dashes, whichever is shown on the teacher's model.

Teacher: "This time letters are written across the line. As you did with letters written in columns, let your eye span include two (three or four) letters to name to yourself, remember, and write without looking back until you are finished writing."

Examples of different groupings for different lessons

s s y,   l l s,   g g h,   f k f,   t m h,   z y n,   t p p,   r o h

fsf – tmr – ghs – hts – ayf – oxy – nce – int – ort – nch – ush

bran	strai	anch	schoo	shril	ottle	opps
Scru	Blan	Cring	Idle	Mund	Dren	Fren

to que,	a slen,	the year,	at ever,	by itse
at chur,	a hamp,	in cas,	on cov,	I list

NOTE: The examples shown on this and the following pages are set in type, but the teacher's models should be written in cursive.

PROCEDURE TWO

DEVELOPING EYE SPAN

Children will have been taught that every word must have a vowel. They should look for all of the consonants preceding and including the vowel for one eye span. Possibly the final consonant can be included if the word has no more than four or five letters. They should name the letters to themselves, just as they did the letters that did not make words.

If the word can be recognized and its spelling is known, children should try to include it in their eye span with the next word which will have letters that may need to be named and consciously recalled. The teacher should demonstrate with hand swings or by forming arched lines how some words may be held in one eye span.

Word lists

Two-Letter Words and Three-Letter Words

in,	of,	you,	but,	at,	be,	can,	was,	his,	ate
for,	us,	it,	has,	did,	me,	on,	her,	son,	he
few,	sky,	and,	one,	she,	ate,	sun,	saw,	try	

(The same words should be rearranged and used in different lessons.)

Four-Letter Words

they – than – inch – must – home – does
isn't – can't – want – wish – will – bent

were,	with,	have,	tree,	walk,	talk
much,	moon,	seen,	hood,	best,	made
tail,	hide,	rope,	soap,	ouch,	boil

Five-Letter Words

child,	cause,	could,	would,	thank,	laugh,
shall,	chair,	house,	think,	scoot,	trail
torch,	twist,	grand,	pinch,	grasp,	scrub,
shred,	sprig,	pitch,	budge,	shrill,	strip

Six- and Seven-Letter Words

With six- or seven-letter words the teacher should demonstrate with arched lines (as shown below) how letters can be grouped.

scratch	spring	stretch	grudge	speech
branch	flinch	stream	strange	glance

Phrases

Practice should begin with short phrases, possibly arranged at first in columns to minimize figure-ground discrimination, and then presented in lined arrangements.

Teacher: "Here are some phrases to copy. Try to extend your eye span to include the little words you may know with as many letters as you can recall in the word you must copy in the way you have learned.

"In the first phrase (shown below), tell yourself to think 'in a *b-o-a-t*,' and then write without looking again until you have finished."

Sample phrase list

in a boat	for a walk	over the wall
on my foot	on my cat	can go by
to see us play	for all of them,	under that one
under the big table	made of wood	up the trail

LESSON PLANS TO INTEGRATE PAST AND PRESENT LEARNINGS

A day's lesson plan, as shown below, should include a sampling of the procedures children already have practiced. It should be prepared in cursive and presented in its entirety.

Lesson Plan

letters:	str, th, one, er, Ga, Ge, Oth, oast, Gl
words:	coat, Get, string, some, Grand, her, stern
phrases:	with a long string, Get this coat,
	my other ones, to see someone, not for me

Words with Suffixes

Children should be told about root words and shown how to perceive them, whether familiar or not, when they precede familiar suffixes. After the root words have been copied in the usual way, the easily remembered suffix is added.

Examples

ask*ing*	stretch*able*	bus*es*	fool*ish*	cream*y*
play*ful*	strand*ed*	soft*ly*	child*ish*	strong*est*

Words with Two or More Syllables

Teacher: "With some two-syllable words, break your eye span between the two consonants in the medial position."

Examples

banyan	glisten	trellis	brandish	slender	happen
squander	bobbin	sudden	spinner	stringent	upper

Teacher: "With some words, include the first one or more consonants with the first vowel or vowels."

Examples

treason,	courage,	gruesome,	country,	Easter
earlier,	builder,	through,	fearsome,	loosely

Teacher: "Here are some words to copy. Use no more than two eye spans that are comfortable for you."

closure	traction	earnest	lonesome
joyous	volume	afford	explode

Teacher: "When suffixes appear in words of more than one syllable, concentrate on all of the preceding letters because the suffix will be easy to recall."

invent*ing*	structur*ed*	hungri*est*
suggest*ed*	conduct*able*	astonish*ment*

Teacher: "Prefixes in some words help your eye span."

*mis*statement	*dis*trustful	*mis*judge
*re*claimable	*un*patriotic	*dis*mount

Teacher: "With long words, group as many of the consonants and vowels together as your eye span lets you remember."

electricity	Androcles	decoration
distribute	flexible	scientifically
birdhouse	nuthatch	immediate

Phrases and Sentences

The teacher should prepare phrases that begin with prepositions (e.g., *into the large mansions, under the airplane, with that elephant*), that begin with articles (e.g., *the long feathers, an endless parade, a new undertaking*), that describe (e.g., *the tall, white flagstaff; that beautiful tree; has long, black feathers*), that are subjects (e.g., *another black boot; some small, ugly gnomes; every single tiger*), and other phrases that are suitable for the practice.

Phrases should be written in sentences for the children to copy, for example:

They live on rocks near the seacoast.
Barnacles live on ship bottoms and on rocks by the ocean.
Years ago, some natives believed in monsters.

If copying needs to be simplified, easier words should be used, for example:

Without food we would starve.
They fled to a new land across the sea.
She ran to the camp to find her friends.

Examples of lesson plans for copying

Words: glance, conduct, sandal, color*ful*, secret*ly*

Phrases: forming small drops,   to paint a picture,   to try again,
with good conduct,   kind things to do,   to figure out

Sentences: The day before Christmas, he saw the new bicycle.
Settlers brought ideas from the Old World.
We had turkey for Thanksgiving dinner.
Food tastes good when we are hungry.

The lesson to copy should be shortened or lengthened according to the time available.

Words: Copy the following words in a column:

clamor	clamoring	investment	invest
holiday	crystal	pilgrim	pilgrimage

Phrases:

hear the breakers	on the beach
by the seashore	to see the waves
can look for shells	to tell us why

Sentences: We go to the beach to enjoy an outing.
When it is not too cold, we go into the water.
A perfect shell is hard to find.

PROCEDURE THREE

COPYING USED INDEPENDENTLY

When copying begins to be automatic and enables children to meet daily demands, they can use it to follow the teacher's directions for independent performances without supervision. Failure is prevented by limiting requirements until the children develop "patterns of performance" that ensure success and confidence when they undertake tasks that require unsupervised copying.

Sample tasks that require copying

The teacher should write on the chalkboard words to be copied under the correct headings.

Name words — Action words

climb	home	swimmer	scream
swim	scramble	glasses	target
trader	tackle	spender	spend
baker	elbow	sprain	cradle

Name	*Date*
Name words	*Action words*
trader	*climb*
baker	*swim*

Some of the words can be in either or both columns, offering an opportunity to discuss meanings.

Describing words — Name words

moist	tall	strange	cowboy
children	hopeless	grass	grassy
strangest	hunter	tables	speedy
skillful	strong	beautiful	unusual

Suggestions for other categorized lists

Food — Clothing   Names of boys — Names of girls
Animals — Birds   Liquids — Solids

With suffixes — Without suffixes

blinking	dream	elephant	clucking
clattered	stormy	wishful	wish
colorless	color	colorful	shapeless
enjoyment	enjoyed	grounded	flying

Present time — Past time

hike	retreat	run	connect
hiked	retreated	ran	stumbled
painted	float	invite	employed
paint	floated	dictate	collect

Words having the same vowel spelling should be copied under the correct headings.

a-e — ai — eigh

sleigh	strain	plain	freight	plate
weigh	claim	weight	weightless	grain
brave	snake	shale	chain	waist

Suggestions for other vowel spellings

oo	ew	ou	/o͞o/		er	ur	ir	/ûr/
ow	ou	/ou/			oi	oy	/oi/	
ee	ea	e-e	/ē/		igh	i-e	ie	/ī/

Phrases that "Tell when," "Tell where," "Tell who," or that are "Subject phrases" or "Describing phrases" should be written by the teacher for copying.

Example

Tell when — Tell what

a long time ago	that tall building
that large duck	a very strong one
at midnight	next Christmas
before too long	my new bicycle

Teacher: "Write *Tell when* and copy the right phrases below it. Then write *Tell what* and copy the right phrases below that."

After the children have learned to transcribe manuscript (or any print) into cursive writing, they can be directed to use cursive to copy phrases by categories as described above from the page(s) of a book.

Copying, as a functional skill, is used for many purposes:

- preparing dictation lessons for study,
- recording homework assignments,
- writing invitations, notices, etc., and
- copying a question (Visual stimuli) to be individually answered in written form (inner Auditory stimuli).

THE VISUAL APPROACH TO READING WITH CONCEPT

Teachers of third-year children (and beyond) should read the Introduction and the Background sections of this book before attempting to use the multi-sensory techniques of THE VISUAL APPROACH.* Instruction for learning to *read written material* from Visual stimuli as taught in THE VISUAL APPROACH should be given at an entirely separate time of the school day from instruction in THE AUDITORY APPROACH. (Refer to page 50.)

Until the visually-presented graphemes can be simultaneously associated with their *names and sounds*, and *feel* in speech and arm, they serve little useful purpose in unlocking words — a skill that helps children with SLD learn to pronounce unrecognized words. The practice time devoted to A—Alphabet Cards of THE VISUAL APPROACH strengthens input-output or Visual-Auditory integration.

A—Alphabet Cards

NOTE: The Alphabet Cards should be used in daily periods of from five to ten minutes. Not all of the cards should be (or could be) used in any one lesson but time should be allowed to practice from ten, at the least, to fifteen or even twenty of them in each day's lesson.

Sometimes the entire class should participate in the practice. At other times, Alphabet Card practice should precede instruction of individual reading groups, thereby allowing for variation in both progress and the number of graphemes that have been learned in each group.

In THE VISUAL APPROACH a grapheme exposed on a card may require association with more than one phoneme. For example, the visually-presented phonogram *ea*, as a vowel digraph, says /ē/ as in *eat* and /ĕ/ as in *head*, and as a diphthong, says /ā/ as in *steak*. It may be *recognized* in a word by some who may *not* be able to recall the exact spelling of the word.

In THE AUDITORY APPROACH a phoneme voiced by the teacher (not seen on the card until *after* the child makes the correct association) may require memory of numerous spellings that demand exact letter sequencing before the phoneme can be used in spelling and writing a word. For example, the auditorily-presented vowel sound /ē/ is spelled *e, e-e, ee, ea, ie*, and *y*. (Refer to page 64.) If the sound of the *ee* can be recalled when a word such as *steep* is seen, the word can be pronounced and the reading can be continued. On the other hand, when the same word is to be written, the various ways of spelling the sound /ē/ must be recalled and the *exact* one for the word *steep* remembered — a much more difficult task than merely naming the word.

Both approaches provide output for each individually performing child and much input for the listeners taking part in the group practice.

*It is recommended that teachers read Slingerland, *Book Two — Basics in Scope and Sequence*.

OBJECTIVES FOR A—ALPHABET CARDS

Grapheme-phoneme (symbol-sound) associations for which to strive are:

1. All consonants, including *c* and *g* followed by *e, i,* or *y*
2. Consonant digraphs and trigraphs
3. Vowels (modified when followed by consonants and at the end of accented and unaccented syllables)
4. Vowel-consonant-*e* units
5. Phonograms (diphthongs, vowel digraphs) as single units
6. Letter combination units such as *ang, tion, unk, ble,* etc.

GRAPHEMES AND PHONEMES
FOR VISUAL-AUDITORY-KINESTHETIC ASSOCIATION

Not all of the grapheme-phoneme units shown below will have been taught during the second year of the continuum. Those that have should be reviewed with continuing children and introduced to newcomers in an SLD classroom. Some of them, shown with asterisks, are not meant for presentation until children reach upper-elementary or junior high levels, but teachers should be familiar with them for exceptional needs that may arise. To introduce unnecessary words is to confuse and distort children's thought patterns when they must put these visual symbol units to use in reading words.

Grapheme or Symbol	Key Word	Phoneme or Sound*
1. Consonants (should appear on white cards)		
b	ball	/b/, not /bŭh/
c	cake	/k/, not /kŭh/ (hard sound)
	cinch	/s/, not /sŭh/ (soft sound)
		(*C* has no sound of its own.)

The children should learn to say, "*C* followed by *e, i,* or *y* says /s/."

d	duck	/d/, not /dŭh/
f	fish	/f/, not /fŭh/
g	goat	/g/, not /gŭh/ (hard sound)
	gem	/j/, not /jŭh/ (soft sound)

The children should learn to say, "*G* followed by *e, i,* or *y* sometimes says /j/."

h	house	/h/, not /hŭh/

* Refer to pp. 52-56.

Grapheme or Symbol	Key Word	Phoneme or Sound
The children should feel only air come through their throats because the sides of the throat should not touch.		
j	jam	/j/, not /jŭh/
k	kite	/k/, not /kŭh/
l	lamp	/l/, not /lŭl/ or /ŭl/ Refer to page 53.
m	mittens	/m/, not /mŭh/ The lips stay closed.
n	nest	/n/, not /nŭh/
p	pig	/p/, not /pŭh/
qu	queen	/kw/, not /kwŭh/
The children should learn to perceive *qu* as a unit.		
r	rug	/r/, not /rŭh/ and not /ûr/ Refer to page 53.
s	sun	/s/, not /sŭh/
	was, rose	/z/, not /zŭh/
t	turtle	/t/, not /tŭh/
v	vase	/v/, not /vŭh/
The children should learn to perceive *v* followed by silent *e* at the end of many words. Refer to page 53.		
w	wagon	/w/, not /wŭh/ Refer to page 53.
x	box	/ks/, not /ĕks/
The children should learn that *x* usually comes at the end of a word or syllable in our language, but it may sometimes appear at the beginning in some words of foreign derivation.		
y	yellow	/y/, not /yŭh/
The children should learn that *y* can be both a consonant and a vowel and that, as a vowel, it has the same sounds that *i* has.		

Grapheme or Symbol	Key Word	Phoneme or Sound
Y as a vowel also can say /ē/. (For practice, *y* as a vowel should appear on a salmon-colored card. See page 54.)		
z	zebra	/z/, not /zŭh/

2. Consonant Digraphs and Trigraphs (should appear on white cards)

ck	Jac*k*	/k/, not /kŭh/
ch	*ch*air	/ch/, not /chŭh/
	*Ch*ristmas	/k/, not /kŭh/
	*ch*ef	/sh/, not /shŭh/
ph	*ph*one	/f/, not /fŭh/
kn	*kn*ife	/n/, not /nŭh/
th	*th*imble	/th/, not /thŭh/

Say to children: "Put your tongue through your teeth and push the air out."

Say to children: "Put your tongue through your teeth and let your throat vibrate or touch while pushing the air out."	*th*is	/t̶h̶/
wh	*wh*eel	/hw/, not /hwŭh/

Say to children: "Blow as if blowing out a candle and feel the air on your hand."

gn	*gn*aw	/n/, not /nŭh/
tch	ma*tch*	/ch/, not /chŭh/
dge	bri*dge*	/j/, not /jŭh/

3. Vowels (should appear on salmon-colored cards)

a	*a*pple	/ă/
	b*a*′ by (at end of accented syllables)	/ā/
	p*a* rade′ (at end of unaccented syllables)	/ŭ/ (schwa sound)
e	*e*lephant	/ĕ/
	m*e*′ ter (at end of accented syllables)	/ē/

Grapheme or Symbol	Key Word	Phoneme or Sound
	r*e* new′ (at end of unaccented syllables)	/ē/
i	*i*nch	/ĭ/
	t*i* ger (at end of accented syllables)	/ī/
o	*o*lives	/ŏ/
	p*o*′ ny (at end of accented syllables)	/ō/
	p*o* lite′ (at end of unaccented syllables)	/ō/
	h*o*ney	/ŭ/ (schwa sound)
u	*u*mbrella	/ŭ/
	m*u*′ sic (at end of accented syllables)	/ū/
	l*u*′ nar	/o͞o/
y	g*y*m, c*y*n ic	/ĭ/
	sk*y*, c*y*′ cle	/ī/
	cand*y* (at end of some words)	/ē/

4. *Vowel-Consonant-e Units (v-e) (should appear on salmon-colored cards)*

a-e	s*afe*	/ā/
e-e	th*ese*	/ē/
i-e	p*ine*	/ī/
o-e	h*ome*	/ō/
u-e	m*ule*	/ū/
	fl*ute*	/o͞o/
y-e	t*ype*	/ī/

5. *Phonograms as Single Units (should appear on salmon-colored cards)*

ai	rain	/ā/
ay	play	/ā/
aw	saw	/ô/
au	author	/ô/
ee	feet	/ē/
ea	eat	/ē/
	head	/ĕ/
	steak	/ā/

Grapheme or Symbol	Key Word	Phoneme or Sound
eigh	sleigh	/ā/
ew	few	/ū/
	grew	/ōō/
eu	feud	/ū/
igh	night	/ī/
ie	pie	/ī/
	chief	/ē/
oa	boat	/ō/
ow	snow	/ō/
	cow	/ou/
ou	ouch	/ou/
	soup	/ōō/
oi	oil	/oi/
oy	boy	/oi/
oo	book	/ŏŏ/
ar	star	/är/
	dollar	/ēr/
er	her	/ûr/
	cherry	/ĕr/
ir	girl	/ûr/
or	corn	/ôr/
	visitor	/ēr/
ur	burn	/ûr/

(usually placed on white cards but can appear on salmon-colored cards)

6. *Letter Combination Units (should appear on white cards)*

ing	sing	/ĭng/, not /ing g/
ang	sang	/ăng/
ink	think	/ĭngk/
ank	thank	/ăngk/
tion	na tion	/shŭn/
sion	mis sion	/shŭn/
	vi sion	/zhŭn/
tle	lit tle	/t'l/
ple	pur ple	/p'l/

NOTE: The letter combinations *tle* and *ple*, and others such as *ble, cle, dle, fle, gle, kle, sle,* and *zle,* have three letters but only two sounds. These are examples

Grapheme or Symbol	Key Words	Phoneme or Sound
	of silent-*e* syllables that begin with any of the consonants. They should be perceived as single units of sight and automatically integrated with their corresponding sound units. (Refer to pages 90-91 and *TWL*, page 47.)	
*ti	sometimes as in spa*ti*al	/sh/
*ci	sometimes as in spe*ci*al	/sh/
*ce	sometimes as in o*ce*an	/sh/

MATERIALS

Teacher's Hand Pack for Classroom Use

PROCEDURES

Graphemes perceived visually must be simultaneously associated with their Auditory counterparts as a Visual-Auditory integrative process if they are to be used functionally in decoding words. Dependable use requires instant multi-sensory recall without prompting by the teacher or reference to clues other than those that may come from within an individual.

The daily period of practice (from five to ten minutes) affords time:

- for automatic Visual-Auditory association linked with the Kinesthetic in arm and speech through over-teaching and review.
- for introducing and teaching unlearned graphemes and including them in the Teacher's Hand Pack for daily review in both the Visual and the Auditory Alphabet Card practice.

At the beginning of the practice, *the teacher* should expose the card and say, "Tell us about these letters," or "Give the sound(s) of this letter unit." Thereafter, to keep the tempo of class performance moving along without interruption, *the teacher* should simply expose the cards one at a time and have children take turns telling about the graphemes. *The child* should 1) name the letter(s) exposed on the card, and at the same time form the letter(s) with an arm swing, 2) name the key word, and 3) give as many of the sounds (phonemes) as have been learned. *The class* should repeat.

---

*Words with asterisks can be introduced for spelling in upper-elementary grades and junior high but not in third grade, except in rare instances. Many of the grapheme counterparts *can be learned for reading* long before they should be expected to be used in spelling. If needed for spelling, they can be learned as Red Flag words.

NOTE: The card in use should remain exposed throughout each performance.

Example

Teacher: Exposes a card, such as *ow*.
Child: "*O-w*, cow, /ou/," forming the letters with arm swings as they are named. "*O-w*, snow, /ō/."
Class: Repeats.

Teacher: Exposes a card, such as *e*.
Child: "*E*, elephant, /ĕ/; *e* at the end of a syllable, meter, /ē/."
Class: Repeats.

Teacher: Exposes a card, such as *ai*.
Child: "*A-i*, rain, /ā/."
Class: Repeats.

Teacher: Exposes a card, such as *sion*.
Child: "*S-i-o-n*, mission, /shŭn/; *s-i-o-n*, vision, /zhŭn/."
Class: Repeats.

Teacher: Exposes a card, such as *ie*.
Child: "*I-e*, chief, /ē/; *i-e*, pie, /ī/."
Class: Repeats.

Teacher: Exposes a card such as *u-e*.
Child: "*U*-consonant-*e*, mule, /ū/; *u*-consonant-*e*, flute, /ōō/."
Class: Repeats.

NOTE: Children who are new to the program should be given turns repeating as individuals, thereby affording extra integrative practice for them at the conclusion of each group or class repetition.

Frequently, Alphabet Card practice should be used with each one of the reading groups into which the class should have been divided. The practice should precede each group's lessons in Unlocking, Preparation, and Reading from the Book. By following this arrangement, each reading group can be introduced to phonograms, digraphs, diphthongs, letter combinations, etc., according to its own level of reading achievement.

On days when the Alphabet Card practice is done with the entire class as a group, only the children who have been taught a greater number of the grapheme-phoneme associations should be expected to tell about them, but their performances should serve as learning opportunities for the others. The less-advanced children should be asked to tell about the graphemes that they have been taught. Such individualized performance opportunities give less-advanced students a chance to learn new grapheme-phoneme associations, and enable all children to strengthen their learning through over-teaching and repetition.

The Yellow Cards are not used in THE VISUAL APPROACH. They are for use in THE AUDITORY APPROACH alone.

No lessons in Alphabet Card practice of THE VISUAL APPROACH require written performances. If the children were to write what they see on the cards, the performance would be *copying* from Visual stimuli, requiring no recall. Writing from Auditory stimuli requires recall of the Visual-Kinesthetic association.

B—Unlocking

Unlocking groups of letters combined to form words is a skill that enables children to decode many unrecognized words. Simply unlocking the pronunciation of words, however, cannot be considered reading. It is *word naming*.

To name a single word out of context teaches no meaning, but only reinforces what the decoder may already understand it to mean. When the word is unlocked as part of a phrase, its meaning clarifies the meaning of the phrase. If the word is unrecognized, the meaning of the phrase will be lost until the word is decoded. Therefore, the ability to unlock words is an important skill for use in independent reading.

Within The Daily Format for lesson planning, B—Blending as well as B—Unlocking are essentially teaching times. The key to independent unlocking is perceiving and recognizing the vowel(s) in simultaneous Visual-Auditory-Kinesthetic association and then resynthesizing the vowel and consonant sounds into the pronunciation of the word.

Children who are following this multi-sensory approach will have learned to unlock one-syllable, short-vowel, phonetic words (*slam, plot*), letter combination words (*tank, think*), phonogram words (*cloud, dream*), and equivalent two-syllable words with suffixes (*slamming, cloudy, thinker, dreamless*). Also, they can be expected to have learned to unlock one-syllable, vowel-consonant-*e* words (*hope, state*) to which suffixes have been added (*hoping, stately*). (Refer to pages 219-220.)

To understand the meaning of written words is the purpose of learning to read. A writer's purpose is to convey thoughts to a reader, and this requires the ability to sequence letters to spell words correctly. A reader's purpose is to comprehend written words without necessarily recalling their spelling or spelling rules. Graphemes (Visual sight-sound symbol units) should be introduced as Visual stimuli for unlocking words before they are integrated into spelling. For spelling, the stimulus is Auditory and the phonemes (Auditory sound-sight symbol units) often have ambiguous spelling that requires much more exact recall of the grapheme if spelling is to be correctly accomplished.

It is easier to recognize and name (unlock) certain written words than to recall the exact letter sequencing of these words, especially when sound units have ambiguous spellings. For this reason, grapheme-phoneme units should be introduced first for unlocking (naming words) and then for *blending* (spelling words).

For any beginner, regardless of age, blending, not unlocking, should be taught as the initial step in the logical progression of learning names and sounds of single letters of the alphabet. Using these single units of sight-sound-feel to form word units, which now have meaning, is the initial step in blending.

Until single letters are blended and written, there is *no word to see*, whereas in *unlocking*, the *word is seen* and its elements can be taken apart and put back together, or *blended*. Therefore, blending should be taught first with purely phonetic words. Once this concept is mastered, new grapheme-phoneme units should be taught first for unlocking words and then for blending words. This task should be learned with purely phonetic words and when cognition of word formation is established, children should be ready to learn to unlock words by determining the vowel sound and then blending all of the letters to form word "wholes."

Beginning in the second year, when many phonograms are introduced in the lessons of B—Unlocking and A—Alphabet Cards,* and from the third year on, as new phonograms are added, the unlocking techniques should be extended to polysyllabic words, and discussion of the effect of vowel placement and accent on the pronunciation of vowels. The place to teach, to explain, and to give practice should be in B—Unlocking of THE VISUAL APPROACH before children are expected to apply these learnings to an Auditory approach for more difficult use in spelling, dictation, and propositional writing.

Use of punctuation marks to unlock meanings in reading material should be introduced often in this division of The Daily Format for lesson planning, where practice can be provided prior to application in reading from books.

OBJECTIVES FOR B—UNLOCKING

Review and strengthen**the unlocking of:
- One-syllable short-vowel, phonetic words, including consonant digraphs and trigraphs, such as *grand, which, flinch, stretch*, and *drudge*.
- One-syllable vowel-consonant-*e* words, such as *stroke, blame, chide*, and *whine*.
- One-syllable letter combination words, such as *clank, fling, strung*, and *strength*.
- One-syllable phonogram words, such as *strain, mound, shawl*, and *spread*.
- One-syllable soft *c* and *g* words, such as *cell, space, gem*, and *stage*.
- All of the above word formations as two- or multisyllabic words when suffixes are added, such as *strength' en, blame' less, whi' ning, stretch' a ble, grand' est*.

Teach (or reteach and review) two-syllable words with:
- Short-vowel syllables having:

    two like consonants in the medial position, such as *muf fin, ten nis*, and *dob bin*.

    two unlike consonants in the medial position, such as *can did, cac tus*, and *ban dit*.

---

*It is suggested that teachers refer to Slingerland, *Book One — A Multi-Sensory Approach*, pp. 154–156 and 157–174, and *Book Two — Basics in Scope and Sequence*, pp. 153–195.

**Children who enter this multi-sensory approach for the first time must be taught what, to the others, requires no more than review and strengthening.

a short vowel in the first syllable and *er* in the last syllable, such as *blis ter* and *ham mer*.

- One short-vowel and one silent-*e* syllable in words such as *mid dle*, *crum ble*, and *top ple*, and with:

  special teaching of words with *ck* in the medial position, such as *crac kle* and *frec kle*.

  special teaching of words having a letter combination syllable and a silent-*e* syllable, such as *wrinkle*, and *jingle*.

- One phonogram syllable and one silent-*e* syllable in words such as *mar ble* and *whee dle*.

- One short-vowel and one vowel-consonant-*e* syllable in words such as *con fide*, *trom bone*, and *ath lete*.

- One phonogram syllable and short-vowel, vowel-consonant-*e*, or another phonogram syllable in words such as *hor net*, *ear shot*, *oat meal*, *par take*, and *crow bar*.

- One of the two syllables a letter combination in words such as *junk et*, *yank ee*, and *trink et*.

Teach the effect of vowel placement and accent when the:

- First vowel is long at end of an *accented first syllable* that does not contain the one consonant in the medial position in words such as *fi' nal*, *si' lent*, *lo' cate*, *no' ble*, *a' pex*, *thy' roid*, and *na' tion*.

- First vowel has a modified sound at end of an *unaccented* first syllable that does not contain the one consonant in the medial position in words such as *po lite'*, *a bout'*, *bri gade'*, *se dan'*, *re quire'*, and *a dore'*.

- First vowel is modified, usually to a short sound by placement in a syllable that contains the single consonant in the medial position in words such as *cab' in*, *den' im*, *tim' id*, *frol' ic*, *pun' ish*, *hab' it*, *lim' it*, and *com'et*.

Teach three-syllable and polysyllabic words with syllable division as learned from unlocking two-syllable words.

Examples

ep' i sode	mu se' um	pho' no graph
tel' e graph	mar' tin gale	in ves' ti gate
pro mo' tion	e vac' u ate	in ves ti ga' tion
ad mi ra' tion	twink' ling	blank' et ting

MATERIALS

Phonetic Word Lists for Children's Use
Small Manuscript Alphabet Cards
Chart Holder

PROCEDURES

The children who have come from primary SLD classrooms presumably will have learned the unlocking technique with one-syllable words. They should be able to:

- *perceive* the letters that spell the vowel sound,
- *name* the letter(s) that spell the sound,
- *blend* all of the letters together to obtain the pronunciation of the word.

Learning to *blend*, introduced in B—Blending of THE AUDITORY APPROACH, should precede learning to unlock words because blending is required to resynthesize letters of a word after its vowel sound has been perceived for unlocking. Only a single vowel, such as *a*, should be used in practice until the "patterning" for the unlocking technique is established and can be applied with other vowels, letter combinations, phonograms, and vowel-consonant-*e* units.

As soon as children can blend words containing short-vowel sounds, ambiguous spelling can be introduced — usually at the second year grade level. Each one of the letter combinations, vowel-consonant-*e* units, and phonograms to be learned should be presented through THE VISUAL APPROACH as graphemes for Visual-Auditory association to be used in decoding practice of B—Unlocking. Perception and Visual-Auditory association is strengthened in the card practice of A—Alphabet Cards.

Sometimes all of the words to be unlocked for review and practice may contain the same graphemes, and sometimes they may contain a mixture of already-learned graphemes in order to strengthen a student's ability to discriminate among vowel sounds.

The words should be written *by the teacher* in manuscript rather than in cursive letters because manuscript more nearly resembles the appearance of the printed letters used in the books that children are expected to read.

Examples

Short Vowels

				Letter Combinations	
crunch	squint	blast		clank	blink
struck	clutch	blend		strung	throng
squelch	drench	swift		shrink	strength

Phonograms

chief	bloom	coarse	sleigh	speech	quaint
grieve	broom	toast	sprain	breeze	crowd
shield	pooch	cloak	freight	breath	sprout
shriek	groove	groan	fright	breathe	growth
niece	sweep	coach	streak	moose	moist

Vowel-Consonant-e

spike	swine	shape	choke	plane	grade
blaze	grope	sphere	stave	crude	prune
drone	breve	sprite	mere	chore	cute

Individual children should be given turns unlocking the words. They should understand, as should the teacher, that unlocking requires *naming but not writing* the words. When children reach the point where underlining the vowel(s) is no longer necessary, they should use a pointer to indicate which word is being unlocked by holding the pointer at the word to keep the point of focus until unlocking is completed.

If the vowel "unit" is to be underlined:

Child:	Underlines the letters giving the vowel sound in a word such as *brain* and says, "*A-i,* /ā/, brain," forming the *ai* with arm swings.
Class:	Repeats, "*A-i,* /ā/, brain."

If the word is to be *pointed* to only:

Child:	Points to the word, such as *freight*, and says, "*E-i-g-h,* /ā/, freight," forming *e-i-g-h* with arm swings.
Class:	Repeats, "*E-i-g-h,* /ā/, freight."

blink

Child:	"*I-n-k,* /ingk/, blink," forming *i-n-k* with arm swings.
Class:	Repeats.

drape

Child:	"*A*-consonant-*e,* /ā/, drape." Follows same procedure.
Class:	Repeats.

NOTE: If a child recognizes the word that he or she is asked to unlock, it should be decoded with the usual unlocking technique to insure automatic use of the "patterning" and to strengthen use of the technique for other words that may not be recognized. Also the child should be told that good performance affords extra input for those children who are listening and learning from his or her performance.

Sometimes the teacher should use nonsense words or syllables for unlocking. To unlock them demands use of the unlocking skill. (Refer to *TWL*, pages 19, 20.)

When the children are able to use the unlocking technique without needing to underline the vowels and this "crutch" can be withdrawn, the teacher should point to words for individual children to unlock by:
- *naming* the vowel,
- giving the vowel *sound*, and
- *pronouncing* the word.

The class should respond by:
- *repeating* the word.

Examples

town

Child:	"*O-w,* /ou/, town."
Class:	"Town."

	hoist
Child:	"*O-i,* /oi/, hoist."
Class:	"Hoist."

	drove
Child:	"*O*-consonant-*e,* /ō/, drove."
Class:	"Drove."

	group
Child:	"*O-u,* /ou/, group" (which does not make a word; tries /o͞o/.) "*O-u,* /o͞o/, group."
Class:	"Group."

	weight
Child:	"*E-i-g-h,* /ā/, weight."
Class:	"Weight."

	strength
Child:	"*E-n-g,* /ĕng/, length" (not len th).
Class:	"Length."

NOTE: It is recommended that copies of *Phonetic Word Lists for Children's Use* be kept in the classroom, one for each child. From appropriate lists of words, individual children should be given turns unlocking words by following the procedures shown above.

ONE-SYLLABLE WORDS WITH SUFFIXES

The children who have had previous experience in this multi-sensory approach should be able to tell themselves to:
- Look across the word and where they recognize a suffix, underline it, knowing that it must be preceded by a root word.
- Unlock the root word in the usual way. (Refer to page 211.)
- Pronounce the word again, including the suffix.

Sample performance

	stainless
Child:	Looks across the word, *stainless,* or runs fingers under the word to note the suffix, if there is one.
	Underlines *less.*
	Draws a vertical broken line to separate the root word and suffix.
	Follows the usual procedure to unlock the root word.
	Pronounces the root word again, including the suffix.

Sample list to be written in manuscript

blowing	twister	weightless
matched	trustful	spoonful
spoiling	quaintly	grandly
soapy	joinable	clasped

VOWEL-CONSONANT-e WORDS WITH SUFFIXES

How to unlock vowel-consonant-*e* words to which the suffixes *ing, ed,* or *er* have been added, such as *baking, raked,* and *roper,* should be explained and demonstrated for the children to *see and hear.* Preferably, this should be done on the Chart Holder with the *Small Manuscript Alphabet Cards.* The demonstration can be done on the chalkboard if a Chart Holder is unavailable. Using a word such as *naming,* the teacher should follow the usual procedure for perceiving and covering the suffix, leaving the root word to be unlocked.

n	a	m	ing

n	a	m	

The remaining syllable is pronounced /năm/ and does not sound like a real, meaningful word. However, *nam* is a vowel-consonant word, and it would have been a vowel-consonant-*e* word if a silent *e* had been part of it before the suffix was added. The teacher should push the *ing* over to the right and insert a card showing an *e,* forming the word *name.*

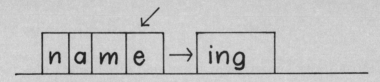

The silent *e* was dropped because a suffix beginning with a vowel was added. The silent *e* is no longer needed to make the first vowel long. The first vowel should be left at the end of the first syllable where it will have its long sound and the *m* should be moved into the last syllable with *ing.*

n	a		m	ing

NOTE: When there are two consonants in the medial position, there is no problem. The word is divided between the two like consonants and each syllable pronounced and blended into the whole word.

After the teacher's verbal explanation and demonstration — an Auditory-Visual performance for the children to *hear* and *see* — students should be given individual turns verbalizing and performing each progressive step. Doing so affords each individual an Auditory-Visual *and* Kinesthetic-gross motor association since body action is included in the performance using the cards on the Chart Holder.

Examples

waving	shaving	choking
lining	riding	tuning
spading	closing	chasing

The same procedure applies to unlocking words that end in suffixes beginning with *e*, such as *ed, er, en*. (There are no suffixes spelled with the single letters *d, r,* or *n*.) Each suffix varies the meaning of a word and children should be made aware of these differences in order to understand what they read. The word *voter* was formed from the word *vote* and the silent *e* was dropped when the suffix *er* was added to form the two-syllable word, *vo ter*, meaning the one who votes. Therefore, the *e* that appears *is part of the suffix* and is not the original silent *e* that was dropped when no longer needed. Telling children that *r* was added to make *vote* into a name would not be teaching "through the intellect."

Examples

waved	spoken	joker	choker
liner	cutest	pruned	ruled

Sometimes the suffix *ed* is pronounced as part of the root word without adding another syllable in such words as *lined, ruled*, and *joked*. Here again, the silent *e* is dropped when the suffix is added. The *e* in the suffix serves to keep the first vowel a vowel-consonant-*e* word with a long sound.

There is no problem in unlocking vowel-consonant-*e* words that have suffixes beginning with a consonant in such words as *closeness, hopeless*, and *bravely*, for example. When the suffix is covered, or recognized without being covered, the root word remains a complete vowel-consonant-*e* word.

TWO-SYLLABLE WORDS

VOWEL PLACEMENT

At some point in the third year of the continuum, or later depending upon background and experience, the children should be given an explanation of the effect that vowel placement within a syllable or word has on the sound of the vowel. They should be told, and shown, with real words that:

- vowels usually have sounds that are the same as their names — long sounds — when they occur at the end of a word or syllable, in words such as *be, she, pa per, se cret, Cu ban, lo cate,* and *Bi ble.*
- vowels followed by a consonant (or consonants) in words and syllables have modified vowel sounds, usually short sounds, in words such as *lum ber, tam per, lock et, twist,* and *branch.*
- vowels followed by consonants in words and syllables usually are returned to their long sounds by adding silent *e,* in words such as *spin–spine, dim–dime, plan–plane, cub–cube,* and *met–mete.*

NOTE: The teacher should have the children discover how words such as *athlete, invite,* and *explode* would be pronounced if they were written *ath let, in vit, ex plod,* and help them to understand why the added *e* is called a silent *e.*

WORDS WITH SHORT-VOWEL SYLLABLES

Explanation and practice for unlocking two-syllable words should begin with words having phonetic, short-vowel syllables and like consonants in the medial position, such as *pollen, gossip, nobbin,* and *annex.* (Refer to *TWL,* page 48.)

A list of words to be unlocked, as shown below, should be placed on the chalkboard before the lesson begins.

pollen	annex	muffin
gossip	rabbit	tennis
nobbin	comment	happen

Procedure

A child should be asked to follow the teacher's directions in demonstrating a way to unlock two-syllable words.

> *pollen*

Teacher: "Every syllable must have a vowel. Underline each vowel (or vowel unit). By doing so, the number of syllables usually will be determined. Tell us what you will do."

Child: "I will underline the vowels."
          Underlines *o* and *e* in *pollen*.

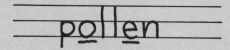

Teacher: "Look at the consonants between the two vowels and you will see that they
          are alike. Draw a vertical broken line between them to separate the two
          syllables. Tell us what you will do."
Child: "I will draw a vertical broken line to separate the syllables."
          Draws the broken line.

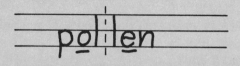

Teacher: "Now you are ready to unlock the word. Unlock each syllable as if it were a
          single word and then blend the two syllables together to pronounce the
          word."
Child: "I will unlock the word. *O*-consonant, /ŏ/, pol; *e*-consonant, /ĕ/, len;
          pollen."
Class: Repeats, "Pollen."

With children who understand the procedure,* the teacher need do no more than listen
and give help or guidance if needed.

*It is recommended that elementary teachers read Slingerland, *Book Two — Basics in Scope and Sequence*,
pp. 161–195.

> *gossip*

Child: "I will underline the vowels." Underlines the two vowels, *o* and *i*. "Divide between the two consonants. *O*-consonant, /ŏ/, gos; *i*-consonant, /ĭ/, sip; gossip."

Class: "Gossip."

NOTE: When children automatically recognize that vowels followed by consonants are modified, usually to the short sounds, another "crutch" may be dropped — in place of saying "*o*-consonant, /ŏ/," they say no more than "*o*, /ŏ/."

> *nobbin*

Child: "Underline vowels *o* and *i*. Divide between the consonants. *O*, /ŏ/, nob; *i*, /ĭ/, bin; nobbin."

Class: "Nobbin."

The same approach should be followed with two-syllable words having two or more unlike consonants in the medial position. (Refer to *TWL*, page 48.)

Short-Vowel Syllables

submit   "*U*, /ŭ/, sub; *i*, /ĭ/, mit; submit."
hamlet   "*A*, /ă/, ham; *e*, /ĕ/, let; hamlet."

Last Syllable Ends in *er*

butter   "*U*, /ŭ/, but; *e-r*, /ēr/, ter; butter."
buzzer   "*U*, /ŭ/, buz; *e-r*, /ēr/, zer; buzzer."
dipper   "*I*, /ĭ/, dip; *e-r*, /ēr/, per; dipper."

Last Syllable a Silent-*e* Syllable

The children should be reminded that, because every syllable must have a vowel, the silent-*e* is used in silent-*e* syllables where there is no vowel sound — *ble, dle, fle, gle, kle*, etc. The silent *e* serves as the necessary vowel that every syllable must have, and the three letters should be perceived as a "syllable unit" with consonant sounds only. (Refer to *TWL*, page 47.)

sizzle   "*I*, /ĭ/, siz; *z-l-e*, /z'l/; sizzle."
kettle   "*E*, /ĕ/, ket; *t-l-e*, /t'l/; kettle."
tremble   "*E*, /ĕ/, trem; *b-l-e*, /b'l/; tremble."

Silent-*e*-Syllable Words Containing *ck*

Although *ck* usually is perceived as a unit, there is an exception to this, as shown below.

In a word such as *trickle*, the *c* stays in the first syllable to modify the vowel to its short sound and the *k* completes the three-letter silent-*e* syllable. (Refer to *TWL*, page 47.)

tac⸾kle   "*A, /ă/,* tac; *k-l-e, /k'l/;* tackle."

tic⸾kle   "*I, /ĭ/,* tic; *k-l-e, /k'l/;* tickle."

Silent-*e*-Syllable Words Containing Letter Combinations

In words containing such letter combinations as *ank* and *ing*, the *k* and *g* do "double duty." In *twinkle*, the *k* is part of the letter combination *ink* to be pronounced /ingk/ and the *k* is part of the last syllable to complete the silent-*e* syllable pronunciation /k'l/. (Refer to page 223 and to *TWL*, page 47.) Otherwise, the word would be pronounced *twin kle* instead of *twing kle*. The same "double duty" is required of the *g* in *jingle* — /jing g'l/. (Refer to *TWL*, page 47.)

twinkle   "*I-n-k, /ĭngk/,* twing(k); *k-l-e, /k'l/;* twinkle."

jingle   "*I-n-g, /ĭng/,* jing; *g-l-e, /g'l/;* jingle."

One Phonogram and One Silent-*e* Syllable

wheedle   "*E-e, /ē/,* whee; *d-l-e, /d'l/;* wheedle."

gargle   "*A-r, /är/,* gar; *g-l-e, /g'l/;* gargle."

poodle   "*O-o, /o͞o/,* poo; *d-l-e, /d'l/;* poodle."

turtle   "*U-r, /ûr/,* tur; *t-l-e, /t'l/;* turtle."

(Refer to *TWL*, page 47.)

One Short-Vowel and One Vowel-Consonant-*e* Syllable

benzene   "*E*-consonant (or *e, /ĕ/,* ben; *e*-consonant-*e, /ē/,* zene; benzene."

capsule   "*A, /ă/,* cap; *u*-consonant-*e, /ū/,* sule; capsule."

inhale   "*I, /ĭ/,* in; *a*-consonant-*e, /ā/,* hale; inhale."

(Refer to *TWL*, page 49.)

ONE PHONOGRAM AND ONE MISCELLANEOUS SYLLABLE

portrait   "*O-r, /ôr/,* por; *a-i, /ā/,* trait; portrait."

hawthorn   "*A-w, /au/,* haw; *o-r, /ôr/,* thorn; hawthorn."

dauphin   "*A-u, /au/,* dauph; *i, /ĭ/,* in; dauphin."

lawyer   "*A-w, /au/,* law; *e-r, /ẽr/,* yer; lawyer."

boycott   "*O-y, /oi/,* boy; *o, /ŏ/,* cott; boycott."

REVIEW

Each new way of decoding two-syllable words should be included in frequent lessons for review after it is taught and practiced.

cam|pus	cole|slaw	graph|ite
rud|der	nee|dle	com|bine
hum|bug	com|plex	trum|pet
jangle	un|screw	wish|bone

NOTE: Only the trained teacher can be the judge of children's readiness to learn new concepts and of the rate at which they can progress in integrating new steps with previously learned ones. All should be put to functional use in reading phrases, sentences, and paragraphs, which will be explained in C—Preparation for Reading and D—Reading from the Book of THE VISUAL APPROACH.

VOWEL PLACEMENT AND ACCENT

By the time the children understand how to unlock two-syllable words and can follow the same procedures for perceiving suffixes in two-syllable as well as one-syllable words, they should be ready to learn the effects of both *vowel placement* and *accent* on the *pronunciation* and *meaning* of words of more than one syllable.

When a two-syllable word contains only one consonant in the medial position, that consonant's *placement* in either the first or second syllable determines the first syllable's vowel sound. If the vowel occurs at the end of the syllable to form an open syllable, the *accent* determines long- or modified-vowel sound.

- In *accented* syllables, vowels have long sounds, as in *lo' tus, tu' lip, Ve'nus, ri' val*, and *de' mon*.
- In *unaccented* syllables:

  A usually is pronounced with its obscure or schwa sound, as in *pa rade', a way'*, and *ca det'*.

  I usually has either its long or short sound, as in *hi bis' cus, bi fo' cal, ve' hi cle*, and *in vi ta' tion*.

  E, o, and *u* usually have half-long sounds, as in *se dan', po lite', re quire', pro pel'*, and *hu mane'*.

At this point the goal of children advancing through elementary grades is to become familiar with vowel placement and accent. When vowel placement is followed by a consonant(s), the vowel sound usually is short, as in *cab' in, rob' in, tram' ple*, and *graph' ite*, but not always, as in words such as *was, want*, and *wasp*, where the vowel is modified but not to a short sound.

When vowel placement is at the end of an *accented* syllable, the vowel sound usually is long.

When vowel placement is at the end of an *unaccented* syllable, the vowel sound usually is modified as explained above.

When they don't recognize words, children should be urged to experiment with the sounds they have learned.

> Teacher: "Would *robin*" (pointing to but not naming the word) be pronounced /rō' bin/ or /rŏb' in?" (pointing to the pronunciations shown on the chalkboard).

Context clues in the reading material should help, as in *Polish countryside* and *Polish the table top* (written on the chalkboard for the children to *see*).

Vowel at the End of First Accented Syllable

Before the lesson begins, the teacher should have placed on the chalkboard words containing one consonant in the medial position. In the initial lesson, children *should be told* that the one consonant in the medial position is in the last syllable. This leaves the first vowel at the end of the accented syllable. The teacher should place the accent mark.

Using a word such as *silent*, the teacher should demonstrate by showing and saying: "I will underline the vowels." Underlines *i* and *e*. "This one consonant (pointing) is to be in the last syllable." Divides. "The accent is to be on the first syllable, like this" (demonstrates and shows the correct way to make the mark).

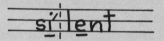

"Because this first vowel is at the end of an *accented* syllable, it will be long and say its own name /ī/, *si*. In the last syllable: *e*-consonant, /ĕ/, *lent*, *silent*."

The class should repeat *si lent*.

The teacher should tell the children that they are to have turns unlocking all the words (shown below) in the same way. They are to speak out clearly and loudly enough to be heard by all in a way that helps everyone learn as they listen and watch. They should be told that they will not have to experiment because they have been told where the accent is and where the medial consonant belongs. (Refer to *TWL*, page 50.)

Examples

silent	fracus	voter	rival
cupid	topaz	unite	*sy*p*hon* (*ph*, a single unit)
vacate	ozone	unit	rodent
Venus	profile	totem	tiger

cupid

Child: "I underline *u* and *i*." Underlines. "I will divide between the *u* and *p* to keep the one consonant in the last syllable." Divides. "Accent is on the first syllable." Places the mark.

Unlocks: "*U* at the end, /ū/, *cu*; *i*-consonant, /ĭ/, *pid*; *cupid*."

Class: Repeats *cupid*. (As soon as the children learn the unlocking technique, the "crutches" may be dropped.)

	syphon
Child:	Underlines *y* and *o*; "*p-h* makes a single sound. I divide between *y* and *p-h*." Divides. Places accent mark after first syllable. "*Y*, /ī/, sy; *o*, /ŏ/, phon, *syphon*, /sī fŏn/.

Vowel Followed by One Medial Consonant

The same procedure should be followed with words having the medial consonant in the first accented syllable. The children should be helped to see that in both syllables the vowels are followed by modifying consonants and that accent does not affect the modified vowel in the first syllable.

Examples

vanish	camel	level	banish	graphic
mimic	tonic	solid	cabin	robin
salad	rapid	denim	comet	seven

	vanish
Teacher:	"In all of these words, the medial consonant will be in the first syllable, which also has the accent."
Child:	Underlines *a* and *i*. Divides between the "*n* and *i*." (Make sure that the child does *not* say, "Between the *i* and *n*.") Places accent mark after *van*. "*A*, /ă/, van; *i*, /ĭ/, ish; vanish."

Vowel at End of Unaccented Syllable

The teacher should follow the same procedure when showing and demonstrating the effect of vowel placement. Begin with unaccented *i*, then *e, o, u,* and last, explain unaccented *a* syllables; follow with practice for their unlocking.

i

It should be explained that *unaccented syllables* ending in *i* usually have short sounds, but in some words they have the *i*'s long sound, as in *Chi nese'*.

Examples with unaccented final-i syllables

di vide′	Ti bet′	di vine′
di rect′	di verge′	di verse′

	divide
Child:	Underlines *i* and *ide*. "The one consonant is to be in the last syllable." Divides between the *i* and *v*. Places accent after the last syllable. "*I*, /ĭ/, di; *i-d-e*, /ī/, vide; divide′."

With three-syllable words, as shown below, the teacher should *name the letters of the accented syllable* for the performing child to mark and then underline the vowels. In a first lesson, all the letters of an accented syllable can be underlined with an extra line under the vowel when they are named by the teacher.

Teacher: "In some words of more than one syllable the *unaccented i* has its long, instead of its short, sound. In these words (pointing), I have shown you the accented syllable and, to help you understand this learning, I am telling you that the unaccented *i* in each word will be long.

"When no one tells you, you must experiment with both the long and short sounds. *Usually*, unaccented *i* is short but it could be long, as in these words" (pointing):

hi*bis*cus   bi*cus*pid   bi*fo*cal   bi*late*ral

Child: Underlines the vowels *i, i,* and *u*. Divides between *i* and *b, s* and *c*. Places accent mark.

Child: "*i*, end of syllable, /ī/, hi; *i* consonant /ĭ/, bis; *u* consonant /ŭ/ cus; hibiscus."

If a child has difficulty recalling all three syllables, he or she should be encouraged to pronounce the first two together before adding the last syllable.

". . . hibis, *u* consonant /ŭ/ cus; hibiscus."

e, o, u at the end of unaccented syllables

The children should be told that *e, o*, and *u* continue to say their own names at the end of unaccented syllables but without any stress ("half-long").

Examples

debate	provide	humane	require
elate	unite	propel	polite

The procedure for decoding should be followed by underlining vowels, dividing the syllables, and unlocking each syllable.

a at the end of unaccented syllables

The teacher should explain that *a* at the end of unaccented syllables has an obscure or schwa sound that is much like the short *u* sound: /ŭ/.*

---

*In the dictionary the diacritical marking is /ə/ but to simplify for, and to aid, children's memories, they should be told to associate the schwa sound with that of the short *u*. Only the teachers of upper-level elementary children need to understand the fine distinction and to be familiar with the diacritical marking. When necessary, explanation can be given to upper-elementary or more advanced children.

Teacher: "A good word for illustration is this one." Places *banana* on the chalk-board and underlines the accented syllable.

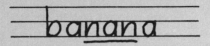

"I have shown you the accented syllable. Remember, when the *a* is at the end of an unaccented syllable, the sound will be the obscure *a* or /ŭ/."

A child should be asked to unlock *banana*.

Child: Underlines *a*, *a*, and *a* and divides between *a* and *n* and *n* and *a*.
"*A*,/ŭ/, ba; *a* consonant, /ă/, nan; *a* /ŭ/, banan'a."

Examples for practice in unlocking

If a child mispronounces a syllable or word, the teacher should *write* what the child says for all to *see*. This helps the child *see* where the mistake is made — the Visual approach. The words should be written in manuscript.

cola	cobra	Laura	toga	vista	magma
parka	lava	Nora	panda	ultra	extra
trauma	opera	casaba	cadenza	angora	America
Santa	tuba	naphtha	Cuba	soda	tuna

As children learn to unlock words with unaccented syllables ending in vowels, mixed lists should be presented to give them practice in applying each new learning.

Sometimes the teacher should underline syllables or should place accent marks. The usual procedure should be followed, and children should experiment to determine correct pronunciation.

A child who has difficulty *hearing* accent is helped when the teacher taps the accent on his or her shoulder for *feeling*.

Polysyllabic Words

After learning concepts for accent and vowel placement in unlocking two- and three-syllable words, children usually begin to apply the same procedures to longer words. Lists of words for unlocking under teacher supervision and guidance should be provided. With experience, children should be led to the realization that the longer the words, the more phonetic each syllable is and the easier unlocking becomes.

There should be discussion which points out that there is rhythm within polysyllabic words, just as there is in sentences, in music or dancing, in the seasons of the year, or in the movement of the ocean. With the older children, the teacher should discuss the heavier and lighter stresses in accent found in sentences as well as words, all of which assist comprehension of what is read.

Examples

ex per' i ment	in sti tu' tion	de ter' min ing
in' tel lect	pho to graph' ic	re mon' strant
se ques' tered	sym pho' ni ous ly	un ac count' a ble
pro ra' tion ing	com pen' di um	dan' de li on

ACCENT AND MEANING

In many words that are spelled the same way, accent determines the meaning. Accent on the first syllable of the words shown below forms name words (nouns), and on the last syllable, forms action words (verbs).

The teacher should place the accent marks. Unrecognized words should be unlocked by the child who, if ready for this "learning," has already mastered the necessary techniques to do so.

Name words	*Action words*
sus' pect	sus pect'
con' tract	con tract'
im' port	im port'
con' vert	con vert'
re' peat	re peat'
ex' ploit	ex ploit'
in' cline	in cline'
re' ject	re ject'
con' vict	con vict'
ref' use	re fuse'
pres' ent	pre sent'
proj' ect	pro ject'
rec' cord	re cord'
con' serve	con serve'

In order to show the different meanings conveyed by accent, phrases for children to read should be prepared at the appropriate level of achievement. The accent mark should be placed on the underlined word in each phrase.

an *im' port* from China	signed the *con' tract*
to *import'* from China	to *contract'* plans for a pool
to *present'* a gift	to *suspect'* that he is
a *pres' ent* for me	the one *sus' pect*
performs many an *ex' ploit*	had gone up the *in' cline* in the pathway
can *exploit'* our plans	try to *incline'* the board by the door
present' the *pres' ent* to her	

SOFT C AND G WORDS

It should be explained to the children that the letters *c* and *g* have both "hard" and "soft" sounds.

About the Letter *C*

C has no sound of its own. It uses either the *k*'s sound /k/, called its "hard sound" or the *s*'s sound /s/, called its "soft sound."
When the *c*:

- occurs at the end of words or syllables, it says /k/, as in *talc* and *ac cessory*.
- is followed by *a, o, u, l,* or *r*, it says /k/ as in *cast, cir cus, coat, crust,* and *clip*.
- is followed by *e, i,* or *y*, it says /s/ as in *cir cus, cell, cy press*.

About the Letter *G*

G has its own "hard" sound /g/ but it does not have its own "soft sound"; it uses the *j*'s sound /j/.
When the *g*:

- appears at the end of words and syllables, it usually says /g/, as in *rag* and *mag net*.
- is followed by *a, o, u, l,* or *r*, it says /g/, as in *goal*, and *grasp*.
- is followed by *e, i,* or *y*, it sometimes says /j/, as in *gem, gym, gen er al,* or *gi ant*. While the letter *c* can use *k* for the required hard sound before *e, i,* or *y* (as in *kitty, kill, kept, Kyle,* etc.) there is no letter but *g* to use for hard *g*. The *g* must be used for words such as *get, give, gear, geese, gift, gilt, gig,* etc. Knowing this, a reader can try both sounds when decoding, but a speller must turn to an authoritative source for exact spelling if it is not known.

Lists of words, such as those shown below, should be placed on the chalkboard for children to unlock with the teacher's guidance. Sometimes discussion helps, as with words containing two *c*'s together, each with a different sound. The same kinds of lists can be simplified or enlarged, depending on children's achievement levels.

Examples — words containing cc

(Children should "divide between the two *c*'s.")

accept	/ak sept/	access	/ak ses/
accepted		accessible	
accepting		accession	
acceptable		accent	/ak sent/
acceptance		accenting	
accepter		accented	
succeed	/suk sed/	accident	/ak si dent/
success	/suk ses/	accidental	
successful		accidentally	
successfully		accede	/ak sed/
successfulness		flaccid	/flak sid/

Words in which neither *c* has a soft sound should be used and sometimes mixed with words having both sounds of the *c*. Make sure that the children understand both concepts.

Examples for upper-elementary children

accommodate	/ak kom mo dat/	accomplish	/ak com plish/
accommodation		accomplishment	
accommodating		accomplishing	
accede	/ak sed/	accuse	/ak kus/
accelerate	/ak sel er at/	accusation	
acclaim	/ak klam/	accord	/ak kord/
account	/ak kount/	accordingly	
accountable		accordance	

EXPANDING A ROOT WORD

Beginning with a single familiar word, the teacher should show how the addition of suffixes or other words gives variation in meaning. A brief discussion of meanings should be encouraged, and the part of the base word that remains constant should be underlined. Examples for children to read are shown below.

sign	*sign*ificant	*sign*alizes
*sign*ing	*sign*ificantly	*sign*alizing
*sign*ed	*sign*ificance	*sign*alized
*sign*al	*sign*et	*sign*alizer
*sign*alman	*sign*et ring	
*sign*ify	*sign*ature	
	*sign*alize	
science	*bomb*	*bomb*ardment
*science*s	*bomb*er	*bomb*ast
*scien*tist	*bomb*ing	*bomb*astic
*scien*tific	*bomb*ard	*bomb*astical
*scien*tifically	*bomb*ardier	*bomb*astically
book	*book*binder	*book*shop
*book*ish	*book*case	*book*stand
*book*ishly	*book*shelf	*book*seller
*book*ishness	*book*shelves	*book*mobile
*book*keeper	*book*rack	*book*craft
*book*end	*book*store	*book*worm
elect	*elect*oral	*elect*orate
*elect*ed	*elec*tion	*elec*tive
*elect*ing	*elec*tioneer	*elec*tively
*elect*or	*elec*tioneerer	*elec*tiveness

PUNCTUATION

The teacher should discuss use of punctuation marks and elicit from the children the reason for using them — to clarify meaning for the readers.

THE APOSTROPHE IN CONTRACTIONS

It should not be assumed that children with SLD will understand the formation of contractions without some help. Through discussion and from the teacher's demonstrations, the children should discover that *contractions* originally were two words which have been shortened, or tightened, into one. The apostrophe is used to indicate this to the reader.

wasn't	couldn't	aren't	isn't	wouldn't
didn't	shouldn't	hasn't	I'm	doesn't
he's	she's	it's	weren't	don't

A list such as the one above should be placed before the children. After each contraction is read by a child, he or she should tell from which two words it was formed, and the teacher should write the two words for all to *see*. It should be pointed out that only the vowel of the second word was omitted.

> NOTE: The teacher should not expect the children to do the writing. The lesson is not for spelling but for clarification of punctuation.

When the concept is clear, more difficult contractions should be presented in which several medial letters are omitted.

Examples

I've	(I have)	should've	(should have)
you've	(you have)	could've	(could have)
you'll	(you will)	won't	(will not)
they've	(they have)	shan't	(shall not)
they'll	(they will)	I'll	(I will)

In the above words more of the medial letters are omitted or the whole contraction changes, as with *shan't* and *won't*. Time should be devoted to discussion, demonstration, and verbalization with both phrases and sentences, all of which serve to unlock meaning.

Verbalizing with Visual Association

The teacher should point to a contraction and say, "I will use a contraction, such as *I've* (pointing) in a sentence. When I call upon one of you, repeat the sentence, using the two words from which the contraction was formed."

Teacher: "I've brought some pictures to show you."
Child: "I have brought some pictures to show you."

The same procedures should be followed with other contractions from the list that can be *seen* by the children.

Copying to Associate Contractions with Whole Word Counterparts

The teacher should place two lists on the chalkboard. One list should contain contractions and the other, whole words. The children should copy both lists and then draw lines from the contractions to the corresponding whole words.

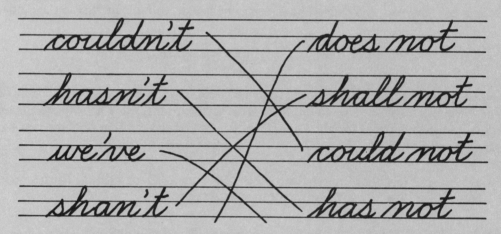

APOSTROPHE TO SHOW OWNERSHIP

The written form that shows ownership is introduced in the primary years of this approach.* From the third year on, the teacher should emphasize recognition of singular-plural possession as a perceptual-conceptual essential for reading comprehension. Discussion and demonstration should extend children's understanding of how punctuation is used to simplify reading comprehension.

It should be explained that words naming a person, place, or thing that own something end in an apostrophe and *s* ('s), or a single apostrophe (') if the word already ends with one of the two sounds of *s*, /s/ or /z/.

A list of both singular and plural words showing ownership should be selected from the following list and placed before the children.

Examples of Singular-Plural Ownership

tiger's	home's	clubs'	books'
tables'	legs'	door's	flowers'
chin's	leg's	doors'	glove's

*Refer to Slingerland, *Book Two — Basics in Scope and Sequence*, pp. 190–192.

table's	roof's	carpet's	turtles'
chins'	roofs'	shelf's	box's
pencils'	house's	shelves'	march's
pencil's	houses'	fork's	marches'
hotel's	buildings'	forks'	apartments'
animal's	animals'	buffalo's	buffaloes'

After each word is named, its singular or plural ownership should be determined by the child. Children should be guided into seeing that if they cover the apostrophe *s* or the single apostrophe, the remaining word tells how many owners there are.

Example

turkey's	turkey█	one turkey owns something
church's	church█	one church owns something
flags'	flags█	more than one owns
ladies'	ladies█	more than one owns
lady's	lady█	one owns

When the plural of a singular word is formed in an irregular way (not with an *s* or *es*) as are *children, men*, and *women*, and the apostrophe *s* is covered, ownership will be shown in the same way.

child's	child█	mice's	mice█
children's	children█	mouse's	mouse█
		goose's	goose█

When singular and plural words are the same, as with *sheep, deer*, and *moose*, the reader must depend upon the wording of the phrase or sentence in which the word occurs to determine singular or plural ownership.

many sheep's wool	a moose's antlers
that sheep's wool	six moose's tails

Reading and Copying for Practice

Phrases such as those that follow should be placed before the children. Individual children should read each phrase aloud, cover the apostrophe or apostrophe *s*, and state whether singular or plural ownership is meant.

this windmill's wheel	this road's gravel topping
all of the farmers' mills	the large stores' sales
several boys' chins	numerous roosters' legs
his foot's bandage	a pet rooster's legs
the house's doors	the houses' doors

UNLOCKING FROM PUNCTUATION MARKS

Punctuation marks, such as commas, dashes, quotation marks, hyphens, periods for various uses, etc., should be shown and their use demonstrated in phrases and sentences, preferably preceding their appearance in a reading lesson. Learning immediately ahead of need adds to each child's ability to comprehend without missing or misunderstanding the meaning, which is the goal for learning to read in the first place.

If a teacher determines that the punctuation in a forthcoming reading lesson calls for reinforcement or teaching, he or she should accomplish this through demonstration and explanation. Procedures should be similar to those already given for the two different uses of the apostrophe. After a good time for this is within the time allotted for B—Unlocking.

Reading

INTRODUCTION*

At this point in the continuum, children usually are familiar with the basic steps used prepare for the lesson of the day as planned within the divisions of The Daily Format—C—Preparation and D—Reading from the Book.** It must be determined by the number of children in a class whether one, two, or three reading groups should be arranged according to the reading levels of the children. Newly enrolled children should be placed in the group to which their reading levels are most adaptable. They begin to learn from observation of their classmates as well as from the teacher's instruction and guidance. Independent, individual performances by these children should not be expected until the teacher feels they will be successful and then they should be encouraged. Usually it takes a month to six weeks for children's patterns of performance to begin becoming secure and for their self-images to change from negative to positive. There should be no pressure or condemnation; only their attention and willingness to try should be expected and encouraged. Teaching "though the intellect" with discussion leads children to understand the purpose of being taught *how to learn to read*.

Unless phrases can be perceived as units conveying fragments of the whole thoughts expressed in sentences and paragraphs, comprehension will be faulty or may be lost entirely. Therefore, the teacher is responsible for showing children how to approach this necessary learning in a consistent step-by-step procedure. The children should understand that it is not always *what is read in school* that is important but the *skills learned from reading that are*.

Children should be told that brains are something like computers. When patterned correctly for reading and writing, they perform correctly. Computers are 'set up" by people to perform by themselves, but brains are even more wonderful. With conscious effort, people can "pattern" their own brains. Teachers help by showing children how to do this.

The children should understand that perception of symbols that can be heard and seen for language and reading may become disorganized in a way not yet fully understood by any-

---

* It is advisable for teachers to read the section on reading in Slingerland, *Book Two—Basics in Scope and Sequence*, pp. 195–221.
** Refer to The Daily Format on pages 8–9 and 10.

one. Children who have this perceptual problem are said to have Specific Language Disability and they can be taught how to cope with this difficulty because it has nothing to do with being smart or intelligent. Their brains can understand and think, store, remember, and do their own planning for future performances. The children can be shown how to help themselves learn to read, write, and spell. It takes effort and the children's will to learn from teachers who have been trained to give them the special kind of help they need.

Teachers use instructional approaches that are effective with most SLD children. Classroom teachers cannot be expected to teach reading from a book that pleases everyone. Nor are there enough school hours to give each child a special lesson in the book of his or her choosing. The teacher's task is to show the children how to learn to read from any book in a way that enables them to read whatever they wish for enjoyment and for their own particular needs. The following pages are written to help teachers learn one effective way to teach SLD children to read.*

C—Preparation

The purposes of C—Preparation** are 1) to remove stumbling blocks by teaching and using new and review words in phrases that convey the meaning of these words, and 2) to develop phrase concept. Preparation is undertaken with the intention of eliminating numerous obstacles in an upcoming specific reading lesson, among them the failure to recognize words or phrase units or to perceive phrase meanings. These failures distract the focus of attention from perceptual-conceptual processing for comprehension. The children will be better able to think ahead while reading when the mechanics of the process do not override the thought behind the words. A felling of success while being *taught how to learn to read* provides children with an on-going motivation that may be lost if they are permitted to struggle (and fail) to unlock, regardless of how motivating are the contents.

The practice with phrases given in C—Preparation is conducted in a controlled situation. Less is demanded of children when they use phrases that are selected and presented by the teacher than when they select their own phrases from a figure-background of many words on the page of a book, which they will learn to do in D—Reading from the Book.

OBJECTIVES FOR C—PREPARATION

Strengthen recognition and comprehension:
- with phrases beginning with prepositions
- with phrases beginning with articles
- with perception of subject phrases
- with perception of action phrases
- with perception of descriptive phrases
- with phrases that tell how, when, where, what, why, etc.

*For more suggestions for reading, refer to Clara McCulloch, *Selections for Teaching Reading Using the Slingerland Approach to Language Arts and The Teacher's Guide*, 1990.
**Refer to pp. 8–9 and 10.

Strengthen eye span as ability to recognize words increases

Extend understanding of how suffixes or inflectional endings change tense, person, gender, etc., and aid comprehension

Increase ability to apply decoding techniques to unrecognized words

Increase ability to use phrase concepts and decoding to aid recall of new or forgotten words

Encourage awareness of punctuation as an aid to comprehension

Encourage rhythm in phrase reading

PROCEDURES

Four steps, as discussed below, should be followed to develop phrase concept. No more than six to eight phrases should be used in any one lesson. Each phrase should be written in manuscript on one line to enable children to perceive phrases as "units" that convey part of the complete thought expressed in a sentence. The teacher should discuss how reading does not begin until phrases can be perceived and understood. Naming or unlocking words gives no meaning other than what the word-namer knows them to mean. Words must be grouped with other words before they convey thoughts from one person to another.

The four steps for practicing phrase reading follow somewhat the same progression as those relating to preschool phenomenal learning of spoken and understood language. In learning to read, the same sensory channel associations — Auditory-Kinesthetic in association with the Visual at the object level for *understood and spoken language* — are extended to include the Visual at the symbol level for *reading*.

In making lesson plans for each classroom reading group, the organization of The Daily Format should be followed:

- A—Alphabet Cards — selected cards to make simultaneous Visual-Auditory association from a Visual stimulus.
- B—Unlocking — selected words from the reading lesson to strengthen independent decoding techniques.
- C—Preparation — selected phrases to strengthen recognition with comprehension of phrases upon which reading depends.

STEP ONE

In early years before children go to school, they learn language by *hearing, remembering,* and *feeling* spoken words associated with visually perceived objects or pictures and emotional feelings. Upon entering school they are *taught* the Visual symbols corresponding to the Auditory-Kinesthetic symbols of the spoken language they have already learned.

The teacher should select six to eight phrases from the reading lesson and write them with heavy strokes in manuscript on the chalkboard (or with a quarter-inch black felt pen on butcher paper) where they can be seen with ease by all of the children in the reading group.

When the lesson begins, the teacher should place the pointer under the first phrase and read it aloud — a Visual-Auditory association *for the children*. Children should repeat in the natural rhythmical flow of ordinary speech and not in a word-by-word monotone. By doing so, they experience simultaneous sensory channel association as they *see, hear*, and *feel* the words of the phrase.

If a word is not understood and needs clarification, for whatever purpose, it should be done at this time.* Then the phrase should be reread *by the teacher* and repeated by the group. The pointer should remain under each phrase as it is read by the teacher and repeated by the children or, in some instances, by a particular child or a new child in the group. The pointer helps to focus attention on the correct phrase.

An opportunity is afforded to emphasize the effect of punctuation marks, such as a comma at the end of a phrase to indicate a pause or slight change in thought, or for words in apposition, or words in a series, and for apostrophes that show ownership or the plural of numbers when written in such phrases as *made several 4's in a row, writes 7's in this special way*, etc.

STEP TWO

A second step in preschool language development occurs when children are ready to make independent, simultaneous Visual-Kinesthetic associations from a single Auditory stimulus. They *hear and associate a named object* with its corresponding Visually perceived object and the Kinesthetic feel of its name.

For reading, a child should be asked to find a phrase named by the teacher and place the pointer under it — an Auditory stimulus for the child which will be followed by Auditory-Visual association for performance. While the other children in the group watch, the child should 1) place the pointer under the correct phrase (keeping it there throughout the performance), and 2) read the phrase loudly enough to be clearly heard by all as it is *heard* and *felt* in speech by the performing child — a V-A-K association.

If the performing child should place the pointer under an incorrect phrase or read a correct phrase incorrectly, the class should *remain silent* and not repeat the phrase. This way, the child has the opportunity to make his or her own correction, or to be given appropriate help. Step Two should never be slighted. It provides practice as the teacher names phrases in no consistent order for all of the children to have one or more turns finding and reading a given number of the phrases.

---

*As an example, on one occasion a third-grade boy, after hearing his teacher read the phrase *swift movement of the stream*, said, "I know what *swift cheese* is but what is *swift movement*?" Clarification *before* reading from the book, rather than while reading, removed an obstacle that would have broken the train of thought while reading.

STEP THREE

A third step occurs in preschool early language development when a child's concept or understanding can be put into words. For example, when a young child is asked to show what says "bow-wow" and points either to a real dog or its picture saying, "dog," his or her performance stems from an Auditory-Conceptual stimulus followed by simultaneous Auditory-Visual (object level)-Kinesthetic association as the child points and speaks.

In Step Three, the teacher should give the *meaning* of the phrase without naming or pointing to the correct one. From the Auditory-conceptual stimulus, the chosen child should 1) select the right phrase and, keeping the pointer under it throughout the performance, 2) read the phrase for all to hear. The class should repeat unless incorrect reading requires the procedure explained in Step Two.

For example, the teacher should direct the children to find phrases by saying, "Which phrase:

tells the name of something?"	shows past time?"
tells the name of someone?"	tells who?"
describes something?"	tells why?"
describes a person?"	tells when?"
indicates happiness?"	tells how?"
refers to a baby?"	indicates something scary?"
tells how someone feels?"	gives a direction?"

Examples of phrases taken at random from third-grade reading books:

a tall traffic officer   for twelve or more minutes
tried to protect himself   the underside of his paws
shivering with fear   the clear, cloudless sky
crawled to his crib   jumped, laughed, screamed for joy
flew away in a helicopter

If more than one phrase answers the same question, those phrases should be found and read, too. The teacher might say, "Find two phrases that tell *what someone did*," or "Phrases that tell what is *happening*."

> NOTE: If the children have difficulty finding or reading phrases correctly, *the teacher* may have given too little practice with Step Two, or the phrases may contain too many difficult words, indicating that the lesson is too hard for the children. Conversely, if there is no challenge to learning, the reading material may be too easy. It is the teacher's responsibility to judge what children are capable of learning at given stages of achievement.

STEP FOUR

From *hearing and conceptualizing* words in association with *seeing or visualizing* objects of the environment and *feeling* the movement of speech while naming them, the developing child learns to initiate his or her own expressive language.

Step Four enables both the teacher and the children to know if phrases can be read and conceptualized independently. Different children should be called upon to read two, three, or four phrases. The reading group should repeat after the reading of each phrase unless it is incorrectly read. Their silence tells the performing child to check for inaccuracy.

If there are many new, difficult, or unfamiliar words in a lesson, they should be practiced for meaning and recognition within the same structured framework used to develop phrase concept.

Step One: The teacher names or reads, with discussion of the meaning and/or punctuation, if any (A-V- with K association).

Step Two: The teacher names or reads and the children find and name or read (A- with V-K association).

Step Three: The teacher gives the meaning and a child finds the right word or phrase, naming or reading (A-Concept with A-V-K association).

Step Four: Different children name the words or read the phrases and the group repeats (V-A-K association).

An example of passages that might have been taken from a story and from which phrases have been selected with suggestions as to their use in the phrase practice of C—Preparation follows. To save space, a concentration of "learnings" is included, many more than usually would be found in any one reading lesson. Reading from a book requires application of learnings into a single integrated performance, to be explained in the next division of The Daily Format, D—Reading from a Book, and for which the following reading material will be used.

SAMPLE READING PASSAGE

"Let's talk about Antarctica," said Suzy one evening after supper while she and her friends were sitting by the fireplace.

Robert said, "What made you think of Antarctica, that cold region, where it is so different from this cabin?"

Suzy answered by saying, "I know we are snug, warm, comfortable, and very cozy by the fireside, but I can see warmly clothed men traveling over snow and ice in a picture on the cover of that book on the table. Snow-covered, high mountains are in the distance. I have learned that Antarctica is a frozen, mountainous land covered with ice and snow. The white mountains and the men's clothing make me believe that they are in Antarctica."

The children began sharing their knowledge. They spoke about the way men lived in that frigid region, about animal life, and about early and present-day explorers, and about whatever they had learned of the southern polar region.

Ronnie knew that Antarctica was the last continent to be explored. Bitter cold, frozen lands, terrible storms, high mountains, and long periods of winter darkness prevented exploration for many centuries. The winters last six months and the sun does not rise. During the other six months the sun never sets. Even so, it is not warm enough to melt all that ice and snow. Because plant life cannot survive, the first explorers had to take enough supplies of food and everything else they needed to last throughout the expedition. When the sea froze, ships could not travel.

In 1910, two men — Amundsen from Norway and Scott from England — leading different expeditions tried to reach the South Pole. Amundsen got there a few days ahead of Scott who, with the others of his expedition, lost his life before he could return to the base from which the expedition started.

Another English explorer, Shackleton, tried to cross Antarctica in 1914. When his ship got stuck in the ice, he and his men were compelled to camp on the ice for five months. There was no help. Finally they managed to reach a place where a big ship could rescue them. Because they tried, as had Scott, and they didn't give up, England honored them — and still does. All of this the children knew.

Tom's grandfather, so he told the children, had known Admiral Byrd, an American, who set up a base called "Little America." That was in the late 1920's. By then, small airplanes were being flown and radios helped explorers send messages. Admiral Byrd took an airplane to Antarctica. From "Little America" he and his pilot flew over the South Pole — the first men to do this.

"Today," Tom said, "people's ability to fly modern planes enables them to land on the South Pole and to visit many unexplored regions."

"Whales, seals, fish, and penguins — of most interest to me — visit Antarctica," said Howard. "They can't go inland because they must live near or in the water where they find their food. I wish I could see the penguins. Next best is to see them on TV or in the movies."

Doris added, "Now there are permanent settlements in Antarctica. Scientists from all over the world — from twelve countries, or maybe more — meet there and work together to learn more about that part of this planet. You should be a scientist, Howard, and go to Antarctica to study the penguins. When I finish school I hope that I can go there."

"You children have learned a lot about Antarctica, more than I knew when I was your age," said Bob's mother.

"Our children will know more than we know about Antarctica," Bob said. Then, before anyone could say more, he jumped up, saying, "How about a surprise before bedtime!"

22

In Sets A and B which follow, examples are shown of phrases that should be selected by the teacher from a reading lesson such as the one just given. Only one set should be used in any one lesson of C—Preparation. The purpose is to have children understand phrasing and not to expect them to memorize every phrase in a lesson when reading from a book.

SAMPLE PHRASES—SET A

sitting by the fireplace

one evening after dinner

"Let's talk about Antarctica,"

Antarctica, that cold region,

are snug, warm, comfortable, and very cozy

showing warmly clothed men

snow-covered high mountains

began sharing their knowledge

SAMPLE PHRASES—SET B

that frigid region

throughout the expedition

they tried, as had Scott,

England honored them—and still does.

a base called "Little America"

In the late 1920's

"Whales, seals, fish, and penguins

helped explorers send messages

The procedures explained previously for Steps One through Four should be followed.
Step One: In addition to naming the phrase, the teacher should clarify, with brief discussion, the various meanings conveyed by punctuation marks. Examples are shown for both Set A and Set B.

PUNCTUATION MARKS*—SET A

Quotation marks and Comma	placed around "*Let's talk about Antarctica,*" indicate exact words spoken by someone. at the end separates the quotation from the rest of the sentence.
Apostrophe and *s*	used to shorten *let us* into one word, *Let's.*
Capital A	used for *Antarctica* to denote the proper name of a place.
Commas	used in *snug, warm, comfortable, and very cozy* to separate describing words by taking the place of the word *and*, and by giving a more euphonious sound. used in *Antarctica, that cold region,* to set apart *that cold region* as a phrase that could be omitted without changing the meaning of the sentence. It enriches. The second comma tells that the sentence is not ended.
Hyphen	used in *snow-covered, high mountains* to combine two words into one that conveys one meaning. (A second meaning, to review, is the hyphen's use to separate syllables of a word when parts must appear at the end of one line and at the beginning of the next.)

PUNCTUATION MARKS—SET B

Commas	used in *they tried, as had Scott,* to stress a phrase by separating it with commas from other phrases of the sentence. The commas call attention to the need of a slight pause and emphasis when reading orally.
Dash	used in *England honored them — and still does.* The dash indicates that the phrase emphasizes or explains the main clause. Only one *dash* is required because the words following the dash end with a period, indicating that the sentence is ended.
Quotation marks	used in *a base called "Little America"* indicate that the enclosed words are a special name for something.
Apostrophe and *s*	used for *in the late 1920's* indicates that more than one year of the decade is being referred to.
Quotation marks	at the beginning, but not at the end, of the phrase *"Whales, seals, fish, and penguins* means that more words will follow to complete the exact quotation. (Refer to Set A.)

*An excellent book for children to enrich their concepts of punctuation is Ellsworth Rosen, *To Be a Bee* (Boston, Mass.: Houghton Mifflin Company, 1969). It may be purchased from Educators Publishing Service, Inc.

Commas   in the above phrase, separate names of sea life in a series, taking the place of the connecting word *and*.

Phrase and punctuation mark concepts help children to *project thought* or *think ahead* in expectation of what is to follow. This approach — to be more fully explained in D—Reading from the Book — is preferable to *looking back* to ascertain the meaning after a word-by-word reading performance.

Step Two: The same procedure as that explained on page 239 should be followed.

Step Three: Refer to pages 240-241 for the procedures of this step. Sets A and B below show how to elicit meanings from the phrases.

PHRASE READING—SET A

A child should be asked to read a phrase (or phrases) that:

"tells when."   (second)
"describes how people feel."   (fifth)
"describes a place."   (seventh)
"tells what someone or something is doing."   (first or sixth)
"also tells what someone or something is doing."   (sixth or first)
"tells what someone started to do."   (eighth)
"suggests something to do."   (third)
"tells about a place."   (fourth)
"quotes the exact words used by someone."   (third)
"has a series of describing words."   (fifth)
"has in it two words combined to give a single meaning."   (seventh)
    "How are they combined?"   (hyphen)
"has capitalization that tells us the proper name of a place."   (third and/or fourth)
"contains a contraction."   (third)
"contains words that the punctuation tells us could be omitted."   (fourth)

PHRASE READING—SET B

Read a phrase that:

"names something."   (first or fifth)
"also names something."   (fifth or first)
"is just one phrase of a direct quotation."   (seventh)   "Explain how the punctuation tells us that."   (Only the first quotation marks are there.)
"has words in a series."   (seventh)   "What kind of words?"   (names)
"contains words that punctuation tells us could be omitted."   (fourth)
    "Why are two dashes not used?"   (The words after the first dash conclude the sentence as indicated by the period.)
"has punctuation that encloses an enriching phrase."   (third)

"has punctuation to show that something has a special name." (fifth)
"has words containing two soft *g*'s." (first)

NOTE: After the first direction is given, the teacher should not be repetitious by continuing to say, "Read a phrase that ___." The children will understand what they are to do and the teacher need give only the last part of the direction as shown above.

Step Four: The same procedure as that explained on page 241 should be followed.

D—Reading from the Book

Children who are learning to read* by following this multi-sensory approach usually are ready for language skill enrichment in elementary grades.** Reading, as a functional skill, begins when phrases can be perceived and comprehended from a background of many words and punctuation marks on a page and integrated with other phrases in sequential order. It is hoped that as the children learn to perceive and integrate, the writer's meaning will be conveyed and the children's thought processes will be stimulated.

Reading independently from pages of a book must be done without guidance. The lessons in this division of The Daily Format are intended to help children learn how to approach this complex task and to give them practice in doing so with a teacher's guidance and help. Rather than "looking back" after reading or trying to read to "find what happened," they need to learn how to "think ahead," or to "project thought," in expectation of what is to be revealed.

A rapid reading rate is not the goal. That develops *after, not before*, children have learned *how to read*. Perception with comprehension is the object of the procedures for teaching children how they can *help themselves learn to read*.

OBJECTIVES FOR D—READING FROM THE BOOK***

- Continued practice for phrasing with concept.
- Development of a smooth eye span as phrases are perceived.
- Ability to perceive broken phrases in which some words are printed on one line and the remaining words on the next.
- Recognition of phrases introduced with prepositions and articles.
- Functional use of unlocking skills learned in B—Unlocking.

*Teachers are advised to read Slingerland, *Book Two — Basics in Scope and Sequence*, pp. 208-221.

**Children who are new to this multi-sensory approach should be given instruction at their level until special instruction and observation of their peers helps them to become successful.

***Refer to Slingerland, *Book Two — Basics in Scope and Sequence*, Objectives on pp. 208-209.

- Awareness of points where eyes should pause, often before prepositions, articles, and punctuation marks.
- Ability to conceptualize from clues derived from understood phrase meanings, root word-suffix variations in meaning, prepositions, punctuation, and parts of speech.
- Ability to "look ahead" or foresee events by "projecting thought" as the reading progresses.
- Awareness of how reading material is organized—introduction, body, and conclusion.
- Development of awareness of characteristics and relationships brought forth by events, actions, or quotations.
- Continued child-teacher study of long stories, social studies, science, arithmetic, or other subjects.
- Individual study for information and/or pleasure.

PROCEDURES

Children should be grouped for reading lessons according to their abilities and reading levels. Not doing so may bring about poor situations for learning and/or outright failure for some. Children with less severe disabilities may advance more slowly if they are misplaced for instruction. Each group should be taught from a book suited to its level of reading achievement.

During a lesson, the children in each group should sit together where they can be *heard* during their individual performances. Phrases used for preparation should be where they can be *seen* for referral, if desired.

A "basal" reading series* should be favored over programmed or phonetically oriented reading books. Too many phonetic elements and specific tasks, introduced too rapidly without time for them to be integrated with previous learnings, can be self-defeating.

Four steps for guiding children toward independent reading are used. They are:

1. Structured reading *with the teacher*.
2. Studying aloud *with the teacher*.
3. Studying silently *with the teacher* present.
4. Studying independently without the teacher but followed by *oral reading with the teacher*.

The goal of independent reading is explained in E—The Goal: Independent Reading. The reading matter on page 242 is intended to illustrate procedures of instruction in this division of The Daily Format, D—Reading from the Book.

*Any level-appropriate, well-written material may be used.

STRUCTURING READING

The lesson should begin with oral phrase reading as directed by the teacher; otherwise it is difficult to determine how the children apply reading skills and what help or instruction they may need. The teacher should give directions, according to the phrasing on the page, such as:

- "Read the first four (or five or two) words to find out *who*."
- "The next three words tell *when*."
- "The next five words form a broken phrase. Do not read until you can include all of the words from both lines in one continuous eye span."
- "Reread that phrase smoothly now that you know all of the words."
- "Read the phrase enclosed with quotation marks," or "What do the quotation marks tell you about this next phrase of five words?"

No more than a paragraph or two should be structured. The better the children can read, the less structured practice they require, except for clarification of special phrasing such as that shown within dashes, commas, or quotation marks. It is advisable to use a little structuring each day without overdoing it. No more than a paragraph or two, to get the lesson started, should be used for structuring the phrasing and for directing children's thinking "ahead." Below are some examples of suggested procedures as applied to the reading matter shown on page 242.

Assuming that the children have read previous pages of the story already, the teacher should have a child summarize what happened at the close of the last reading session. A child might say, "The children had a picnic supper and lots of fun. Then they were told to go into the big room in the cabin. They were to sit around the fireplace. After a rest, there would be a special treat before bedtime."

The teacher should ask, "As you read on, think what you will be hoping to find out." The books should be placed in the children's hands.

Teacher: "Read the first four-word phrase to get an idea of what the next part of this story will be about."

Children: Read silently.

Teacher: "What *one word* tells you?"

Child: "*Antarctica.*"

Teacher: "Read the phrase with good rhythm."

Child: Reads, "*Let's talk about Antarctica.*"

Teacher: "What are the first punctuation marks?" . . ."Yes, quotation marks. When you saw them, what did you want to find out?" . . ."Yes, the one who was speaking. The next phrase tells when she was speaking."

Child: Reads, "*One evening after supper.*"

Teacher: "Read the next five words."

Child: Reads, "*While she and her friends.*"

Teacher: "Who is *she*? . . .Yes, *she* stands for Suzy. How do you know?"

Child: "It said, *said Suzy.*"

Teacher: "Read the last phrase and think what it tells us."

Child: Reads orally, "*Were sitting by the fireplace*. It tells us *where* they were sitting."

Teacher: Chooses a child to read the whole paragraph with good phrasing.

Child: "'*Let's talk about Antarctica,' said Suzy one evening after supper while she and her friends were sitting by the fireplace.*"

If a child does not phrase well, he or she should reread. The teacher and the children should understand that *learning* sometimes requires *doing it again*, and, perhaps, again.

NOTE: If a child had started to read the whole phrase after being asked the *one word* that named what they would be talking about, the teacher should stop the child immediately by saying, "My direction was to name the *one word*, not to read the whole phrase." The child should be given time to make his or her own correction by saying, "Antarctica." If the child did not recognize *Antarctica*, a reminder that it names a far-away region to the south often helps. Also, by unlocking a first syllable, memory is aided. With *Antarctica*, the child should say, "*A-n-t, a, /ă/, ant*," which usually triggers recall of the whole word. The teacher should tell tne number of *letters in a syllable* if it is not immediately perceived by the child.

Still another way to trigger recall is for the teacher to point to one of the two phrases in which *Antarctica* appeared for phrasing practice of C—Preparation, prior to reading from the book. (Refer to page 243.) The object is to show various ways to recall a word by allowing a reasonable time for response and *not by calling upon a second child* to take over before the first has had time to "pattern" his or her own thinking.

Teacher: "In this next short paragraph, who will be talking? . . .Yes, *Robert*. What will you find out if you read on?"

Child: "I'll read to find out what he said."

Teacher: "Read the first four words and then the next two."

Child: "*What made you think   of Antarctica?*"

Teacher: "Remember, those commas tell something."

Child: "The phrase between them could be omitted but it adds more meaning to the sentence: *that cold region*."

Teacher: "Read the next five words and then the last three."

Child: "*Where it is so different   from this cabin.*"

Teacher: "Reread this same second paragraph with good rhythm and phrasing."

Child: "*Robert said, 'What made you think of Antarctica, that cold region, where it is so different from this cabin?'*"

Teacher: "Was Robert giving or asking for information and how do you know?"

Child: "The words tell me he was asking and so does the question mark."

Teacher: "From his question, what can we expect the next paragraph to tell us?"

Child: "I think it will tell why Suzy thought of Antarctica."

Teacher: "This time, let's study the next paragraph aloud."

STUDYING ALOUD

Unlike *structured study*, in which the teacher tells the children how many words comprise each phrase in a sentence as it is being read, *studying aloud* requires the performing child to perceive the phrases independently and to read orally in a voice that can be heard by all, phrasing and rephrasing where necessary to ensure comprehension. Throughout the lesson, children should keep the sides of their hands under each line of words while it is being studied or read aloud, as shown in the picture below.

When hesitations, inaccuracies, or faulty phrasing occur, the children should reread phrases correctly and then include them *in a rhythmic rereading of the entire sentence*. The performing child benefits from individualized guidance and personal attention while the others in the group experience added input until they have their own turns to study aloud while the teacher listens and helps. The portion used for studying aloud should be reread orally by a child (or several may have turns) before the silent study begins.

The teacher should call upon different children to read aloud without previous study. When a need to rephrase or unlock interrupts the smooth, rhythmic flow of the words, the child should reread the sentence, knowing that to do so *is a way of studying*.

Teacher: "Think who will be answering Robert's question, and why."
Child: "Suzy will because she is the one who suggested talking about Antarctica."
Teacher: "Remember to pause after a comma and to think why it is being used."
Child: Reads aloud: *"Suzy answered by saying, 'I know we are snug, warm, comfortable, and very cozy by the fire side but I can see . . . .'"*

Probably the child would recognize incorrect phrasing when saying, "*side but I can see,*" and realize that *side* belonged with *fire* to form a whole word that had to be divided with a hyphen when all of it could not be written on one line. The child should rephrase to, "*and very cozy by the fireside.*"

The teacher might take this opportunity to call attention to the word *but*, which introduces the next phrase, *but I can see.* He or she should explain that *but* often implies something is going to be different, and they should find out what that difference in thought is going to be. After reading the next phrases, and rereading the whole sentence, a child should explain that although the children in the story are in a warm place, the cover on a book shows men in an opposite kind of land.

Child: *warmly clothed men traveling*
          over snow and ice   in a picture on the cover
          of the book   on the table

The teacher should call the children's attention to the number of prepositions that introduce the phrases above. They should understand that prepositions such as *in, on, over, at, under, by,* etc. usually introduce a phrase and should not be included at the end of one. Also, they should be asked *how* the men were clothed (*warmly*) and the kind of clothes they wore (*warm*).

Continuing, the child might misphrase by saying *snow-covered, high   mountains*, and, realizing the words should stay together, reread *snow-covered, high mountains* in a way that conveys meaning. If the child fails to perceive the need for rereading, the teacher should request that he or she do so and place the rhythmic accent on *mountains*. The child should read on to find *where* the mountains are — *are in the distance.*

Teacher: "Did you find out *why* Suzy thought of Antarctica?"

The teacher should elicit from the children that Suzy saw a picture on the cover of a book that made her think how comfortable they were, while for others it could be different — as in Antarctica.

Teacher: "Who else did Suzy talk about?"
Child: "Herself. She said, *'I have learned that Antarctica   is a frozen,'*" and hesitating over the word *mountainous*, stops reading.
Teacher: "Cover the suffix *o-u-s* with your thumb. Do you recognize the root word? . . .Yes, it is *mountain.* The suffix says /ŭs/ and makes *mountain* into a describing word."
Child: "It says *mountainous.*" Continuing, the child rephrases, saying "*is a frozen, mountainous land   covered with ice and snow.   The white mountains   and the men's clothing   make me believe   that they are in Antarctica.*"
Teacher: Asks one of the children who studied aloud to read the whole paragraph again using good phrasing.
Teacher: "Did that paragraph tell what people were *doing*, or *describe* something, or *name* things?"

Discussion should bring out the idea of *describing*. Different children should read describing sentences. The teacher should explain punctuation marks and discuss the way paragraphs are separated from each other.

Using a different approach for study and comprehension, the teacher should ask a child to read only the first sentence of the next paragraph to get an idea of what it is about.

Child: "*The children began sharing   their knowledge*."

Teacher: "What one word tells what they began doing? . . .Yes, it is *sharing*. What did they share?"

Child: "They shared *knowledge*."

Teacher: "If they *shared knowledge*, what can we expect the whole paragraph to be about?"

Child: "Maybe it will tell what they talked about. I will keep that thought in my mind as I read."

Teacher: "Before we study this paragraph, read the first sentence in the next one."

Child: Reads aloud, "*Ronnie knew that Antarctica   was the last continent to be explored.*"

Teacher: "What will this paragraph probably be about?"

Child: "Perhaps it will tell why it has been the last one to be explored."

Teacher: "What will you make your mind do as you begin to read each paragraph?"

Child: "We will think ahead about the idea we get from reading the first sentence in the paragraph."

The lesson should continue until the teacher judges that the children are prepared to *study silently* with continued guidance and direction while they work independently.

STUDYING SILENTLY

The children should be directed to apply the same approach to *studying silently* that they used for *studying aloud* with the teacher. A given number of sentences or a paragraph should be studied silently before individual children are called upon to read orally. They should be expected to read smoothly and with good phrasing after having time to perceive and comprehend phrase and sentence meaning. From previous guidance by the teacher in the first two steps of the day's lesson, the children should have developed their skills in:

- phrasing for clarity in comprehending;
- rhythmic wording with smooth eye span;
- unlocking where needed, and if within the child's capabilities;
- partial unlocking of unrecognized words by using the first letters or first syllable of a word to trigger recall; and
- rereading silently for clarity and rhythmic phrasing before being called upon by the teacher to read aloud.

When the silent study is completed and the teacher has directed individual children to read passages aloud, questions or projected thought should be answered and/or discussed. Succeeding sentences should be studied silently and then read aloud to give practice in perceiving and comprehending. The ideas and thoughts conveyed in the phrases and sentences should be integrated into the overall theme of the reading matter.

During this study, the teacher should devote full time to the group, giving direction, guidance, and encouragement to build self-confidence and self-reliance.

> NOTE: Words that children cannot unlock independently because they are non-phonetic to the children or irregularly spelled Red Flag words, should have been included in the phrase practice of C—Preparation. If they were not, the child should be told the word, or be shown how some part of the word, such as the beginning letters or the first syllable, can be unlocked sufficiently well to aid recall of the entire word — an approach that can be applied to other words that are unrecognized. (Refer to the note on page 250.)

The following is an example of the procedure for a day's lesson that moves from *structured study* to *studying aloud* and then to *studying silently.*

> Teacher: "Study the next paragraph by yourself but ask for help if you need it. As you read the first sentence, try to find what the paragraph is going to be about before you study it. If you finish your study of the whole paragraph, reread what you studied."

After a reasonable time, a child should be called upon to read aloud, summing up in a few words the main thought of the paragraph.

> Child: "This paragraph is about the first two men who went to the South Pole," or "A man from Norway and one from England were the first to go to the South Pole."
>
> Teacher: "Read the paragraph aloud."
>
> Child: Reads orally.

The child should be expected to read with good phrasing, having had time to study and to ask for specific help if needed.

The teacher should ask what was learned about the two men before having the group continue their study of the next paragraph or two.

> Teacher: "You will see the name of another explorer as you read on. I will write it for you to unlock.

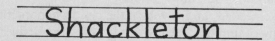

> Child: "*A*-consonant, /ă/, shac; /kle/, shackle; *o*-consonant, /ŏ/ or /ŭ/?" (The teacher should say /ŭ/ and the child should complete unlocking the word.) "*U*-consonant, /ŭ/, ton, Shackleton."

The teacher should call attention to the words *compelled, managed,* and *honored* and their suffixes before the study begins. After the study, a child should read orally and a brief discussion of the content should follow.

> Teacher: "In this next paragraph, another man from our country did something different. Read to find what that was." (Admiral Byrd made a base in Antarctica and flew over the South Pole.)

The teacher must be the judge of the amount of silent study and immediate oral reading that is required before the children *study independently*.

STUDYING INDEPENDENTLY AND THEN ORALLY

After the preceding three steps have been accomplished in preparation for *studying independently*, the children should return to their desks from the group arrangement to study an assigned number of pages as directed by the teacher. They should study without further help until called together for *oral reading* of the studied assignment.

> NOTE: By following this plan, the teacher is able to work with another group of children whose achievement level requires reading material adapted to its needs. This group should have guidance and help from the teacher without interruption from the children who have just received his or her full attention.

As the children study independently, they should seek answers to questions, follow projected thought, determine where the "body" of the reading matter ends and the conclusion begins, etc. They should strive for good phrasing and independent use of unlocking techniques. When they hesitate or fail to comprehend, they should reread. When finished, they should use their free time as previously directed by the teacher for other requirements, and/or choices of their own. When the teacher calls them together for *oral reading* of *independently studied* material, they should be ready.

> Teacher: "Before you go to your own seats to study to the end of this chapter (story, or to page ____, etc.) read the first three words of this next paragraph to get an idea about what they tell us."
>
> Child: "*'Today,' Tom said.* Tom is going to say something and begins by saying *today*. We will have to read to find what he is talking about."
>
> Teacher: "In the next paragraph, read the words in a series in the first sentence and tell us what idea comes into your mind."
>
> Child: "*Whales, seals, fish, and penguins.* We'll be reading about living creatures (or sea life, or life in Antarctica, etc.)."
>
> Teacher: "In the next paragraph, who will be talking? . . .Yes, it will be Doris. After you read to the end of the paragraph, be prepared to tell us what kind of girl you think Doris is from what she says. I will ask you. Also, find where you think the conclusion of this chapter begins and how your thoughts are projected into the next chapter. We will talk this over when you have had time to study and we come together to read orally."

ORAL READING

At a later, convenient time for the teacher, the group should be reassembled for *oral reading* of the assignment. If the entire story or article has not been covered, it should be continued in the next day's lesson with the same procedures used with the first part: phrase practice in C—Preparation, followed by the steps for study in D—Reading from the Book. If, however, the story or article is unduly long and the teacher deems it advisable to move on to something of fresh interest, the final part can be completed with the teacher as described below.

For oral reading, individual children should be called upon to take turns reading while the others listen and keep the place by placing the sides of their hands under each line.

Teacher: "At the beginning of the next paragraph, did anyone find what Tom meant when he said *today*?"

Child: "He was talking about *now* or this particular day and not about the past."

Child: "He said that people can land at the South Pole in airplanes of *today*."

Teacher: "What was said to make you know that penguins are not found at the South Pole?"

Child: "Penguins have to live near the ocean to get their food and the South Pole is inland."

Teacher: "Remember, I said I would ask about Doris. Did you get an idea about what she may be when she grows up?"

There should be discussion based on the children's response to reading the paragraph quoting Doris.

Teacher: "You must have noticed where the thread of thought or events changed and the conclusion or ending began. Someone read that part."

Brief discussion should be encouraged and a child should be called upon to read aloud the sentence that introduced the conclusion.

Teacher: "Someone read the sentence that "sparks" or *motivates* us to read the next chapter."

Child: Reads with good phrasing: "*Then, before anyone could say more, he jumped up, saying, 'How about a surprise before bedtime!'*"

Teacher: "Let us reread orally the part you studied" (or the whole chapter). Different children should be given turns to read.

On other occasions, with different reading matter, if there is time at the end of a lesson, or if it seems advisable not to extend a particularly long story over too many days, a teacher-children oral reading session should complete the unfinished portion without any previous study, as suggested below.

The teacher should begin by reading several sentences using good phrasing before naming a child to continue. Without interruption or pause, the child should read two or three sentences before another child is named to continue the reading. At intervals, the teacher should read again at a rate to enable children to keep the place and feel the tempo of performance. Each oral reader should speak in a clear voice that all can hear as they follow, ready to continue if called upon.

When rephrasing or unlocking is necessary, the performing child should not hesitate to do so, or the teacher may request that it be done. Sometimes the teacher should name the unrecognized word if it is being learned and requires more practice. Often, after the first sentence of a paragraph has been read, the child should tell what may be expected of its contents. When exact words of a conversation are quoted, children should be encouraged to perceive something about the speakers from what their words convey as well as from what the words say they do. By hearing each other read in turns — not at a fast, but at a consistent pace — SLD children are helped to acquire a pattern of performance to follow when reading independently.

E—The Goal: Independent Reading

Reading matter for various levels of abilities should be available at all times. The children should be encouraged to spend at least ten, fifteen, or more minutes of the day reading something of their own choosing.

Independent reading as a tool or skill for studying various subjects begins in the elementary grades. In later school years it becomes even more important, and for some children it will be necessary throughout life. Therefore, they must learn *how* to learn to read. Reading for pleasure should be encouraged. This is a time when a teacher's aide can give support by naming unrecognized words as children practice independent reading.

The same procedure as that used for studying aloud or silently, and for teacher-children oral reading explained previously, should be followed in the reading done for social studies, health, or other subjects. The children need experience both in applying the projection of thought to first sentences of paragraphs and in unlocking words containing known phonetic elements and syllabic organization.* Teacher-children oral reading with reading matter other than "readers" is helpful to SLD children when they have assignments for different subjects.

Over the years, children are not likely to recall the reading content of each day's lessons in varying subjects, but it is hoped that by forming patterns of approach and performance, they will *learn how to learn to read* well enough to enable them to do so independently and to meet the daily needs of their individual lives.

---

*Frequently children turn to the teacher to ask, "Is this a word I can do (unlock)?" If the answer is in the affirmative, the child should unlock it. If not, the teacher should name it and the child should repeat it and continue without further pause.

RESOURCES FOR FURTHER INFORMATION

TEACHER EDUCATION COURSES, CURRENT WORKSHOPS, RESEARCH AND PROGRAMS

Slingerland Institute, One Bellevue Center, 411 108th Avenue SE, Bellevue, WA 98004

BOOKS AND INSTRUCTIONAL MATERIALS

Educators Publishing Service, Inc., 31 Smith Place, Cambridge, Massachusetts 02138. Publisher and distributor of books for professionals and for teachers of children with Specific Language Disability (dyslexia).

VIDEOS (AVAILABLE FROM EDUCATORS PUBLISHING SERVICE, INC.)

The following videos may be rented or purchased:

>The Slingerland Screening Tests for Identifying Children with Specific Language Disability (3 one-half hour cassettes)

>The Slingerland Multi-Sensory Approach to Language Arts for Specific Language Disability Children in Primary Grades (38 minutes)

>Specific Language Disability: A Medical and Educational Overview by Dr. Wilbur Mattison (45 minutes)

There are many other videos available. Call EPS for more information.

THE ORTON DYSLEXIA SOCIETY

National headquarters: Chester Building, Suite 382, 8600 La Salle Road, Baltimore, MD 21286-2044. A nonprofit educational and scientific organization open to professionals and non-professionals. Branch organizations in twenty-five locations in the United States, Canada, and Bermuda.
Publications include:

>*Annals of Dyslexia* (annual journal)

>Monographs

>Reprints (articles and conference papers of interest to researchers, teachers, and parents)

>*Reading, Perception and Language* (papers from the World Congress on Dyslexia 1974) edited by Drake Duane, M.D. and Margaret Byrd Rawson

>*The Significance of Sex Differences in Dyslexia* (proceedings from Symposium 1980) Norman Geschwind, M.D., et al.

A BIBLIOGRAPHY OF
SUGGESTED READING TO OFFER BACKGROUND
FOR UNDERSTANDING CHILDREN WITH
SPECIFIC LANGUAGE DISABILITY (DYSLEXIA)

Bakker, Dirk J. "Hemispheric Specialization and Stages in the Learning-to-Read Process." *Bulletin of the Orton Society*, Vol. 23 (1973), pp. 15–27. Also available as Orton Society Reprint No. 51.

_____. "Hemispheric Differences and Reading Strategies: Two Dyslexias?" *Bulletin of the Orton Society*, Vol. 29 (1979), pp. 84–100. Also available as Orton Society Reprint No. 82.

Buckley, Evelyn. *Diagnostic Word Patterns Tests 1, 2, and 3*. Cambridge, Mass.: Educators Publishing Service, Inc., 1978.

Critchley, Macdonald and Eileen A. Critchley. *Dyslexia Defined*. London: William Heinemann Medical Books Ltd., 1978.

Duane, Drake. "A Neurologic Overview of Specific Language Disability for the Non-Neurologist." *Bulletin of the Orton Society*, Vol. 24 (1974), pp. 5–36. Also available as Orton Society Reprint No. 61.

Duane, Drake and Paula Dozier Rome, eds. *The Dyslexic Child*. New York: Insight Publishing Co., 1981. Also available as an Orton Society Monograph.

Epstein, Herman T. "Some Biological Bases of Cognitive Development." *Bulletin of the Orton Society*, Vol. 30 (1980), pp. 46–62.

Epstein, Herman T. and Conrad F. Toepfer, Jr. "A Neuroscience Basis for Reorganizing Middle Grades Education. *Educational Leadership*, Vol. 35, No. 8 (May 1978), pp. 656–660.

Geschwind, Norman. "Asymmetries of the Brain: New Developments." *Bulletin of the Orton Society*, Vol. 29 (1979), pp. 67–73. Also available as Orton Society Reprint No. 80.

_____. "Anatomical Evolution and the Human Brain." *Bulletin of the Orton Society*, Vol. 22 (1972), pp. 7–13. Also available as Orton Society Reprint No. 41.

Gillingham, Anna and Bessie Stillman. *Remedial Training for Children with Specific Disability in Reading, Spelling, and Penmanship*. Cambridge, Mass.: Educators Publishing Service, Inc., 1956; rev. ed., 1960. (The 5th edition [red, 1956] is keyed to pronunciation symbols in *Webster's New International Dictionary, Second Edition*; the 7th edition [green, 1960] is based on symbols in *Webster's Third New International Dictionary*.)

Goldberg, Herman K. "Neurological and Psychological Aspects of Reading Disabilities." *Pennsylvania Academy of Opthalmology and Otolaryngology, Transactions*, Spring 1965. Also available in Orton Society Monograph No. 1.

_____. "Ocular Motility in Learning Disabilities." *Journal of Learning Disabilities*, Vol. 3, No. 3 (March 1970), pp. 160–162.

Goldberg, Herman K. and Gilbert Schiffman. *Dyslexia*. New York: Grune and Stratton, 1972.

Hall, Eleanor Thurston. *Learning the English Language*, Books 1 and 2. Cambridge, Mass.: Educators Publishing Service, Inc., 1974.

Hier, Daniel B. "Sex Differences in Hemispheric Specialization: Hypothesis for Excess of Dyslexia in Boys." *Bulletin of the Orton Society*, Vol. 29 (1979), pp. 74–83. Also available as Orton Society Reprint No. 81.

Leong, C.K. "Dichotic Listening with Related Tasks for Dyslexics — Differential Use of Strategies." *Bulletin of the Orton Society*, Vol. 25 (1975), pp. 111–126. Also available as Orton Society Reprint No. 69.

Liberman, Isabelle Y. "Speech and Lateralization of Language." *Bulletin of the Orton Society*, Vol. 21 (1971), pp. 71–87. Also available as Orton Society Reprint No. 39.

——————. "Segmentation of the Spoken Word and Reading Acquisition." *Bulletin of the Orton Society*, Vol. 23 (1973), pp. 65–77. Also available as Orton Society Reprint No. 54.

Masland, Richard L. "Brain Mechanisms Underlying the Language Function." *Bulletin of the Orton Society*, Vol. 17 (1967), pp. 1–31. Also available as Orton Society Reprint No. 18.

Money, John and Gilbert Schiffman. *The Disabled Reader*. Baltimore: The Johns Hopkins Press, 1966.

Oliphant, Genevieve G. "Program Planning for Dyslexic Children in the General Classroom." *Bulletin of the Orton Society*, Vol. 29 (1979), pp. 225–237. Also available as Orton Society Reprint No. 88.

Orton, Samuel Torrey. *Reading, Writing and Speech Problems in Children*. New York: W. W. Norton and Company, 1937. (Available from Educators Publishing Service, Inc.)

——————. *"Word-Blindness" in School Children and Other Papers on Strephosymbolia (Specific Language Disability—Dyslexia) 1925–1946*. Compiled by June L. Orton. Orton Society Monograph No. 2, 1966.

Penfield, Wilder and Lamar Roberts. *Speech and Brain Mechanism*. Princeton: Princeton University Press, 1959.

Schnitker, Max. *The Teacher's Guide to the Brain and Learning*. San Rafael, Calif.: Academic Therapy Publications, 1972.

Slingerland, Beth H. *Screening Tests for Identifying Children with Specific Language Disability*. Cambridge, Mass.: Educators Publishing Service, Inc., 1974.

——————. *Book One — A Multi-Sensory Approach to Language Arts for Specific Language Disability Children: A Guide for Primary Teachers*. Cambridge, Mass.: Educators Publishing Service, Inc., 1971.

——————. *Book Two — Basics in Scope and Sequence of a Multi-Sensory Approach to Language Arts for Specific Language Disability Children: A Guide for Primary Teachers*. Cambridge, Mass.: Educators Publishing Service, Inc., 1976.

——————. *Why Wait for a Criterion of Failure?* Cambridge, Mass.: Educators Publishing Service, Inc., 1978.

Stuart, Marion. *Neurophysiological Insights into Teaching*. Palo Alto, Calif.: Pacific Books, 1963.

Tarnapol, Lester and Muriel Tarnapol. *Brain Function and Reading Disabilities*. Baltimore: University Park Press, 1977.

Thompson, Lloyd J. *Reading Disability*. Springfield, Ill.: Charles C. Thomas, 1966.

ADDITIONAL BIBLIOGRAPHY OF
SUGGESTED READING TO OFFER BACKGROUND
FOR UNDERSTANDING CHILDREN WITH
SPECIFIC LANGUAGE DISABILITY (DYSLEXIA)

Ballesteros, D. & Royal, N. (1980) "Slingerland SLD Instruction as a Voluntary Magnet Program." *Bulletin of the Orton Society.*

Bender, L. with Grugett, A.E. (1987) "Highlights in Pioneering the Understanding of Language Disabilities." *Annals of Dyslexia* Vol. XXXVII

Bowler, R. (1987) *Intimacy With Language*. Baltimore, MD: Orton Dyslexia Society.

Burrows, D. and Wolf B. (1983) "Creativity and the Dyslexic Child: A Classroom View." *Annals of Dyslexia* Vol. 33.

Calvin, W. and Ojemann, G. (1980) *Inside the Brain*. NY: New American Library.

Clark, Diana (1988) *Dyslexia: Theory and Practice of Remedial Instruction*. Parktown, MD: York Press.

De Hirsch, K. (1984) *Language and the Developing Child*. Monograph 4, Baltimore, MD: Orton Dyslexia Society.

Duffy, F. and Geschwind, N. eds (1985) *Dyslexia: A Neuro Scientific Approach to Clinical Evaluation*. Boston, MA: Little, Brown and Co.

Epstein, H. (1985) "Multimodality, Crossmodality, and Dyslexia." *Annals of Dyslexia* Vol. XXXV.

Fulmer, S. and R. (1983) "The Slingerland Test: Reliability and Validity." *Journal of Learning Disabilities* Vol. 16 No. 10.

Galaburda, A. (1993) *Dyslexia and Development: Neurobioligal Aspects of Extra-Ordinary Brains*. Cambridge, MA: Harvard University Press.

Galaburda, A. ed. (1989) "Ordinary and Extraordianary Brain Development: Anatomical Variation in Developmental Dyslexia." *Annals of Dyslexia* Vol. XXXIX.

Gardner, Howard (1983) *Frames of Mind*. N.Y., NY: Basic Books, Inc.

Geschwind, N. (1982) "Why Orton Was Right." *Annals of Dyslexia* Vol. 32.

Kavanagh, J. (1991) Parkton, MD: *The Language Continuum*. York Press.

Levine, M. D. (1987) *Developmental Variation and Learning Disorders*. Cambridge, MA: Educators Publishing Service, Inc.

Liberman, L. and Liberman, A. (1990) "Whole Language Versus Code Emphasis: Underlying Assumptions and their Implications for Reading." *Annals of Dyslexia* Vol. XXXX.

Masland, Richard L. and Mary W. (1988) *Pre-School Prevention of Reading Failure*. Parkton, MD: York Press.

Orton, Samuel T. (1987) *Reading, Writing and Speech Problems in Children and Selected Papers*. Austin, TX: Pro-ed.

Pennington, B. (1989) "Using Genetics to Understand Dyslexia." *Annals of Dyslexia* Vol. XXXIX.

Richardson, S. (1989) "Specific Developmental Dyslexia: Retrospective and Perspective Views." *Annals of Dyslexia* Vol. XXXIX.

Sears, S. and Keogh, B. (1993) "Predicting Reading Performance Using the Slingerland Procedures." *Annals of Dyslexia* Vol. XLIII.

Shaywitz, S. et al (1990) "Prevalence of Reading Disability in Boys and Girls." *JAMA* Vol. 264 #8.

Slingerland, B. (1983) *Language Not Learning Disability.* Cambridge, MA: Educators Publishing Service, Inc.

Vellutino, Frank R. (1987) "Dyslexia." *Scientific American* Volume 256 Number 3.

RESEARCH AND STUDIES ON SLINGERLAND INSTRUCTION AND SLINGERLAND SCREENING PROCEDURES

Adelman, J. (1984). *A Remediation Program for SLD Adults Using an Adaptation of the Slingerland and Orton-Gillingham Approaches*. Unpublished Master's Thesis, San Jose State University: San Jose, CA.

Casper, J. (1983) *An Experiment in the Treatment of Specific Language Disability Using the Slingerland Multi-Sensory Method*. Unpublished manuscript.

Crumbley, L. (1985). *First Grade Reading and Spelling Achievement in Slingerland and Non-Slingerland Classes*. Doctoral Dissertation, Brigham Young University: Provo, UT.

Elkind, J.; Cohen, K.; & Murray, C. (1993) "Using Computer-Based Readers to Improve Reading Comprehension of Students with Dyslexia." *Annals of Dyslexia* Vol XLIII.

Engels, K. (1983) *Teacher Evaluation of Reading, Spelling and Penmanship Programs as a Function of Use or Non-Use of the Slingerland Multi-Sensory Method*. Master's Thesis, College of Notre Dame: Belmont, CA.

Fruth, C. (1984) *The Comparison of Scores Attained by Selected Armstrong Students on Standardized Tests*. A Paper Submitted in Partial Fulfillment of the Requirements in Educational Research. College of Notre Dame: Belmont, CA.

Fulmer, S. & Fulmer, R. (1983) "The Slingerland Tests: Reliability and Validity". *Journal of Learning Disabilities* 16 (10) 591–593.

Gundacker, J. (1992) *Direct Instruction in a Literature Based Program for Third Grade Slingerland Students*. Master's Project, California State University, Fresno: Fresno, CA.

Heinz, S. (1993) *An Investigation of the Pattern of Performance on the Slingerland Screening Tests Among Yup' ik 2nd through 6th Grade Children in the Kuspuk School District*. Doctoral Dissertation, The Union Institute: Cincinnati, OH.

Hofeling, S. (1991) *A Research Study to Determine the Effects of the Slingerland Approach on Decoding Skills of Non-Dyslexic Elementary Students*. A Research Project Report Submitted in Partial Fulfillment for Masters of Arts in Education. University of Phoenix: Phoenix, AZ.

Johansen, R. (1985) *A Comparison of Scores on the Slingerland Screening Test and the Wide Range Achievement Test*. College of Notre Dame: Belmont, CA.

Keogh, B.; Sears, S.; Royal, N. (1988) "Slingerland Screening and Instructional Approaches for Children a Risk in School". *Pre-School Prevention of Reading Failure*. by Richard and Mary Masland.

Knisley, J. (1991) *The Effectiveness of Slingerland Multisensory Approach to Teaching Language Arts*. Cambridge, MA: Educators Publishing Service, Inc.

Lehnherr, Pat (1988) *A Comparison of Slingerland and Basal Reading Instruction*. Master's Thesis, Marycrest College: Davenport, IA.

Lovitt, T. & DeMier, M. (1984) "An Evaluation of the Slingerland Method With Learning Disabled Youngsters". *Journal of Learning Disabilities* 17 267–272.

McCulloch, C. (1985) *The Slingerland Approach: Is It Effective In An SLD Classroom?* Master's Thesis, Seattle Pacific University: Seattle, WA.

Meyers, M.J. (1983) "Information Processing and the Slingerland Screening Tests". *Journal of Learning Disabilities* 16 (3) 150–153.

Moon, V. (1982) *Implementation of the Slingerland Multi-Sensory Approach to Language Arts for Specific Language Disability Children*. Master's Project, Provo, UT: Brigham Young University.

Munro, J. (1981) *Follow Up Study of Student Attitudes Toward Armstrong School Program*. Master's Thesis, Belmont, CA: College of Notre Dame.

Psychology Dept. (1988) *Slingerland Screening Tests: A Normative Study on a Canadian Urban Population*. Toronto, Ontario, CAN: Metropolitan Separate School Board.

Roantree, R. (1982) *A Comparison of the Effectiveness of Slingerland and Conventional Methods for Specific Language Disability College Students*. Unpublished Master's Thesis, College of Notre Dame: Belmont, CA.

Royal, N. (1987) *The Long Term Consequences of Specific Language Disabilities: The Secondary School Years*. Doctoral Dissertation, University of San Diego: San Diego, CA.

Rust, J. (1982) "Local Norms and Two Year Reliability for the Slingerland Tests". *Reading Improvement* 19 (1) 6–9.

Simultaneous Multi-Sensory Instruction Program Assessment Report. (1983) Anchorage School District: Anchorage, AK.

Slingerland—Whole Language: A Delightful Application of the Senses. (1991) Kerrville, TX: Kerrville Independent School District.

White, N. (1986) *The Effects of Simultaneous Multi-Sensory Alphabetic-Phonic, Direct Instruction Approach on the Teaching of Spelling*. Doctoral Dissertation, University of San Francisco: San Francisco, CA.

Wolf, B. (1984) *Growth of Slingerland Trained SLD Students as Shown on the Fourth Grade and Sixth Grade California Achievement Tests: Reading*. Unpublished Data: Bellevue, WA.

Wolf, B. (1985) *The Effect of Slingerland Instruction on the Reading and Language Achievement of Second Grade Children*. Master's Thesis, Seattle Pacific University: Seattle, WA.